Agents of
Transformation

Agents of Transformation

A Guide for Effective
Cross-Cultural Ministry

Sherwood G. Lingenfelter

Baker Books

A Division of Baker Book House Co
Grand Rapids, Michigan 49516

© 1996 by Sherwood G. Lingenfelter

Published by Baker Books,
a division of Baker Book House Company
P.O. Box 6287, Grand Rapids, MI 49516-6287

Printed in the United States of America

Library of Congress Cataloging-in-Publication Data

Lingenfelter, Sherwood G.
    Agents of transformation : a guide for effective cross-cultural ministry /
Sherwood G. Lingenfelter.
      p.   cm.
    Includes bibliographical references and index.
    ISBN 0-8010-2068-9 (pbk.)
    1. Missions—Anthropological aspects. 2. Intercultural communication.
3. Christianity and culture. 4. Missions—Theory. 5. Evangelistic work. I. Title.
BV2063.L433   1996
266'.023'01—dc20   95-47638

To my mother,
    who taught me the disciplines of work and faith,
and to my father,
    who taught me to love, study, and teach the Scriptures

Contents

Preface

he thesis of *Agents of Transformation* is that Christian cross-cultural workers will desire to be agents of biblical transformation, rather than agents of sociocultural change. An agent of sociocultural change brings new economic, social, and cultural interests and facilitates the change process so that members of a local community adopt ways of education, economy, and lifestyle common to the industrialized nations of the world. While change agents may have a positive effect in the development of communities in the two-thirds world, and some Christian workers may legitimately serve in this role, the primary objective of much Christian cross-cultural ministry is to help people come to know Christ, and thereby to become his disciples.

An agent of transformation is one who brings the good news of the gospel to members of a community and who brokers that message in such a way that those who accept it become disciples of Jesus Christ and learn to live spiritually transformed lives within the context of their community and culture. The outcome of this process should not be the replication of western churches and communities, but rather the establishing of vital and dynamic indigenous communities of faith that exert a positive effect on the wider culture in which they are found.

In *Transforming Culture* (Lingenfelter 1992) I have presented the argument that all human beings are prisoners in their distinctive cultural cells of disobedience. The biblical basis for this argument is derived first from the epistles of Paul to the Romans and Galatians, in which Paul says God has given Jews and Gentiles over to their prisons of disobedience so that he might have mercy on them all (Rom. 11:32). Walt Russell's (1993) exegesis of the concept of "flesh" in Paul's epistles further supports this notion of prisons of disobedience. Russell claims that we can understand Paul's contrast of "flesh" and "spirit" only in relationship to their respective social communities. In those terms, Paul teaches that we must be delivered from the communities of the flesh into the "community of the spirit." The community of the spirit is the community of faith formed by those who are followers of the Lord Jesus Christ.

The theory of cultural bias in the social sciences (Douglas 1982; Thompson, Ellis, and Wildavsky 1990) provides support, albeit unintentional, of the biblical notion of cultural systems as prisons. First Douglas and then colleagues who have followed her lead have argued that all human beings are constrained by cultural bias inherent in the particular social environment in which they live and work. From these structural arrangements people embrace a particular set of values and foundational premises regarding nature, society, and others. Individuals who take exception to the predominant cultural bias face the dilemma of subverting their community's beliefs and values, or of moving into another sociocultural system, or of withdrawing altogether. Contending that these social environments are universal and that it is impossible for human beings to live apart from them unless one becomes a hermit, Douglas concludes that it is impossible to become free of cultural bias.

The opening chapters of this volume examine the nature of culture, cultural bias, and social environment. The assumption with which we begin is that self-awareness and other awareness in relationship to cultural bias is essential for effective cross-cultural service. Missionaries and Christian leaders who are unaware of their cultural biases and the biases of others will inevitably be ineffective as agents of transformation. Through the history of the Christian church, believers have struggled against the hounding of society to conform the gospel message to the pervasive bias of the day. In the early centuries the church called such changes heresy. In contrast, many modern Christians view these changes as contemporary enlightenment. Whatever term is employed, accommodating the gospel to the bias of any system leads to cultural conformity rather than biblical transformation. The challenge of Paul in Romans 12 is that Christians not be conformed to this world, but rather be transformed by the renewing of their minds in Christ Jesus.

To become agents of transformation requires significant self-awareness with regard to one's cultural bias. The opening chapters of this book set forth the nature of society and the five distinctive social games that circumscribe human behavior.

Chapters 4 through 11 provide the reader with substantive analytical tools first to examine one's social context and cultural bias, and then to compare and contrast it with that of others. Each chapter sets forth a series of binary sets of questions through which the researcher may investigate characteristics of any social environment and discern the nature of social interests and bias. Three chapters furnish tools to analyze economic characteristics of one's social environment, three examine the structures of authority and leadership, and two address aspects of the cosmology and ritual life of a community. Once the reader has mastered these concepts for self-analysis, the tools may be used to investigate and illuminate the social arrangements and cultural biases of others. Each chapter concludes with a case study of an international mission organization, UNION, Ltd., to demonstrate how these tools may be applied to the analysis of a specific ministry context.

Fieldworkers who master these tools of research are competent to assess both their own and local community biases and are equipped to help new believers become agents of transformation in their society. Once mission leaders and new believers understand their respective biases, and together see the gospel transforming their respective perceptions of the world, they may engage others in dialogue and convey the gospel to them in a way that leads to freedom and transformation.

Chapter 12 presents the interaction of the eight variables, showing how the analysis furnishes useful and powerful insights toward the resolution of tensions and conflict in mission and national church partnerships.

Chapter 13 returns to the issues of change versus transformation. The nature of culture and cultural bias is defined with reference to logic of ideas and the structuring of power relations around personal and social interests. The reader is invited to understand the value biases of our social games, the ways in which we are tempted, and the ways we fail to obey the teachings of the gospel of Jesus Christ. The analysis shows how our expression of the church and our expression of obedience are in fact conformed to a particular social game and cultural bias. The hope of the believer is found in the call to "pilgrimage," living in the world as aliens and strangers (1 Pet.), dead to sin, yet very much engaged in the life of the community as witnesses of and ambassadors for the kingdom of God.

The last three chapters explore the issues of cultural bias as they relate to a pilgrim lifestyle and to service to others as agents of transformation. The thesis is that we must be eager to learn and meek in our efforts to teach others (Matt. 11:29) Jesus instructed his disciples to learn from him as he lived and served among them. He practiced spiritual disciplines, the tools by which we may obtain freedom from the grip of particular aspects of our bias. The final chapter provides a case study of

Philippine Christians applying biblical ideas to challenge the ideas and interests of their traditional society. This case models in many ways the process by which one may serve as an agent of transformation.

This book is the result of more than six years of research, writing, and testing the diagnostic tools for research in the classroom and in the field. Many of my mission colleagues and students have contributed to this work through their questions, dialogue, and struggles to employ these conceptual tools in research. If these research tools are of value, much of the credit must go to those who have worked with me to define the issues and concepts and to sharpen the questions for research.

I also owe special debts to many who have assisted in the preparation of the final manuscript. Steve Barber contributed the graphics of the text, taking my rough notes and turning them into many helpful visual representations. Pete Silzer contributed editorial and textual suggestions. Marvin Mayers thoroughly reviewed the manuscript, and his comments led to many of the organizational revisions that have made the book reader-friendly.

Clyde Cook, Biola's president, has kept the mission of world evangelism always before us, and his support by giving me time to write has been critical to this endeavor. His spiritual leadership and mentoring have been a continuing source of challenge and encouragement. Wendy Walker typed many versions of the text, and her readiness to help always made the improvements easier. Peg Fosmark typed many of the dictated segments as I worked on revisions, and her unfailing secretarial support makes it possible for me to teach and write while serving as the chief academic officer of Biola University.

I am also grateful for the missionaries of Wycliffe Bible Translators, Grace Brethren International Missions, Liebenzeller Mission of Germany, United World Mission, YWAM, and the Assemblies of God, who have provided opportunities for me to teach these principles. Through teaching them I have learned much about the challenges and practice of cross-cultural ministry.

Market, Government, Mosque, and Church

The Social Contexts of Change

ver the history of civilization, political, economic, and religious forces have swept repeatedly across the globe. Great warriors conquered vast territories, establishing empires that have flourished for a time under their successors and then collapsed. Merchants and traders followed the imposed peace of empire, building thriving marketplaces that matured as great ports and cities along their trade routes. Even when empires collapsed, these ports and cities furnished the commercial backbone of the successive empires. The great religious traditions of the world—Confucianism, Christianity, Islam, Buddhism, and Hinduism—spread upon the political and economic foundations of empires. Christianity, for example, spread readily throughout the peaceful, commercial cities of the Roman Empire in Asia Minor and Mediterranean Europe. Beyond the boundaries of empire, in the tribal and peasant hinterlands, both commerce and evangelism encountered the walls of cultural traditions and political hostility.

People living in the twentieth century have witnessed two world wars and seventy years of tension between western democracies and the Communist bloc in Eastern Europe and the former Soviet Union. Industrial capitalism has swept the globe, dominating the west and the Communist bloc. With the collapse of the Soviet Union, political capitalism has emerged as the preeminent economic philosophy for the twenty-first century. The vast military power of the United States, its European allies, and the Commonwealth of Independent States has resulted in a period of unprecedented, albeit tentative, peaceful coexistence among the nations of the world and the expansion of world trade. As a consequence of these changes, nation-state governments have penetrated the aboriginal corners of the world and have opened the villages and hinterlands to commerce and missions.

Christianity has flourished in the twentieth century. Aided by modern technology, missionaries have penetrated the remotest areas of the globe with the gospel, and thousands of people groups have responded. At the Lausanne Conference in Manila (1989) Christian leaders organized to develop strategies to plant churches in every people group of the world. This goal will be accomplished, since it is God's purpose, and his people have committed to the task.

The advances of Christian and Muslim evangelism in the final half of this century have replayed before our eyes the historical relationship among empire, commerce, and evangelism. While empire and commerce create prime conditions for gospel witness, they also produce significant changes in their own right, and are forces for secularization of the culture and the church that takes root in it.

Sipin Island: A Microcosm of Change

In the early 1990s I visited a mission team on Sipin Island, located in the South China Sea. Not more than twenty square miles of land area, Sipin is a dormant volcano covered with coconut palm trees planted by the inhabitants. They produce dried coconut, called copra, for export. The island is populated predominantly by two different groups of people: the Sipinese, who are Muslim, and the Layan, who are animist and Christian. The hamlets of Sipinese and Layan peoples are scattered across the rural areas of Sipin Island. A fairly large town on the eastern side of the island is the government center, the marketplace, and the point to which people come to visit the island.

Visitors to Sipin usually come by boat, a five- to eight-hour trip from the city on Merchant Island to the north. Unlike most visitors to Sipin, I flew there in a single-engine aircraft, landing on an airstrip located about twenty minutes' walk from the town and municipal pier. The missionary team had settled in a Sipinese hamlet where they were studying the language with the goal of translating the New Testament and an abridgment of the Old Testament for these people.

The people in the hamlet, and the mission family, live in wood, bamboo, and thatch houses situated on the edge of their gardens and dry rice fields. The Sipinese house contains two rooms—a cooking section with a hearth, a dirt floor, and a place to store utensils, and a room with a raised bamboo floor in which family members sleep and entertain guests. Each hamlet contains several families who are kin, usually brothers and occasionally a sister, their spouses, and children. These hamlets are dispersed across the mountainside of the island, so that people live near their rice fields, and on land that they or a kinsman owns.

There is little evidence in these hamlets of contact with the outside world. In the hamlet near the airstrip a careful observer may detect the Muslim presence by a small, partially walled mosque. The mosques are distinguished by their construction of wood and corrugated metal, a significant investment for these poor copra farmers. As the place of prayer, these mosques play an important role in the daily life of the Sipinese people.

The town, in contrast, is the locus of interaction with the people and interests from the outside world. The first and prominent feature of the town is a long main street lined with shops built from plywood and corrugated metal. Hand-painted signs over their doors and colorful posters on their walls and windows advertise the wares within. On that Saturday, a great crowd had gathered in the street. Men and women bumped one another on the pier as they loaded, unloaded, and watched the boats coming and going—copra farmers seeking the best price from several local buyers, and fishermen trading their catch to shopkeepers to whom they had debt and selling to customers in the market. The restaurants, billiard halls, dry goods store, hardware store, bakery, and food shops were teeming with people, while young men played basketball in a court in the center of town.

The second prominent feature of the town is the government complex, the center of which is the municipal hall. At the end of the long street, uphill from the shore through the marketplace, are the office of the mayor, the post office, and the telegraph shop. A few hundred yards away from the municipal office is a school. The school is staffed by a principal and several teachers, mostly immigrants from other areas. Just a few hundred yards from the school is the hospital, staffed by a director and two nurses who are stationed permanently there. Doctors visit occasionally to conduct several days of clinic and to treat seriously ill patients.

15

The municipal hall, the school, and the hospital represent the arm of the national government as it extends to Sipin Island. Those local officials testify that Sipin Island is among the least preferred assignments in the nation because of its isolation. Yet, one takes the best opportunity available. Many of the teachers and civil servants hope for a better placement in the future.

During a walking tour of the town, we discovered a less prominent but important institution—a small, brightly painted mosque. Students were gathering for Saturday classes, and an elderly Sipinese man greeted us. Inside the mosque an imposing figure, clothed in a white robe and a white head cover, presided over the class: an *imam* (expert teacher) born in Baghdad and serving as a missionary. Seeing me outside the door, Mr. Baghdad apparently sensed an opportunity to model for his students. He asked me about my religion, and when I responded, "Christian," he opened his Koran and began to preach in English. For about twenty minutes, using text and verse from the Koran, he proclaimed that Jesus did not rise from the dead, that he was not crucified, that he was not the Son of God, but merely a prophet. Without pausing, Mr. Baghdad attacked each of the foundational tenets of my Christian faith, illustrating in a brief half-hour exchange the daily contest between Islam and Christianity among these people.

On Sunday I discovered a fourth feature of this small town when I attended a church of Layan believers. The church was built much like the local mosque and was situated on the edge of town. About thirty people gathered that morning for worship. Two young women led the group in singing translated hymns and choruses. A young man played the guitar. All were dressed in their Sunday best and enthusiastically participated in the service. They were extremely warm in their welcome to us, and the Bible-school-trained pastor preached in Layan and in English in recognition of our presence. This little community of believers, strong in their faith, formed a close, somewhat besieged group of Christians. A few of the northern shopkeepers occasionally attended this fellowship.

The Social Contexts of Change

In this isolated town the market, the government, the mosque, and the church embody four distinctive patterns of social relationship and cultural bias. Individualism is the dominant cultural theme of the marketplace, while hierarchy is the ethos of the government bureaucracy. The structure of Islam, embodied in the law and the absolute rule of its teachers, lends itself to authoritarianism and fatalism among its adherents. Sectarian egalitarianism characterizes the tribal and hamlet clusters in the rural areas of the island and in the Layan church.

The marketplace is the place in which people take risks. The owners of the shops are for the most part immigrants from other parts of the nation. Many entrepreneurs come from the north, set up their own little stores, and import goods to make a profit. They are individualists. They live simply and work hard. Many own their own generators; others rely on kerosene refrigerators and lamps. Seeking to make money, these shopkeepers provide a significant service for the Layan and the Sipinese people.

The municipal government plays out the hierarchical ethos of the national government. Almost all of the people who work in the school and the hospital have come from other islands and are part of an elite who have been trained and educated for their respective positions. Although most did not choose Sipin, some will become part of the community, while others will leave for higher positions.

The social dimensions of the market and the government are of special interest to us, because they represent different but complementary social systems. The market is the place were rivalries are explicit, goals are clear and competitive. Shopkeepers desire to make money, and therefore spar for better prices and better products with the other merchants on the street. In competition with one another, they all want to succeed. They share concerns that the exchange system be protected and that thieves do not break in and steal from them. They want prices to be reasonable, so they can make a profit, yet not be forced out of business by someone drastically cutting prices. The idea of standard measures and respect for contract is part of their thinking and relationships. Very much like people in markets in the United States, they experience anxiety about buying and selling for profit as a normal part of their life. They know that prices are always changing, and selling in the wider market is frequently a risk. These people cope with change and the exigencies of a larger market on a routine basis.

The government of Sipin Island is much like bureaucracies everywhere. Government officials are concerned about keeping the peace. The schoolteachers, hospital staff, and the mayor act in a similar manner. All the people are their friends. They seek to serve the wider interests of the community—Layan, Sipinese, and shopkeepers are equally important. The people in the government work to soften the internal rivalries, promote harmony for the larger good, and insure that things get done in the proper way.

The responsibilities of the people in the government are defined through their roles: mayor, teacher, nurse, or post office clerk. Fixed instructions—rules about what they are supposed to do—guide each member in his or her daily tasks, and good civil servants follow the rules as integral to the system to which they belong. Yet, these officials tolerate differences and seek to meet the various concerns and interests of the community. As part of the larger bureaucratic system of the nation, town officials try to keep the outside government officials satisfied and the local people content with modest government services. A stable social system is a premium value; they want to protect their jobs, as well as the peace and quiet of their community and the larger government.

Twenty years ago the town did not exist. Today, the town and all its activities have become a new social arena for the people, creating dynamic yet distinctive social environments in which they interact.

The mosque represents another influence from the outside world and defines relationships, structure, and value for Sipinese apart from their domestic groups. Among the Sipinese, each mosque usually has three local *imam* who conduct regular prayer and worship. *Imam,* trained in the Koran and Islamic law, exercise authority in the local mosque. Some Sipinese *imam* had been trained in Merchant City, and these men have authority over the younger or less experienced teachers. The law of Islam defines explicit and strict rules and practice. Scholars from other countries visit the community from time to time to insure orthodoxy among the local people. These visiting scholars represent orthodox authority on practice and faith. When Mr. Baghdad was present, the practice of correct doctrine was intense and structured. When outside *imam* are not present, people respond in a more relaxed, cultural way.

Islam, by its ideology fatalistic, teaches that God acts according to his right, his character, and his will. People must learn to accept the will of God and to follow the rules of Islam without question. The authoritarian dimension of Islam, accompanied by a distant God and a distant Mecca to which people may go perhaps once in their lives, tends to reinforce fatalism. The life of the mosque reflects both the community and the authoritarian system of Islam. Being Muslim does not confer membership in a local kinship group. Belonging to a local Sipinese kinship group, however, makes it almost mandatory that one be Muslim.

18

The Layan church reflects both the external influence of Christianity and the sectarianism of the wider rural community. The Layan and the Sipinese represent distinct and separate ethnic groups. Within each linguistic group, kinship plays the key role in the affiliation of people. This is clearly evident around the airstrip where the mission team had settled. Two Sipinese family groups live to the north and south of the airstrip. Brothers and their wives occupy hamlet clusters near the mosque where they worship and on land that they utilize for farming. Each family unit produces its own food and cash income. In the daily routine of their economic lives they pursue respective individual family interests. However, kinsmen living within a hamlet visit one another, engage in cooperative labor, assist when neighbors are sick, worship together, and stand in strong family support against other families in the region who might threaten their particular interests. Elder brothers have a bit more authority than younger brothers in their mutual relationships, yet each is free to follow his own way. Whereas the Islamic religion is hierarchical, Sipinese families tend to be egalitarian in their relationships with one another. In that regard the Sipinese and the Layan are very much alike. Individual family interests come first, while the extended family serves their broader concerns and support needs.

The Layan church has retained the egalitarian and sectarian ethos of its kin groups and hamlets. Joining the church is voluntary, and the church emphasizes belonging, being together, and being one. In the Sunday service I observed that the pastor, his wife, and his nephews and nieces all participated. Men and women together led in the opening worship. In his sermon the pastor diminished himself at times, and identified strongly with the members. The congregation laughed with him, as he promoted a sense of camaraderie and unity.

The church building is a primitive type of fellowship hall, with an emphasis on function. We sat on rough but serviceable benches. The building and the benches were built by the members and the pastor, working together. The pastor and the members dressed nicely but simply; no one was ostentatious or obviously poorer than others present. From the sermon and conversation, one perceives a sense that the outside world around them is polluted, that it is dangerous to live in a world that is either animist or Muslim, and that Christians are engaged in a spiritual battle to cope with people who oppose their faith.

In summary, we have discovered four distinctive social environments on Sipin Island: the market, the government, the mosque, and the rural hamlets and the church. Through our examination of each of these particular social settings, we have observed distinctive sets of values and world views that characterize each. The marketplace embraces individualism and the values of competition and profit. The government emphasizes hierarchy and values that encompass all groups in the society and seeks harmony among the whole. The authoritarian mosque is exclusive and separatist, defining the followers of Islam as the true people, while all others are subject to them; the distance of God and Mecca and the inexorable law lead to a fatalistic world view. The Layan church is a small voluntary organization, sectarian in its outlook and egalitarian in its values. The church and the hamlets of the Layan and the Sipinese farmers are very much alike in that regard. Living in a hamlet, like belonging to the church, is voluntary, although kinship is a key attractor for members. The kinship groups, like the Layan church, do not grow large, since their land limits the total number of people who can effectively survive in a hamlet. The people are predominantly poor and mobility is often essential for survival.

The Government and the Market: Forces for Change

Each of the social environments on Sipin Island exerts its own distinctive pressures on the larger society. Looking at changes in Sipin Island over the past thirty years, one sees clearly that the government and the marketplace have played prominent roles in the lives of the people.

The national government exerts pressure to enhance national unity among its diverse cultures and peoples. To accomplish its objectives the government seeks to educate people with regard to the importance of the national culture and history, and to promote an ideology of national unity and loyalty. Education also serves as a means to power in the national culture. Without education a person cannot obtain a job in any of the government agencies or in the major business sector of the nation.

Other government services such as the postal service, the courts, hospitals, and health care, and the infrastructure for economic development, serve to incorporate people into the hierarchy by satisfying their individual and collective interests. Because the government provides services of value and importance in the lives of individuals, the hierarchy plays an increasingly important role in the lives of every community.

Through its emphasis on individual competition and profit, the marketplace brings to bear different pressures in the lives of the people. When a Sipinese man produces copra and sells it in the market, he can spend the money as he pleases. In his small hamlet every family is responsible to produce its own food. However, one of the explicit values of kinship is that a brother in need may ask for and expect to receive assistance. In the egalitarian context of the hamlet, hoarding for oneself is bad form and sharing is a routine part of life. The presence of money, however, and the many opportunities to spend money in the marketplace, create tension for these people.

The marketplace champions material interests and individual expenditures while undermining traditional values for sharing. Because money is scarce but goods are plentiful, people experience tension between their individual interests and the demands placed upon them by members of their local kinship group. Materialism and secularism tend to grow out of the marketplace.

Muslim and Christian Missionaries: Agents of Change

Islamic traders and missionaries entered these islands as early as A.D. 1400. To secure their economic interest, the Islamic traders sought to convert the indigenous tribal peoples to Islam. "Missionaries as well as merchants, the Muslim traders spread the faith throughout the Malayo-Indonesian region" (Peacock 1978, 19). Over the next three centuries, local kings became Muslim converts in order to tax Muslim merchants utilizing their ports. The chants and religious exercises of Islam also appealed to the animistic and Hindu mysticism of the contact cultures. By 1600 Islam had penetrated the interior of many islands, where teachers converted Hindu hermitages into Muslim schools, and established an expanding system of religious education that persists today.

On Sipin Island, Islam continues to be a powerful force. In its present form, Islam claims loyalty to God and to Islam above loyalty to the nation and any tribal or communal identity. The mosque is the center from which Islam spreads in the community, and the *imam* is the primary agent teaching the doctrines of Islam. International missionaries, such as Mr. Baghdad, serve to disciple the local teachers and to evangelize non-Islamic neighbors. To become a Muslim is to learn Arabic and to accept the culture and ideology of other Muslims. Conversion to Islam should be a total cultural conversion, with the intent of assimilating converts into the Islamic way of life.

Christianity, in contrast, is multicultural, emphasizing translation and transformation rather than cultural incorporation. Yet, in spite of this characteristic the Christian missionary, like the Islamic missionary, becomes an agent of cultural change. The church planted by a missionary most often looks much like the institutions to which the missionary belonged in his home culture. Because the culture of the Christian church is complex and varied, the expressions of the church that grow out of evangelistic ministry are just as varied. We have described the little Layan church on Sipin Island as sectarian, emphasizing high group commitment and egalitarianism among its members. In all likelihood the missionaries who established this particular church came from a strong sectarian, egalitarian denomination.

However, some Christian evangelists come from strong individualist-oriented churches and promote individualism among their converts. These evangelists believe that faith is a private thing and that every individual must make his or her own decision, have a personal, unique spiritual experience, and receive a special, sometimes prophetic message from the Lord in relationship to one's individual faith. The process of discipling new believers is an individual one and the outcome is to promote a loosely structured fellowship in which the converts are primarily and individually responsible for their relationship to the Lord and the expression of their unique faith.

Christian missionaries also come from church backgrounds that are hierarchical in nature, such as Roman Catholic or Anglican. When people are baptized into either of these churches they become part of an institutional culture. For example, I have observed among peoples of the interior of Sabah, East Malaysia, that converts enter into the Anglican church community and hierarchy. Pastors in these churches serve under the direction of a bishop from the city of Kota Kinabalu and are assigned by the bishop for ministry in these isolated areas. New converts are incorporated into the church liturgy and structure and participate in the corporate institutional relationships of that particular denomination.

The cultural impact of Christian missionaries most frequently takes the shape of the institution that supports the missionaries for their evangelistic and educational ministry. When those institutions are individualistic, the converts and the Christian values emphasized tend to focus on individualism. Should the mission of the church be either sectarian or hierarchical in orientation, the churches planted, the values taught, and the institutions established reflect those of the missionaries' home base. The social impact of the gospel tends to follow the social values of the Christian leaders who brought the message.

The Five Social "Ways of Life"

n their seminal work on cultural theory Michael Thompson, Richard Ellis, and Aaron Wildavsky (1990) argue that there are five, and only five, distinctive "ways of life" that characterize human social and cultural experience. These five ways of life are generated by a congruence between particular patterns of social and interpersonal relationships (social games) and patterns of shared values and beliefs (cultural bias). Further, these five ways of life coexist with one another in every society and compete with one another for adherents. Each way of life is dependent upon the existence of the other four and draws power from competition and complementarity with the other ways of life. Each of the five, which they term individualism, egalitarianism, hierarchy, fatalism, and autonomy, are constrained by the necessity of congruence between a particular set of values and beliefs and a particular pattern of interpersonal relationships (pp. 1–5).

In *Transforming Culture* (Lingenfelter 1992) I have utilized Mary Douglas's (1982) typology of grid and group to define four distinctive social environments. Thompson, Ellis, and Wildavsky build upon this same typological analysis, so I will review it briefly.

Grid refers to the degree to which individuals are constrained in social relations by the elaboration of social roles and the regulation of role behavior by explicitly defined rules and expectations. Traditional or contemporary bureaucracies provide excellent illustrations of high grid social relationships. Nearly everyone in contemporary society has experienced the bureaucratic shuffle, in which one is sent from one office to another to address a specific problem, and no one seems to have the authority to make the decision. Each person in the bureaucracy has a narrowly defined role and responsibility. The person being shuffled has a question that falls outside of the role and responsibility of the persons consulted. None of the persons involved have the freedom or the inclination to address the problem, but rather send the inquirer on to another office where perhaps there will be a person who has the authority to act on that issue.

High grid social contexts are those in which *role* and *rule* dominate social relationships. Low grid social environments are those in which individuals have fewer role choices, and behavior within each role is open for negotiation. In a context of low grid, individuals have the freedom to define and structure their relationships on a personal and situational basis.

The variable of *Group* defines the degree to which people value collective relationships with one another and define those relationships in terms of insider/outsider distinctions. Where the definition of and value for group is exceptionally strong, the survival of the group becomes more important than the survival of the individual members within it. Where the definition of group is weak, individual interests frequently supersede the interests of collective arrangements. For example, when the children of Israel left Egypt, Moses provided for them the Torah, which established strong insider/outsider distinctions. The people of Israel were not to marry outsiders, and they were forbidden to allow outsiders into their worship, with exception given to those outsiders who were distant kin. The descendants of Esau were allowed to enter the congregation of worship after the third generation, whereas the descendants of Moab were forbidden unto the tenth generation. Such strong focus on group identity and the distinction between insider/outsider leads to a pattern of social relationships of incorporation and exclusion.

In *Transforming Culture* (1992) I have described four distinctive social environments emerging from Grid and Group—Individualist, Collectivist, Corporate, and Bureaucratic types (see fig. 2.1). These social environments define the character of social life that leads to the ways of life or the five prototypical "social games" that people play. The fifth option occurs because of the possibility of being a social dropout, as typified in the lifestyle of a hermit.

It is important to state that we are defining five *prototypes* of the social games that people play. A prototype is a model from which people can make copies that are significantly varied in substance and content yet similar in structure. I have found it useful to label these five prototypes

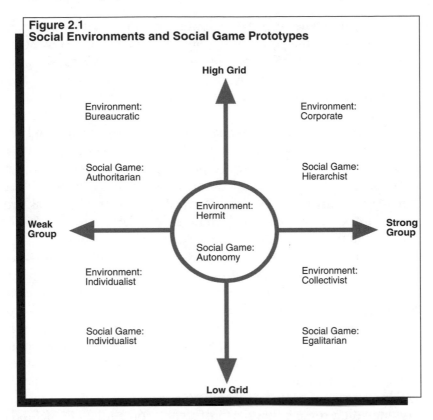

Figure 2.1
Social Environments and Social Game Prototypes

as the individualist game, the egalitarian game, the hierarchist game, the authoritarian game, and the autonomy game. Each prototype may be developed in a given culture with its own language, ideology, and socioeconomic content. For example, Aaron Wildavsky (1984) describes the exodus and transformations of the people of Israel as moving from Slavery (authoritarian game) to Anarchy (individualist game) to Equity (egalitarian game) to Hierarchy (hierarchist game) under the leadership of Moses.

In contemporary industrial societies, the stock market is an expression of the individualist game. On Wall Street individuals compete openly, buying and selling for profit in the daily fluctuation of the market.

In contrast, corporations, such as General Motors, are variants of the hierarchist game. General Motors operates with stockholders, corporate officers, middle management, and organized labor in a cohesive integrated system to produce profit for the stockholders and wages for management and labor. Members of General Motors are dependent upon the success of the whole organization for their personal and collective financial success, and the power of the hierarchy is moderated by accountability to the corporate group. Thompson, Ellis, and Wildavsky propose that the market and corporate worlds are interdependent upon one another and constitute the dominant games of the total social matrix.

Legal or administrative bureaucracies, in contrast to corporate organizations, encompass large numbers of people in an isolating and impersonal hierarchy. These administrative bureaucratic systems are variants of the authoritarian game in which people participate as employed individuals, but without the incorporation and collective support of the corporate social environment. Characterized by high grid but weak group, this social game tends toward despotic rule and cautious compliance or fatalism on the part of those who work within the system.

In contemporary American society environmentalist groups (Sierra Club, Earth First), religious groups (Amish, Brethren), and political groups (Libertarians, National Organization of Women) have organized to oppose the cultural mainstream of the nation. These opposition groups critique mainstream society and challenge its values and processes. Each is a variant of the egalitarian game, which places high value on unity, conformity to the ideals of the group, and the rejection of distinctive leadership and hierarchy.

The autonomy game has many expressions in contemporary society, including some university professors, some urban homeless, and some individuals or families who choose to live in isolated areas. All embrace some of the characteristics of life ascribed to the hermit. The hermit prefers to live in a state of relative isolation, rejecting the value of social relationships and relying upon his or her personal resources for survival. Hermits have existed for as long as we have records of human society. Their lifestyle is deemed strange by members of society, and hermits in turn take a critical stance toward social life and values. Henry David Thoreau provides a famous illustration in American history, yet thousands of men and women have chosen a hermit existence in the history of civilizations. Sometimes, as in the case of Thoreau, the hermit lifestyle is only temporary, while in other cases individuals enter a social wilderness, living and dying without social recognition or support.

The case study of Sipin Island in chapter 1 illustrates for us that four and perhaps all five of these social games may be found within a twenty-minute walking distance on the island. Although I did not observe a hermit, I am sure if I had inquired more carefully, one could have been identified. The Sipin market is clearly a variant of the individualist game and the municipal government of the hierarchist game. Mr. Baghdad and the mosque are modeled on the authoritarian game, and the little Layan church on the egalitarian game.

Thompson, Ellis, and Wildavsky contend that what we have described for Sipin Island is characteristic of human societies. They claim that the dichotomy between the market and the government is essential to their respective existence, that they complement one another everywhere they occur. These two social games, with their respective values and ideology, feed upon one another to survive and to perpetuate themselves. All five social games, these authors explain, exist in complementary relationship with one another; the authoritarian and egalitarian games provide an escape for people who find the competition of the market and the rules of the corporate hierarchy personally distressing.

Each of these social games depends upon the others, and all are sustained by the dynamic interaction among the whole. Faced with choices, individuals and communities embrace one or more games from which to live their lives. For example, the Sipinese and the Layan on Sipin Island live on small farms in which they grow rice, produce copra for market, and fish for their daily subsistence. In their daily economic routines Layan and Sipinese play the individualist game, having little that they share in common. However, few families try to subsist in complete isolation from others. Most engage in an egalitarian game of extended family support and exchange for labor, lifecycle celebrations, and personal crises.

The Sipinese have adopted the religion of Islam so that at particular times of each day when they participate in prayer at the mosque they for a time play an authoritarian game. The Layan Christians carry their extended family egalitarian game over into their church life.

These same village people, Layan and Sipinese, utilize the market and the corporate government institutions at the specific moments when a particular interest or need prompts such interaction. In times of illness the hospital is an important place to seek help. All children attend school for a certain part of their young lives and so each family engages in the hierarchist game of education. The government provides mail services, legal identification, and the court system through which one may seek to settle some conflict with others not in one's own kinship group.

While Sipinese and Layan interact with all of these social arenas and games, they prefer one with its particular values and beliefs as their way of life. They explain and rationalize their social and economic world from this perspective, and feel most at home with the rules and strategies of that one game. They also interpret and judge the behavior of people in all other games from the cultural bias of that specific game.

Cultural Bias: The Magnetic Attractor

According to Mary Douglas, cultural bias originates in the social environments and cultural games we have described. Relying on Douglas's argument, Thompson, Ellis, and Wildavsky (1990, 56–65) assert that the cultural bias of each game prototype stems from a "distinctive way of looking at the world." They explain that each of the social games embraces a particular myth about the characteristics of nature and specific preferences regarding blame, envy, scarcity, risk, and other dimensions of social value (see table 2.1). For example, in reference to "blame," they describe how individualists attribute blame to bad luck or personal incompetence, whereas hierarchists assign blame to social deviance. Egalitarians, in contrast, blame the system that is external to them as both monstrous and evil. Fatalists in the authoritarian game give blame or credit to the exigencies of fate.

Each group elaborates similar preferences in reference to risk. The individualist sees risk as potential opportunity and seeks to capitalize on the better chances while avoiding those risks that would result in loss. The hierarchist endeavors to manage risk so that whatever action taken is done within acceptable bounds. The egalitarian sees risk in terms of potential catastrophe and is ever conscious of the real and perceived dangers to self and to the larger society. The authoritarian/fatalist is passive: danger is inevitable; one takes whatever steps one can to avoid it, yet submits with despair in the face of real or potential danger.

The hermit also has a particular cultural bias and way of life, the autonomy game. Hermits blame no one, because they take no part in social struggles. Regarding risk, they are much aware of the common dangers all around and accept them as ingredients of daily life and existence. Because hermits are disengaged, they are often socially irrelevant. Envy is an emotion without meaning, since hermits are satisfied with their isolation and means of existence.

28

Table 2.1
Preferences and Cultural Bias
(Thompson, Ellis, and Wildavsky 1990)

Preferences	Individualists	Hierarchists	Egalitarians	Authoritarians
Blame	Bad luck or personal incompetence	Blame shedding to deviants	"System" blame External = monstrous Deviant = evil	Blame and credit fate
Envy	Flaunt advantage Envy spurs ambition	Institutionalized inequality controls envy; public splendor v. private monotony	"Plain" living; difference is right or wrong, appropriate or illegitimate, natural or unnatural	Good luck, bad luck says it all
Economic growth	Seek to create new wealth, new combination	Flow of wealth to top for capital investment and growth; system is *old* wealth	Equal distribution rather than growth	Happy to see wealth; hopeful
Scarcity	Rejects idea of scarcity; promotes full use of resources	Scarcity an opportunity for control, power, and group gain	Resource "depletion" a fault of system; promotes maximal preservation	Individual preservation of property and resources
Risk	Risk is opportunity; see opportunity, avoid profitless risk	Experts define acceptable risk and management; seek to manage whole system	Accentuate risks of technology/change; predict catastrophe (safety "inside"); cry wolf, but also spot real dangers	Passive avoidance of risk Helpless in face of danger
Apathy	Apathy implies consent; cost of participants not worth engaging	Apathy=consent; poor turnout implies weak civic responsibility	Decry lack of public involvement	Participation doesn't make a difference; voting is immaterial Winners all the same

Each of these five social games is potentially present in every socio-political context, often in variant cultural forms. In small-scale communities social pressure tends to eliminate competing games. But, as population increases, larger-scale societies allow greater social choice, which results in individual and group variability.

Why do people choose one game over another, and why do their choices change over time? Thompson, Ellis, and Wildavsky suggest that people sometimes experience discontent with the conventional wisdom (cultural bias) of their way of life. Looking for other alternatives, they find the conventional wisdom of another game more attractive. Discontent, coupled with alternatives, prompts people to move from one game to another. Drawing upon the analogy of a flock of starlings, Thompson, Ellis, and Wildavsky propose that people, like starlings, circulate among the four quadrants that make up their social space. They report that starlings in flight circulate between four aerial quadrants of space while hovering as a flock in one place, and then they move en masse to a new location. This characteristic of flight—hovering, circling, leaving for another location—is achieved as individual birds fly in continuous motion in a quadrant until it becomes too crowded, at which point some birds move into a less crowded environment.

People seem to make their choice of social game based upon personal comfort and fit with the bias or conventional wisdom of the environment in question. For example, a Christian who has grown up in a strong sectarian, Baptist church may, after going through college and graduate school, become uncomfortable with the strong insider/outsider distinction and what will appear to him or her as rigid, exclusive commitments to a particular theological position and behavioral standards. For this individual, the social fit in the church of one's youth is no longer comfortable. On many points, the person challenges or takes exception to the conventional wisdom of that group. Seeking a church more consistent with his or her present views, the believer may move to a charismatic Calvary Chapel. The person finds Calvary Chapel an open atmosphere, fostering individual expressions of faith and one's personal walk with God.

Collective celebration and charismatic gifts may be revitalizing for this former Baptist. In some cases, however, the openness and the flexibility of the charismatic environment may prove too much. Seeking more of a structured game, yet freedom from sectarianism, the believer may move again, choosing a more hierarchical expression of the Chris-

30

tian faith as typified by the Anglican or Presbyterian denominations. The most radical departures from Protestantism are those few individuals who move from a sectarian group to Roman Catholicism. Major ideological conflicts between Catholicism and Protestantism make such a choice a shocking one in the Protestant world.

According to the theory, Protestant denominational movements are created by people who frame their Christian faith in terms of one of the five prototypical games. Protest movements are precipitated by individuals or groups who experience discomfort with the theology of the group from which they come. However, each interpretive theology is inextricably linked with a cultural bias that originates in the prototype game being played. Individual protesters do not create new games but merely move from one to another. Particularly influential individuals, however, such as the Reformation fathers, may draw others to follow their teaching and leadership.

The theory suggests that society is dynamic, with people creating variants of the game prototypes or even shifting from one social game to another over a lifetime. The coherence derives from the complementarity of the social games and the cultural biases available to the participants. The individualist and hierarchist games are typically the central and dominant paradigms, while authoritarian and egalitarian games constitute border or peripheral options. Authoritarian fatalism provides a haven for the passive who are content to let the hierarchists and individualists run the show, while egalitarianism serves the agenda of activist protesters who join together in sectarian groups in opposition to the flawed yet powerful center.

The Economic Variable: Three Systems of Production

The five social ways of life present a two-dimensional picture of social life and culture. To understand the complexity of societies and culture it is necessary to add a third dimension: economic production and distribution. In the history of human societies, economic production has gradually shifted from tribal hunting, herding, and horticulture, to peasant agriculture and commerce, to industrial market societies. Following the definitions of Eric Wolf (1982), we can say that tribal subsistence economies emphasize production and distribution activities organized around kinship obligations. In contrast, peasant tenant farmers work land owned by a landlord and produce a surplus crop, a share of which goes

31

to the ruling owner. In peasant tributary systems craft specialization and surplus agricultural production feed a wider commercial economy, in which the rulers enhance their personal lifestyle and splendor of their kingdoms or states.

Industrial market societies are distinct from the previous two types of production in that most workers sell their labor to persons and corporations who own the productive facilities, the product, and the profit that comes from the sale or distribution of the products. Specialized labor is much more predominant in the industrial system than is typical in the peasant or tribal societies. In spite of these significant economic differences, the five prototypical social games are present in each of these economic systems and manifest the same interdependence and complementarity that we have described for industrial societies (see fig. 2.2).

Some anthropologists and missiologists (Service 1962; Hiebert and Meneses 1995) have utilized these broad socioeconomic distinctions to create typologies through which they compare cultural systems. While these typologies are useful, they oversimplify significant social distinctions that occur in each level of economic complexity. The argument here is that the social game prototypes provide significant opportunity for and expression of variation in cultural bias at each economic level. No single bias can be used to typify behavior in tribal, peasant, or urban industrial cultures.

The story of Abraham illustrates four of the game prototypes in a tribal subsistence economy. The story begins with Abraham playing the individualist game, separating himself from his father and kinsmen with whom he had lived for many years. He had his own God, a large number of servants, and wealth in gold and livestock. As a seminomadic tribal herder, Abraham lived an individualist lifestyle, negotiating relationships with other people with whom he came in contact as he moved from mountain to valley seeking pasture for his flocks.

The peoples with whom Abraham came in contact played by one of the other three games. He ordinarily made his livelihood trading livestock and dairy products for grain in symbiotic relationship with "hierarchist game" agricultural towns nearby. In a time of local famine Abraham and his nephew Lot moved down into Egypt for a time to buy grain. Egypt was an authoritarian kingdom populated by kinship-based, agricultural towns that paid tribute to the rulers and priests. The ruling pharaoh, whom Abraham feared, took Sarah, Abraham's wife, to be part of his harem. The Scripture reports that God sent a plague upon Pharaoh's

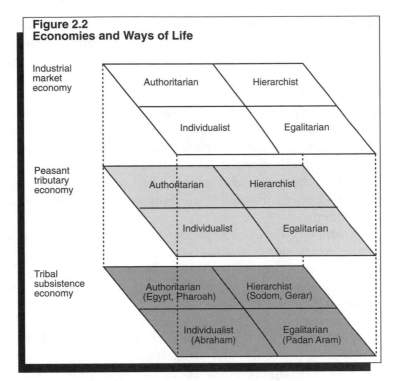

Figure 2.2
Economies and Ways of Life

Industrial market economy
- Authoritarian
- Hierarchist
- Individualist
- Egalitarian

Peasant tributary economy
- Authoritarian
- Hierarchist
- Individualist
- Egalitarian

Tribal subsistence economy
- Authoritarian (Egypt, Pharoah)
- Hierarchist (Sodom, Gerar)
- Individualist (Abraham)
- Egalitarian (Padan Aram)

house because of Sarah, prompting Pharaoh to send Abraham out of Egypt with gifts of sheep, oxen, donkeys, and servants to appease the wrath of God.

After their return from Egypt, Abraham's and Lot's families fought with one another as is common in tribal systems, and Lot chose to move into the valley of Sodom and Gomorrah and establish relationships with the people of these agricultural, hierarchist city-states. When Lot was captured by five kings in their war against Sodom, Abraham pulled together a coalition of kinsmen and friends and liberated not only Lot, but also the kings of the city-states to which Lot had attached himself. Abraham then moved with his herds near the city of Gerar, where he became involved in another conflict over Sarah with Abimelech, the ruler of a hierarchist town populated by his kinsmen.

In spite of Abraham's economic relationships with people in towns and with other clans of herdsmen, he refused to intermarry with these groups. When it came time for him to seek a wife for his son, Isaac, he sent his servant back to his extended family in Padan Aram. There he arranged to find a wife from among the kinsmen who had continued their egalitarian, collectivist tribal lifestyle in Abraham's absence.

A similar analysis is possible for the peasant and industrial levels of economic production. Careful study of fourteenth-century Europe, or of the Ming dynasty in China, or of the Mogul period in India, will show all five social games and cultural biases present and contending for adherents among the peasant peoples of each of these great civilizations. Individuals and groups within these ancient states and civilizations structured their lives within the same constraints of social game and cultural bias as did the people of Abraham's day, or as does the Christian seeking to find a denomination in which to worship and fellowship in industrial America.

In summary, the five social game prototypes and the three major systems of production provide a framework within which to understand the complexities of the social and economic worlds of people. Although the cultural elaboration of human life is highly variable over time, certain common themes and variations are repeated. These similarities arise from human social relationships and economic interests. The five prototypes circumscribe the social management of food, labor, sharing and distribution, protection, and advancing one's social interests. While the ideas of human experience are exceptionally variable, these social games and cultural biases reflect and demonstrate substantive common ground across cultures.

Understanding Social Environment

The concept of social environment is central to everything that follows in this book. Every society has many social environments existing within it, and each social environment reflects at least one of the game and cultural bias prototypes described in chapter 2. Since every social environment has its own distinctive features and characteristics, each must be studied separately if the fieldworker is to understand the dynamics of relationships and values within that environment in the context of the larger culture. The illustrations from Sipin Island (chap. 1)—the market street, the government complex of municipal office, hospital, and school, the Layan church, the Sipinese hamlets, and the mosques—spell out the kinds of variation possible in any society. Each has a specific location, people who are committed players, rules that regulate the relationships or the game played in that specific environment, and interested spectators.

If you are to understand the people, the society, and the culture in which you are working, it is essential that you engage in a program of systematic observation and research. Reading about interests, economic relations, and cultural biases will be useful, enlarging one's understanding, but the only way to grasp the meaning of these concepts is to apply them in data collection and analysis. The study of social environments provides that engagement. The first step in the application of these learning tools is to identify a specific social environment to be researched. The features of any social environment include the following: space, people, relationships, activities, and time.

35

Aspects of a Social Environment

Space: The Playing Field

All social activities occur in space that has social meaning for the participants. The size and features of this space vary significantly in reference to the type of social activity characteristic of that environment. Some typical social environments include village, neighborhood, fire station, factory, and church. Each of these encompasses a very specific defined social space and has within it all the other features we have identified.

The first step in understanding the social environment is to map the space characteristically used by the participants. For example, if the social environment is a village, one would map all of the distinctive features marked by the members in the village as key components of the village community. Figure 3.1 illustrates a village on the island of Yap in Micronesia. The map includes households, village gathering places, men's houses, agricultural resources, and other key components of village life.

A fire station, factory, or church constitutes a different kind of social environment from a village. A map of a fire station reveals sleeping quarters, eating quarters, offices, and firefighting equipment, while a map of a factory does not ordinarily show sleeping facilities. The fire station has a great deal of equipment, but the equipment is primarily stored for activity that will occur at some future time outside of the station. A factory has equipment that is utilized daily to manufacture products. The church also has offices, equipment, and frequently a place for eating, but the activities for its membership are focused on worship and learning rather than on productive labor.

The space dimension of a social environment provides the playing field upon which people engage in meaningful social action. It is essential to understand the components of that social space to know how people classify and define that space and to understand the significance of space in terms of meaningful action. Mapping is the tool by which the fieldworker is able to systematically study space and its meaning.

People: The Players

The people who consider a particular playing field a legitimate place in which they spend meaningful time are the subject of our research. It is people who establish relationships with one another and engage in activ-

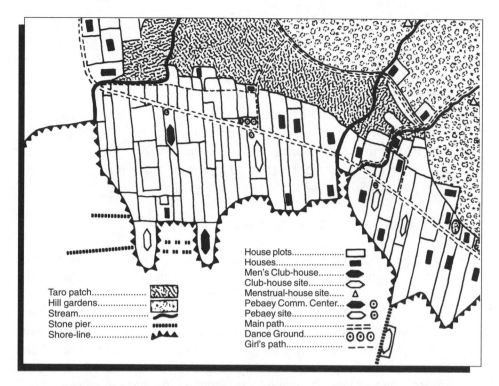

Map of Wonyan Village in Yap, Western Caroline Islands

ities together. The people may organize themselves in diverse ways. Some will form strict rules of membership, as in a Muslim mosque, and include only those who are willing to participate in accord with those rules. Others may have open, loosely defined criteria upon which relationships are established and broken. Still others may seek to engage whoever is available, such as in the marketplace on Sipin Island. For the study of a social environment one must identify those people who are regular players and who therefore maintain meaningful relationships over time.

In every social environment some people take roles that are peripheral to those of the central players. We may call them spectators, substitutes, or occasional participants in the game. The substitutes and the occasional participants have more vested interest in the activities in the social environment than do those who are merely spectators. However, even spectators may have a vested interest when players have a special relationship to them. Other spectators may be quite casual in their observation and engagement with the people who constitute the social environment.

37

The importance of spectators is that they often watch the game with interest and concern about the outcome, and sometimes they invest time and personal resources so as to be more than bystanders. For example, the spectators to a fire station know that if they have a fire in their own home, they can telephone the station and receive assistance in a very short time. People who live around a factory may establish businesses to support the needs of factory workers in their transit to and from their jobs. People in the neighborhood of a church may from time to time participate in its activities or be affected by those activities in a positive or negative way. Spectators then are not merely bystanders.

Relationships: Rules of the Game

Every social environment has within it socially specified relationships. These relationships may be defined in terms of social roles and/or a collective organization of a group. The definitions by which people order their relationships and engage in activities with one another constitute the rules of the game. It is through rules, values, and understandings that people engage in their regular meaningful activities and manage their interests and crises. Wonyan Village (fig. 3.1) is constituted wholly of privately owned land. People who live in the village do so because they have ownership rights to parcels of land and are thereby able to build houses, plant gardens, and harvest food and other resources from their particular parcels. Public-access roads and buildings are maintained by the people who reside within the village and who privately own the land segments subject to public access. The villagers also have rules about who may utilize the roads and paths and what kind of activities are appropriate on them. For example, loud talking or shouting is prohibited within the residential area. People must walk in single file on public roads and footpaths.

Some of the parcels of land in this village (fig. 3.1) have been identified as chiefly lands. The eldest member of the family that owns a titled parcel speaks for the authority vested in the land and exercises authority within the community in the role of village chief. The village is divided into sections, and residents of each section are responsible for organized cooperative labor within those sections. The social space then defines not only personal space, but also collective responsibilities and obligations.

In contrast, a fire station in an urban neighborhood is a different spatial unit than a village. It has no permanent residents, but rather is occupied twenty-four hours a day, during three different shifts. The firefighters sometimes sleep at the station, often eat at the station, and always work at maintenance activities in the station. However, when the station chief receives a call to extinguish a fire within its region of responsibility, the shift on duty immediately responds and does everything within its power to extinguish that fire. Within the fire station there are specific roles assigned to members of the shift. These roles include captain, engineer, paramedic, and firefighter. Each has designated responsibilities within the organization of the station. Daily activities and firefighting work are governed by some very specific rules known by all of the participants.

Each social environment then has its roles, its organization, and its rules of the game. It is essential to identify the roles of each player, to understand how their relationships are structured, and to discover how they engage in their regular activities.

Activities: The Game

Every social environment has some focal purpose and common activities. The village and urban neighborhood provide a place of residence for families and a structure within which families may relate to one another for larger community interests. Wonyan Village (fig. 3.1) serves not only as a residential community, but also as a place within which people feel safe, a place that defends its members against hostile outsiders, a place where people cooperate together for communal activities such as fishing, dancing, and the construction of community gardens. They hold common meetings and make decisions of relevance to the whole at the local meeting house. Some activities that are important to the members of this community are conducted in relationship with other villages. For example, this village participates with other villages for its weekly worship in the regional Catholic church and for the children's education in the regional government school.

The fire station, in contrast, has none of these residential functions. The station is primarily where people work for wages with the expressed objective of protecting residences and businesses in the surrounding community in the happenstance of fire or accident. The training and the routine of the participants are focused continually upon the anticipation of catastrophic events. The routines and regulations of this community have as their end coping with catastrophe. All other social activities are secondary to this objective. Yet eating, working, and sleeping in the same place, training, and celebration are all part of the routines of the participants within this social environment.

Members of each social environment construct rules to govern the specific space, time, and activities of meaning and purpose for the participants. In some situations activity may be limited to a very specific time and place. In an environment such as a factory activities are focused primarily on production of particular manufactured goods. The participants come only at a scheduled time, engage in activities on the basis of contractual arrangements with the owners, and perform functions that are defined by the manufacturing process. Eating, celebration, and other activities may occur, but when the specified time for labor is completed, the members disperse to homes and locations that may or may not have any relationship to other participants within the factory social environment.

Time: The Calendar

Activities within every social environment are governed by some kind of calendar. The calendar spells out the particular arrangement, sequence, and time frame within which activities and relationships occur. The calendar may be very carefully defined or hardly defined at all. However, time is a crucial component to social activities and must be considered for an adequate understanding of social environment.

In a village, for example, time may be tied to an agricultural cycle, whereas in an industrial neighborhood, time may be tied to government holidays and the functions of manufacturing and education of participants within the neighborhood. The agricultural village will respond to environmental constraints on planting, cultivating, and harvesting, while the urban neighborhood will be affected far more by issues of transportation, distance from employment, holidays, and other urban considerations.

In a jungle village time is crucial to understanding variation in the rules and relationships that are part of the social environment. Among the Deni Indians in Brazil, for example, most daily activities are conducted independently by individuals as they scatter into the jungle to hunt, fish, and gather produce. However, two or three times a month, the chief in the village calls its members early in the morning to participate in a collective feast. If the people agree, over the next day or two the members of the village engage in a collective celebration, including public games, sharing meat gained by hunting and fishing, gathering in the village plaza to share and eat food prepared in their respective households, and dancing and singing through the night. For this brief period of time all of the players in the village act in concert with one another with a common purpose of celebration. Once this event is over, individuals resume their independent activities with little or no cooperation with other members in the community.

In the social environment of a fire station time is also a significant component of work and social life. As long as there is no fire, work activity within the station is regulated by specific rules and routines. Each individual has a job assignment, space, and responsibilities; work not completed on one shift will be passed on and continued by equivalent members on the following shift. However, when members of a shift are called to respond to a fire or other catastrophe, the organization of work changes to meet the impending crisis. The hierarchy present at the station is disbanded for a collective team process in which every member tackles a particular problem at the scene of the crisis, and all work individually and collectively to attack the fire and bring it under control. In the time of crisis, the organization of work and rules of the game change. As within the Deni village, time becomes an important component for understanding the organization and structure of social activities.

Time is also crucial to understanding the social environment of a factory or of a church. In a factory work is scheduled according to hours and shifts; in some situations laborers work in shifts around the clock for five or six days a week. Most factories shut down on Sundays, and the passerby will find the parking lots empty, the gates locked, and the machinery quiet. The church operates on almost the mirror opposite calendar. During the week passersby will find the parking lots empty and few persons other than staff members on the premises. On Sundays, however, the parking lots will be full and the church a focus of worship and educational activity.

Strategies for Research

The best strategy for research is to select a social environment that is accessible and that promises to interest and challenge you. An accessible environment that is uninteresting will soon tire and bore you. A challenging environment that is inaccessible will cause great frustration. You need to find people who are open to observation and questioning over an extended period of time. Observation and interviewing are essential to effective learning.

The first step in understanding a social environment is to map the space that is significant to the participants. In a fire station that would mean mapping each floor, noting the appropriate places for equipment and identifying spaces assigned to people of particular roles such as captain or paramedic. *The more detailed the map is the more useful it becomes.* To map the kind of furnishings in each office in a fire station and the kinds of equipment provided for each separate role, clarifies further the meaning and detail of significance to the participants. Using the linguistic labels employed by participants also helps to better define how they understand social space.

Time frame and calendar of activities is the second major step in researching a social environment. One begins the calendar by sketching out the major events that participants deem important in their social environment. As one continues research over time one can continue to elaborate on the calendar so that the final result is a detailed picture of how time is utilized by participants within the social environment, and how activities are structured and distributed through time. It is also useful to examine how social rules may change in reference to specific activities and specific times defined by the participants. For the fire station the time of catastrophe invokes a new set of rules and relationships. For the Deni the time of celebration invokes a new set of group expectations and relationships. In the Deni and the fire station calendar, then, time marks distinctive variations in routine and relationship.

The objective of your research is to practice the use of concepts presented in following chapters of this text so that they may become useful tools, empowering you to become a more effective learner. As with any set of skills, they are mastered only with diligent practice! You cannot hope to use these research tools with skill and precision unless you are willing to commit to the discipline of practice.

Property Interests and Cultural Bias

Case of Naomi and Ruth

Meanwhile Boaz went up to the town gate and sat there. When the kinsman-redeemer he had mentioned came along, Boaz said, "Come over here, my friend, and sit down." So he went over and sat down.

Boaz took ten of the elders of the town and said, "Sit here," and they did so. Then he said to the kinsman-redeemer, "Naomi, who has come back from Moab, is selling the piece of land that belonged to our brother Elimelech. I thought I should bring the matter to your attention and suggest that you buy it in the presence of these seated here and in the presence of the elders of my people. If you will redeem it, do so. But if you will not, tell me, so I will know. For no one has the right to do it except you, and I am next in line."

"I will redeem it," he said.

Then Boaz said, "On the day you buy the land from Naomi and from Ruth the Moabitess, you acquire the dead man's widow, in order to maintain the name of the dead with his property."

At this, the kinsman-redeemer said, "Then I cannot redeem it because I might endanger my own estate. You redeem it yourself. I cannot do it." (Ruth 4:1–6)

Case of the Banquet Guests

Jesus replied: "A certain man was preparing a great banquet and invited many guests. At the time of the banquet he sent his servant to tell those who had been invited, 'Come, for everything is now ready.'

"But they all alike began to make excuses. The first said, 'I have just bought a field, and I must go and see it. Please excuse me.'

"Another said, 'I have just bought five yoke of oxen, and I'm on my way to try them out. Please excuse me.'

"Still another said, 'I just got married, so I can't come.'

"The servant came back and reported this to his master. Then the owner of the house became angry and ordered his servant, 'Go out quickly into the streets and alleys of the town and bring in the poor, the crippled, the blind and the lame.'

"'Sir,' the servant said, 'what you ordered has been done, but there is still room.'

"Then the master told his servant, 'Go out to the roads and country lanes and make them come in, so that my house will be full. I tell you, not one of those men who were invited will get a taste of my banquet.'" (Luke 14:16–23)

Concepts of Property

People in every social environment utilize space and materials to facilitate their interests and daily activities. In the two case studies people are engaging in transactions that reference space and materials. Boaz, in the village of Bethlehem, is seeking to purchase land, and a kinsman has prior rights. A wealthy townsman in the environs of Judea has prepared a great banquet, only to discover that two invited guests have purchased land and oxen, and are thus too preoccupied to attend. The rules by which people access space and materials are what we term property.

In this chapter we will investigate how the factors of grid and group influence values and rules in reference to property in different social environments. The purpose of this chapter is to provide the reader with diagnostic criteria from which he or she can investigate property relations in a specific social setting. How important are group relationships? To what extent do people hold private, exclusive interests? Who exercises control over land, livestock, houses, machinery, wealth, and other resources? Using the diagnostic criteria, the student of a society should be able to identify the characteristics of a selected social environment and to understand the social game and the particular values that people hold in relationship to property.

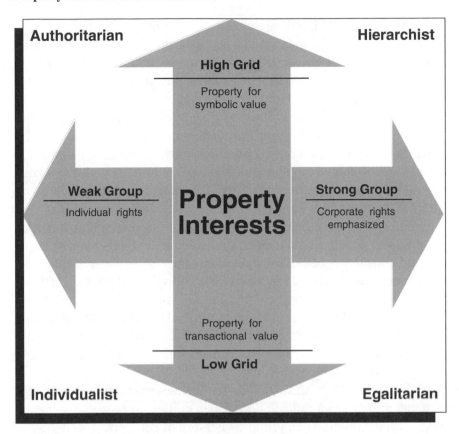

All societies make use of energy resources to meet their basic subsistence needs. These energy forms include the physical elements necessary for the production of food and shelter of its members. In traditional societies, the land, vegetation, and the water are the primary resources that people employ for the production of food and shelter. Societies differ in how they define rights to these resources. Some hold only rights of exploitation, such as hunting and fishing, whereas in others, people hold rights to the space and materials themselves.

Control over energy forms is a basic feature of every social environment. Individual actors exercise control over the physical matter in their environment according to the rules of a local social game. We shall define *ownership* as an entitlement to control certain physical resources.

Physical resources in themselves do not constitute property. Property is rather a compound of two elements—a thing and human labor. In most societies it is the addition of human labor to materials that transforms

45

them into property. Land becomes property only after people have worked to delineate boundaries that separate one parcel from another. A farm is the result of human labor on the land, turning it into a socially meaningful productive resource. The farm may produce either food for subsistence or a cash crop that may be marketed for money and profit. Likewise, a pottery bowl is a transformation of clay into an object that has a socially meaningful use. Property may also apply to items of a more abstract nature, yet have economic utility. A book, for example, is the product of human thought and labor, but in itself has no direct contribution to subsistence. However, like the cash crop, it may be utilized for profit from which a person meets his or her subsistence needs.

Ownership is the process by which an item of property is incorporated into an economic system, so that some individuals have rights to use and consume it and other individuals are denied those rights. The farm, for example, is owned by a particular individual or group, and those people alone have the rights to work the farm and consume its products. The pottery bowl is first owned by the individual who produces it, and he or she has the right to keep and use the bowl or to dispose of it through gift, trade, or sale. Once the bowl is transferred, the new owner holds title to it and authority over its use.

In the cross-cultural study of land tenure and other forms of property, students of American Indian and African cultures discovered societies with a strong emphasis on group ownership of economic resources. In African societies lineages and clans hold rights to land. Among American Indian groups, members of a tribe or a band shared hunting and collecting rights. Some scholars postulated a form of primitive communism as a basic economic system of these societies. Others argued that these peoples had many private interests in property and that their social systems were a mix of private and corporate interests.

The rights of individuals and of groups are important factors in the ownership of property. In some societies where group rights are strongly emphasized, a person's rights to property may be subordinate to group relationships. This is clearly illustrated in the opening case study of Boaz, Naomi, and Ruth—the parcel of land could only be sold to those with rights of redemption, and Ruth the widow was part of the package. In other societies where the survival of the individual may have greater value than the survival of the group, property may take priority over the relations among persons. In the parable from Luke's Gospel, two of the invited guests use recent purchases of property to excuse themselves from attending a banquet.

In all societies, we find varying notions of private and corporate ownership. However, the degree to which each is emphasized appears to be correlated to the strength of the value of group in the social environment. Where group emphasis is weak, private ownership predominates. Where group emphasis is strong, private ownership is subject to larger corporate values. In these latter situations, the group may grant only *usufruct* or use rights to individuals. In situations of weak group emphasis, individuals may hold property in a *fee simple* relationship, which entails completely private ownership and access.

As we explore the nature of property relationships in each social environment, we must investigate how people transform materials by human labor into objects of social value and how they distribute rights to such property between individuals and groups. We must also examine the rules and values by which people hold and exchange these property rights. The binary sets of questions that follow provide a tool for measuring the strength of commitment in a specific social environment to high or low grid values, and strong or weak group values. Through the application of these questions, the researcher may determine the presence or absence of particular features of social behavior, and thereby identify the game prototype being employed in that social environment.

Diagnostic Criteria for the Study of Property

The diagnostic criteria that follow illustrate paired grid or group variables. These criteria represent contrasting components of reality which ordinarily may not both be present at the same time in the same social environment. They are mutually contradictory and therefore exclusive of the other, although most people can live with contradictions in their lives and show little concern. Strong grid/group variables are given a value of +1, and weak grid/group variables are given a value of −1. If neither variable is significantly present in a social environment, the null value (0) is assigned. By assessing the presence (+1, −1) or absence (0) of these variables in a social environment, the researcher may diagnose the relative emphasis of grid/group factors relating to property in a specific social environment.

Under circumstances of rapid cultural change, or in situations where people from different social environments come together for a common purpose, such as a boarding school, tensions may exist between participants seeking to create a single social environment. The goal of research is to describe as accurately as possible the social values and expectations that characterize a social environment, and where conflicts and contradictions exist, they should be documented. When a researcher finds both aspects of a contrasting pair of variables present, half values (+ or −.5) may be given for each variable, or the participants may be analyzed as rival interest groups (A and B) within a single social environment. The case study by Donna R. Downes at the end of the chapter illustrates how a researcher may employ these contrasts to analyze a social environment.

Grid: Property for Symbolic Value or Transactional Value?

In a high grid social environment, property becomes a symbol of position and role in society. Individuals occupying high status positions have greater access to material goods and labor than those individuals in low status positions. As one gains higher position in the social grid, one's public and private control over resources and property increases. People often build a property estate with the objective of enhancing their value as persons and achieving recognition within the social structure. To hold property is to confirm values of high symbolic significance in the social system.

In a low grid social environment, people view property more as a means to an end than as a symbol of one's role. Role is relatively unimportant since the number of roles is restricted and most if not all individuals have opportunity to achieve those roles. People place emphasis upon individual performance and competitive exchange with others in social relationships. These exchanges may occur in strong or weak group context, but they are predominantly egalitarian in their motivation and outcomes. Social distinctions do arise because of the differences in individual skills and effort. However, these differences are not institutionalized; rather they are constantly in flux as individuals compete with one another.

Is property awarded for proper behavior (+1) or achieved by shrewd investment (−1)?

The case of Naomi and Ruth shows Boaz and a kinsman in dialogue about purchasing Naomi's property. To acquire that land the kinsman-redeemer must fulfill two social obligations: marry Ruth and maintain the name of the dead with his property. The man with first rights to redeem the land withdrew, allowing Boaz to fulfill this obligation. The story of Joseph (Gen. 39–41) provides another illustration. When accused of sexual misbehavior, Joseph was stripped of all his material possessions and placed in prison. When he was rewarded for interpreting the pharaoh's dream, he was granted the second position in the kingdom, given control over all of the pharaoh's agricultural land and labor, and married to a daughter of a high priest of Egypt.

The low grid contrast to these two cases is the story of Jacob (Gen. 27–31). Jacob accused his father-in-law, Laban, of exploiting him, thus becoming wealthy, first through his bride service for Laban's daughter, Rachel, and then in his continuing labor, caring for Laban's flocks. Yet, in spite of Laban's efforts, Jacob became wealthy, and the text says that he did so by deceptive as well as righteous means, breeding the flocks to obtain an increase in the spotted varieties that belonged to him.

Is property attributed with symbolic value (+1) or only utilitarian value (–1)?

The palaces of Pharaoh and the priests in Egypt symbolized the power of their offices in the Egyptian hierarchy. Gold, silver, and precious stones have customarily been associated with high status in high grid social environments. Individuals acquire these items to gain public recognition of their wealth.

The symbols of the low grid social environment are rarely vested in property but frequently in other nonmaterial rights. For Jacob and Esau, the blessing of their father was far more important than the materials of their inheritance. Getting wealthy may not confer a particular social rank, but more important is the thrill of achievement and the benefits of adequate food, shelter, and comfort.

Is property secured for protection (+1) or invested at risk (–1)?

Securing property and protecting it from outside threat is a key attribute of a high grid social environment. While the rules for the redemption of land in Naomi's Bethlehem kept outsiders from buying up Hebrew land, they also insured a widow of lifelong care and guaranteed a man's name in perpetuity, even if he had no children of his own.

The low grid environment plays to the motivations of individuals for autonomy in the managing and expansion of their property interests, sometimes at significant risk. Jacob gained considerable satisfaction from outwitting his father-in-law, Laban, by cross-breeding Laban's and his livestock, thereby increasing the number of his own speckled herds. Yet, in returning to his homeland, he placed hundreds of head of livestock as gifts in front of his caravan to induce his brother, Esau, to accept him peacefully and to mediate the expected great risk of his return.

Is property a right of occupation/class (+1) or a right of labor/resources invested (–1)?

Particular kinds of property are often connected to occupation and class identity. The Egyptians and Hebrews distinguished themselves in the time of Joseph on the basis of their property and occupations. The Hebrews were shepherds and owned large flocks. The Egyptians were farmers and owned productive resources and grain. Each scorned the other, rejecting the other's occupations and social identities. Yet, each of them was dependent upon the other, living in a symbiotic relationship of exchanging meat for grain. The higher the grid in the social environment, the greater the identification of occupation and identity with particular property values.

In his flight from Laban, Jacob justified taking his wives and his flocks on the basis on the years of labor that he had given to Laban. Laban accused him of stealing his daughters and his property, but Jacob declared that he acted within his rights. In the low grid social environment individuals see their material possessions as a right of labor or investment.

Does self-esteem come by possessing/preserving (+1) or by exploiting/managing (–1)?

The story of Joseph in the Old Testament again reveals the use of property as an instrument to create or to diminish self-esteem. When Joseph interpreted Pharaoh's dream, Pharaoh rewarded him immediately with his signet ring, fine robes of linen, a gold chain, and a horse and chariot. Joseph, when he revealed himself to the older brothers who had sold him into slavery, gave his younger brother, Benjamin, five sets of clothes and a large quantity of silver, while the others received only a set of clothes. George Eliot's novel, *Mill on the Floss*, provides a classic illustration of the linkage of self-esteem and property; the tragic events ending in deaths in this family focus first upon the loss of the wife's inheritance of furniture, dishes, and linens through debt foreclosure, and then upon the loss of the husband's mill property that had been in the family for generations.

Joseph's father, Jacob, grew up in a low grid social environment, where strategy and the game was as important as the results. Jacob took pride in first negotiating for Esau's birthright, then tricking his father to give him, rather than Esau, the father's blessing, and finally outmaneuvering Laban to expand the number of his livestock. These men all struggled in a somewhat hostile environment to build families of power and wealth. Yet, they lived in tents, migrated from place to place, and held nothing of the wealth characteristic of high grid social distinctions evident in Egypt. Jacob's family in Egypt is an embarrassment, at the bottom of the social hierarchy; yet, in the semi-arid pastures of Palestine he is the distinguished head of a prosperous family.

Group: Corporate or Individual Rights Emphasized?

In a strong group social environment people hold property as a resource committed to the survival of the group. Corporate ownership becomes a key feature of property relations, and the group organizes itself to manage its resources for the benefit of the whole. Corporate groups have a lifespan that exceeds the life of individuals in them. To understand the nature of corporate interest and the scope with which these interests are protected and deployed in a social environment, we will examine features of title, use rights, rights to produce, maintenance, and disposition of property.

In a weak group social environment, the individual becomes a primary focus of social activity. People employ material goods and labor primarily for the survival and enhancement of individuals and their families. Groups are temporary in nature, serve the interest of the individuals who comprise them, and exist only long enough to satisfy those interests. In such a social environment, individuals carefully protect their property rights from the encroachment of others and commit resources to a group only to the extent that such serves their private interest.

Do people value corporate title (+1) or individual title (−1) of ownership?

The land of Naomi was not hers to dispose of as she wished; only a kinsman of her husband had the right to purchase it, reflecting the corporate rights of the clan to the land of its members. Not just any kinsman could purchase the land. The closeness of kinship established one with the right of redemption.

In the story of the rich man's banquet, the men placed their purchases of land and oxen above the interest of their neighbor. Their apparent disregard of the invitation to the banquet suggests an individualist orientation. The American concept of fee simple land ownership and the emphasis on the privately owned house and land derives from a weak group

51

social environment. Americans who travel to Europe and encounter land rights that have been held for generations by European aristocracy see such practices as in conflict with basic human rights.

Are use rights dispersed by the group (+1) or allocated by individual owners (–1)?

Use rights refer to the right to develop and produce from land or other resources. Boaz bargained for the use rights to the property of Naomi. The title of the land remained in Naomi's deceased husband's name, and the children born to Ruth were to legally continue the name of the deceased (Ruth 4:10). Boaz obtained the use of the land and the right to Ruth's sexuality. The first child, however, was considered Naomi's (Ruth 4:14–17).

These practices are alien to weak group social environments. Use of land and resources are either the right of the first to improve, as among the Deni in Brazil and in the homestead acts in early America, or the right of the one who purchases title. Many Americans resent their government's right of public domain and collective requirements such as zoning laws, which they see as an encroachment upon their personal rights to property.

Are rights to produce held corporately (+1) or individually (–1)?

Boaz did not have an exclusive right to his first child by Ruth. The child belonged to Naomi, and the land continued to be listed in the genealogy of her deceased husband. Naomi also continued to have rights to a share of grain produced on the land. A similar illustration of corporate control of produce is seen in contemporary Hong Kong. Individuals born into Chinese villages located in Hong Kong's New Territories receive distributions of royalties from clan property owned by the villagers and leased to the government or to private owners. As long as a villager keeps his name on the village list, he shares in the profits of this land lease arrangement, regardless of where he lives in the world.

Jacob and Laban negotiated their respective shares of the flocks. When Jacob arrived at Laban's house he had nothing. After years of working for his wives, Jacob negotiated with Laban that all the speckled of the flock, a small minority, would belong to Jacob. From that time on, Jacob held individual title to these animals and their offspring. The Deni in Brazil hold similar values, with each individual holding exclusive right to the produce of one's labor, whether in the fields or in some other exploitation of jungle resources.

Are responsibilities for property maintenance/risk collective (+1) or individual (–1)?

One of the obligations of the kinsman-redeemer was to "maintain the name of the dead with his property." The group as a whole had responsibility for the survival and well-being of its members. Once Boaz had redeemed the land, he took the responsibility to maintain it and all of the obligations incumbent with it, including marriage to Ruth the widow. The man with first rights of inheritance refused because he did not want the responsibility of the widow, enforced by the consensus of the elders in Bethlehem.

Americans are familiar with the scene of a middle-class neighborhood in which all of the houses on a block have well-groomed and maintained lawns except for one. One resident on the block may allow his yard to grow up in weeds, the paint to peel from his house, and the property to become a repository for various items that his neighbors consider junk. While all of the neighbors are frustrated with this lack of conformity to public social values, they feel helpless to impose upon the individual their collective values and recognize, albeit regretfully, the right of the individual to neglect or to maintain his property as he wishes.

Where group has high value, collective maintenance is an integral component of access to corporate property. The irrigation systems in Joseph's Egypt were the collective obligation of the families who shared in the rights to water. The work days that rural evangelical churches often have to encourage their members to participate in the maintenance and upkeep of their collectively owned church campus provide a contemporary illustration.

Is the decision to dispose of property collective (+1) or individual right (–1)?

The dispersal of land to the various clans of Israel cited in the Book of Joshua illustrates the collective ownership and distribution of land based upon genealogy. Further, Boaz could not claim the property of his kinsman, Naomi, since another held first rights within the group. Yet, when his fellow clansman rejected the obligation to marry Ruth as part of the inheritance, Boaz was able to exercise his secondary right of inheritance and to marry Ruth.

Many western missionaries at the turn of the century attempted to buy clan-owned property in Africa and Asia. While they discussed these matters with the respective leaders in these settings, and the leaders agreed to provide for them a piece of property at a given fee, the understandings between these individuals engaged in the transaction were at odds. The western missionaries felt they were purchasing the land in perpetuity, whereas the members of corporate clans saw this transaction as the temporary allocation of use rights that would revert to the clan when the missionaries' business was finished. The consequences of some of these misunderstandings remain as conflicts today.

In contrast, when title to property is fee simple, the disposition is the simple decision of the individual who holds it. The New Guinea Big Man may distribute a surplus of pigs or yams to individuals with whom he expects to achieve the maximum political return. He is not constrained by group interest other than those rules that are identified as the rules of the game. Alliance in many New Guinea societies is defined as an agreement between individuals. Therefore, they distribute property individually. Each man seeks to accumulate as many allies as he wishes within that social context. Similarly, Americans sell their property to achieve profit or another interest that enhances their individual standing and survival at that moment.

In the case study that follows, Donna R. Downes has employed these diagnostic criteria to analyze the social environment of UNION Ltd., a multinational mission organization. Downes examines the values of western and African team members in terms of the grid and group diagnostic questions.

UNION Ltd.: A Case of Mission and National Partnership by Donna R. Downes

Introduction to the Social Environment

UNION Ltd. is a parachurch mission organization based in Africa and considered by the national government as an independent corporate entity. UNION Ltd. is a field ministry of UNIWORLD International, a U.S.-based mission organization. The UNION Ltd. staff at the time of the study was made up of two African families and five American families. These seven families constitute what is called the UNION Ltd. team. All are international missionaries who raise the majority of their support in America, have been educated in American universities or seminaries, and are equally compensated monetarily (with the exception of small differences in increments given for years of missionary service).

They share an office facility and live in commuting distance from the office in the capital city of the host country.

In addition to the UNION Ltd. team several national employees serve as secretaries, accountants, gardeners, and guards. These employees were not considered part of the social environment under analysis. The exclusion of these national workers seemed appropriate at the time, but is perhaps a shortcoming of the study, since they do constitute part of the daily working environment of the team.

UNIWORLD International prides itself on its distinctive in being a team-oriented organization. UNIWORLD never deploys individuals to worldwide ministry—only teams. The organization believes that this group of diverse individuals models the type of international partnerships necessary to build the church around the world. UNIWORLD International values strongly group goal-setting and achievement.

First, for the purposes of this research, I divided the UNION Ltd. team into two separate categories—western and African. The differences that occur on the team are not always a result of a division between these two categories. However, perhaps 50 percent of the problems to be addressed have been identified as related in some way to cultural differences. Second, on-site participant observation and a variety of formal interviews and informal conversations provided the means by which the data were gathered on each of the eight grid/group variables measured.

UNION Ltd.: Property

The UNION Ltd. team holds a variety of properties in common: an office with computers, typewriters, desks, furnishings, and miscellaneous equipment; a team car; and team ministry materials. The team also has corporate assets of good will or reputation upon which it builds clientele and ministry. No living quarters are owned as team property, although both African members are purchasing their houses. All members own personal cars, house furnishings, computers, and televisions.

THE GRID DIMENSION

African members hold a high grid perspective (+4.5) on property, endowing it with a symbolic value that often boggles the minds of western counterparts, who are low grid in their outlook (−3) (see table 4.1). African team members emphasize personal office location as a right and reward of (+1) their role. The idea of having computers, nice furnishings, and modern business equipment is a symbol of the stability (+1)

55

of the UNION Ltd. organization as a mission. The security and appearance (+1) of the facility suggests identity with and permanence in the local context and economy. "We need to work on planting grass and some

Table 4.1
Property Variable in UNION Ltd.: Western v. African Missionaries

High Grid		Low Grid			
Property Held for Symbolic Value		**Estate Held for Transactional Value**		**Westerners**	**Africans**
+1	Reward for right behavior	−1	Outcome of individual effort	.5*, -.5	1, 0
+1	Attributed with symbolic value	−1	Utilitarian value only	0, −1	1, 0
+1	Secured for protection in crisis	−1	Invested at risk	0, −.5	1, 0
+1	Right of occupation/class identity	−1	Right of labor/ resources invested	0, −1	1, 0
+1	Self-esteem = possession/ preservation	−1	Self-esteem = management/ exploitation	0, −.5	.5, 0
	Sum of Grid Variables:			**−3.0**	**+4.5**

Strong Group		Weak Group			
Corporate Interests Emphasized		**Individual Interests Emphasized**		**Westerners**	**Africans**
+1	Corporate title of ownership	−1	Individual title of ownership	1, −.5	1, 0
+1	Group dispersed use rights	−1	Owner allocated use rights	1, −.5	1, 0
+1	Corporate rights to produce	−1	Individual rights to produce	1, 0	1, 0
+1	Collective obligation— maintenance, security	−1	Individual maintenance, security	1, 0	.5, 0
+1	Collective control of disposal	−1	Individual decision to dispose	1, 0	1, -.5
	Sum of Group Variables:			**+4.0**	**+4.0**

*A score of +.5 or −.5 signifies that a particular variable was present, but was subject to either the more powerful contrasting value in that social environment or a contested value held by enough participants in the social environment to be of consequence.

flowers," said one African teammate, "so that people will see we're not just going to move out tomorrow."

Allocation of office space is an indicator of one's social and educational status (+1). The African who led the team for four years insisted on having a second-floor office because of the prestige of being upstairs. Although the office was too small for meetings, the location was important for his self-esteem (+.5). The westerners conceded after a lot of hard negotiation over efficiency versus appearances.

The westerners view UNION Ltd. property with a functional, transactional perspective. Ownership is a burden: they would rather rent an office. Having an office is appropriate to the role (+.5) of each staff member, yet one negotiates for (−.5) such office space or earns it by proving physical need. The size, location, and allocation of individual office space is best determined by how the team can make use (−1) of it, not by the status such space might confer. While both westerners and Africans care about the security and maintenance of the property, westerners value a better work environment (−.5). Social and educational status are not valued. The job is all that matters (−1). Self-esteem is tied to efficiency (−.5) rather than to possessions.

Over the years of UNION Ltd.'s ministry in Africa, several of the African team members have stressed the importance of purchasing the office property. The westerners have held firm in their opposition to tying themselves down. UNIWORLD as a mission discourages such ownership. For Africans the ownership of land and the placement of buildings upon that land confers an adult status and respect on the owners. Both of the African team members were constantly building or adding to their rural holdings, not because the properties were particularly functional for them (since they do not live there), but because such buildings show a great deal of status in and identification with the community.

Most of the western missionaries in UNION Ltd. own computers and use them for a variety of personal and ministry tasks. African team members acquired computers for their individual offices, but neither knew how to use them. The older man eventually sold his computer because he had no secretary to do his typing and little interest in acquiring the skill since "office work should be done by secretaries." The younger man, however, eventually learned how to operate his computer and has made good use of it.

THE GROUP DIMENSION

While a few differences occur in the way Africans and westerners in UNION Ltd. view group interests in team property, their overall score is the same (+4) (see fig. 4.1). All agree that members *share ownership* (+1) and have the right to use corporate property (+1); they cannot disperse such property without a collective decision (+1). The group taxes a portion of each member's monthly missionary income (+1) for the purchase and corporate maintenance (+1) of such property. Westerners take a more possessive (−.5) attitude toward equipment for which they raised support than do the Africans. Each has a library-card system for checking out personal books (−.5). They are also more guarded in maintenance and loaning of cars or homes while on vacation. African members feel less obligation to maintain corporate property (+.5), and often loan their cars and occasionally their homes, risking their resources (−.5).

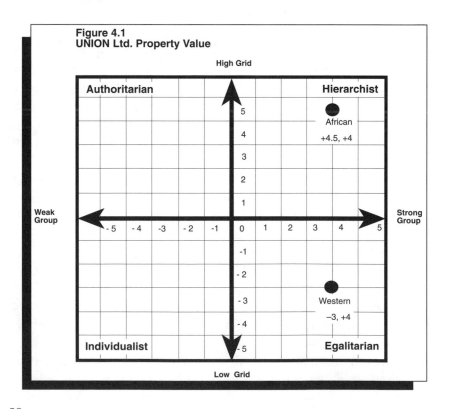

Figure 4.1
UNION Ltd. Property Value

Conclusions

The matrix in figure 4.1 shows striking grid differences between African and western members regarding property values. The westerners show values strongly centered in the egalitarian game, while the Africans prefer the values of the hierarchist game. If the analysis had focused upon their respective family social environments, the westerners would have had much weaker group values, perhaps falling in the individualist game quadrant. Some of this individualism is evident in the westerners' treatment of their personal ministry property, even when transactions occur between them and their teammates.

Research Questions 4.1
Grid and Property

High Grid	Low Grid
+1 *Award for right behavior.* Do people reward for proper role behavior by granting control over valued property? Does one inherit from parents or kin by fulfilling certain duties to them? or	−1 *Achieved by shrewd investment.* Do people extend their property resources primarily by hard work? Do they compete for property by use of coercive measures or manipulative behavior?
+1 *Attributed with symbolic value.* Does ownership of particular property hold symbolic value for the owners? Do some items of property have greater value than others? In what social ways are symbolic values expressed and reinforced? or	−1 *With only utilitarian value.* Do people have an egalitarian view of property, minimizing differences of holdings? Do people emphasize the utilitarian aspects of property, so that holdings are primarily a means to an end?
+1 *Secured for protection in crisis.* Do people seek to protect and secure property through legal title, regular maintenance, attention to the visual impact, and securing against theft and vandalism? Do people manage their property to provide for themselves and their heirs at some future time? or	−1 *Invested at risk.* Do people expend their property resources to provide for subsistence and immediate wants? Do individuals risk their property holdings and seek satisfaction from the challenge of investment for uncertain but anticipated gain and competitive social rewards?
+1 *Right of occupation/class identity.* Does one occupy certain space (land, home, office) because of election, appointment, or succession to a role? Are rewards of property given to those who occupy higher roles in the hierarchy? or	−1 *Right of labor-resources invested.* Do people assert their rights to property based upon their labor invested? Are distributions of and disputes about property settled in terms of equity of investment?
+1 *Self-esteem by possessing/preserving.* Is an individual's self-esteem connected to the possession/preservation of property (e.g., clothing, furnishings, or dishes for a woman, or automobile, tractor, or boat for a man)? or	−1 *Self-esteem by exploiting/managing.* Is self-esteem gauged by success in exploiting and managing one's property resources through transactions with others? Do people recognize skill and daring in competitive investment of resources, win or lose?

Research Questions 4.2
Group and Property

Strong Group	Weak Group
+1 *Corporate title of ownership.* Are certain resources (land, water, forest, reef) or durable property owned corporately with title formally vested in an identifiable group? How does the group pass use to the next generation and constrain transfer of title to outsiders? or	−1 *Individual title of ownership.* Do people assign ownership of land, water, and other resources to private individuals? Do people hold clear, individual title to durable structures and goods?
+1 *Group dispersed use rights.* Does the group allocate the use of property to members? For what time period? How does the group assert its rights beyond that time? What is expected in return from members? Does the group allow nonmembers access to property, and how does it regulate such access? or	−1 *Owner allocated use rights.* Do individual owners have the right to use their property exclusively for their own interests, to rent the property, or neglect to use it at all? Is society limited in its power to restrict individual property use and exploitation?
+1 *Corporate rights to produce.* Does the group tax members for their produce from corporate land? Do kinship obligations include rights of ancestors or local leaders to first fruits? Do corporate rights take the form of tenant fees, taxes, shares, or dividends gained? or	−1 *Individual rights to produce.* Do individuals exercise control over the produce generated from their property (land, other real estate, stocks, royalties, or productive equipment)? Is consuming, selling, investing, or discarding produce an individual matter?
+1 *Collective obligation-maintenance.* To what extent do the members of the group hold one another accountable for the security, maintenance, and upkeep of their property? or	−1 *Individual maintenance, security.* To what extent is maintenance and security of property left to the discretion and motivation of individual owners?
+1 *Collective control of disposal.* Are members constrained by the group from the temporary or permanent disposal of corporate property? What claims does the group exert upon individually owned property? or	−1 *Individual decision to dispose.* Are individuals free to sell or otherwise dispose of their property as they wish?

Labor Interests and Cultural Bias

Case of Bricks Without Straw

But the king of Egypt said, "Moses and Aaron, why are you taking the people away from their labor? Get back to your work!" . . .

That same day Pharaoh gave this order to the slave drivers and foremen in charge of the people: "You are no longer to supply the people with straw for making bricks; let them go and gather their own straw. But require them to make the same number of bricks as before; don't reduce the quota. They are lazy; that is why they are crying out, 'Let us go and sacrifice to our God.' Make the work harder for the men so that they keep working and pay no attention to lies." (Exod. 5:4–9)

Case of Day Laborers in a Vineyard

"When evening came, the owner of the vineyard said to his foreman, 'Call the workers and pay them their wages, beginning with the last ones hired and going on to the first.'

"The workers who were hired about the eleventh hour came and each received a denarius. So when those came who were hired first, they expected to receive more. But each one of them also received a denarius. When they received it, they began to grumble against the landowner. 'These men who were hired last worked only one hour,' they said, 'and you have made them equal to us who have borne the burden of the work and the heat of the day.'" (Matt. 20:8–12)

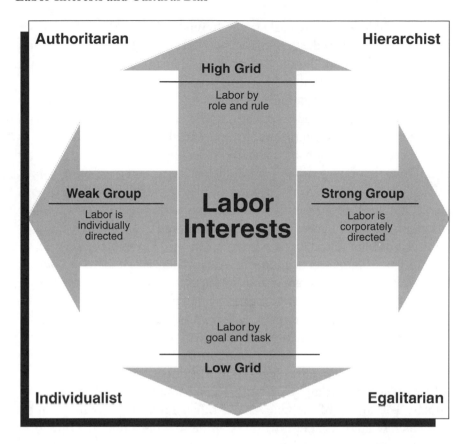

Work and Labor

All human beings regardless of the economic level of their societies engage in work. Even Adam and Eve in the garden in Eden had to collect the seeds and the fruits that provided their daily sustenance. The curse of Adam for violating the command of God (Gen. 3:17–19) was to be subject to painful toil, to eat the plants of the field, and to live by the sweat of his brow. From the simplest collecting societies to the most complex industrial societies, human beings all must engage in work to survive.

Social anthropologist Eric Wolf (1982, 74) has distinguished between the concept of work and the concept of labor. Wolf defines *work* as those activities in which individuals, singly or in groups, expend energy to produce energy. Adam and Eve, collecting seeds and fruits in the garden of

Eden, expended their physical energy to renew their strength for further daily activities. Their descendants expended energy through the toil and sweat of farming and herding to produce the subsistence and general livelihood of agricultural and herding peoples.

Labor, in contrast, is defined as a social process carried on by two or more people in organized cooperation. The concept of labor focuses on human relationships and the cultural organization of work. The laborer always stands in relationship to others. Adam and Eve collected together in a domestic organization of production. Jacob and his father-in-law, Laban, worked together as kinsmen to produce and sustain their livestock, which in turn provided for their subsistence and their wealth. Joseph was sold as a slave into Egypt and worked as a slave in the household of Potiphar and then as a prisoner in jail. Upon Joseph's release from prison, Pharaoh placed him in the position of supervisor over all of the labor in Egypt, second only to the pharaoh. Joseph leaped from slave to executive administrator of Egyptian production.

In the two cases introducing this chapter, the laborers stand in an explicitly defined relationship to others in a social process, each defined by an institutionalized social organization. Pharaoh has the ultimate authority over the Israelite slaves, and instructs his slave drivers to cut off their supply of straw, yet require them to maintain their production quotas. The owner of the vineyard also has authority over the men he hired as day laborers; these workers agree to work under the direction of a foreman for the standard day wage. The purpose of this chapter is to explore the differences in these and other cases of the social organization of labor and productive activities.

Production is defined as that complex set of mutually dependent relations among nature, work, social labor, and social organization. In the illustrations, we have noted several different means of production. Isaac and Rebekah and their sons, Jacob and Esau, constituted a domestic unit of production in which the extended family provided the sole means of social organization of labor. When Jacob fled to his mother's brother, Laban, Jacob became part of Laban's extended kinship group and joined as a laborer with Laban and his sons for their flocks and herds. Jacob increased his wealth working in Laban's kinship group, and finally, with two wives, two concubines, and twelve sons, he returned to his home territory in Canaan. Jacob and his married sons constituted a kinship unit for production, with extensive herds to support their large families.

The stories of Joseph and the Israelite slaves who must make brick without straw illustrate a tributary mode of production. In that context, they serve as subordinates to the pharaoh and his officials. Joseph became the instrument through which Pharaoh gained almost total control of his subjects—first taxing Egyptian farmers 20 percent of their grain harvest as tribute to be stored in his warehouses, then in time of famine selling that grain back to them for profit. By the end of the seven years of famine farmers had exhausted all their gold and silver reserves and turned their lands over to Joseph and Pharaoh. It is from such a position of power that a later pharaoh, who did not know Joseph, held the Egyptian farmers as his serfs engaged in tributary service and exchange, and the Israelite descendants of Joseph and his brothers as slaves.

These three means of production, the domestic, the kinship, and the tributary mode, provide the dominant variations in productive activities throughout human history. The case of the day laborers in the Gospel of Matthew illustrates a fourth type of organization, a capitalist mode of production in which labor is a marketable resource, sold for wages. Only in the last two hundred years with the Industrial Revolution in Europe has this form of the organization of labor begun to dominate human societies; the industrial systems of modern nations have turned exclusively to systems of wage labor to operate private or government-owned industrial machinery.

The reader is cautioned to recognize that variation in social environment may occur within each of these different systems of production (see chap. 2). For example, in Egypt the predominant mode of production was tributary, and Joseph served as the head over all the grain production in Egypt. However, Egypt is a vast area that includes many different peoples. If we were able to explore all of Egypt during that time, we could certainly identify variations in the social environments of production in Egypt. Perhaps the Hebrews, with their emphasis on herding, were more individually directed than the Egyptian farmers who were dependent upon irrigation. There is no correlation between social environment and these four types of production. The case of day laborers in the time of Jesus illustrates this clearly; the dominant organization of production in the Roman Empire was tributary, yet the population of poor in Judea was large enough to provide a pool of day laborers for seasonal work in a vineyard. It would be false to conclude that this case of wage labor implied a more widespread capitalist wage system of production in Judea.

To explore the diversity in labor games in social environments, it is essential that we identify diagnostic criteria that are not contingent upon the different social modes of production. For example, all societies have domestic groups that serve the subsistence needs of the people. The social environment of domestic groups may be high or low grid, or high or weak group, as we will see in a later chapter. Our purpose here is to identify factors of grid and group that operate at all levels of economic complexity and that enable us to discern focal values that arise out of the organization of labor in a given social environment. It is the nature of cooperative work, the labor game, that informs us of the values and characteristics of labor.

Grid: Labor by Role and Rule or by Goal and Task?

Working by role and rule defines the primary features of a high grid social environment. *Role* refers to the specialization of labor into tasks marking differences in skill, authority, and compensation; the most ancient role specializations grew from the development of skilled artisans such as potters, weavers, silversmiths, and blacksmiths. When dynastic rulers organized major public works projects, they added levels of administrative supervision, bureaucracies, to the already existing craft specializations. In the modern context bureaucratic specialization has become so complex that the job market has literally thousands of distinctive roles for prospective employees. *Rule* refers to the regulation of a worker's schedule, productivity, relationships, and compensation by those who direct the labor process. Appointing a foreman, setting a time to begin and to end work, defining a quota for production, and establishing a daily or an hourly wage for compensation are common rules in a high grid environment.

In a low grid social environment, the goal of the work activity leads to objective requirements for the organization of that work and social labor. The job to be done sets the work agenda, and the schedule, productivity, relationships, and compensation grow out of the task and the persons who must do it. A self-employed Realtor in a city like Los Angeles or Philadelphia may organize his or her work and relationships on the basis of personal goals and the requirements of selling property. Since he or she is self-employed, the requirements of the work itself become

66

the primary driving factors. The same is true for a self-employed farmer or rancher, a pastoral nomad like Jacob, or a farmer and hunter like the Deni in Brazil. All are self-employed, yet each must turn to others for labor assistance.

Is labor organized by rule/role assignment (+1) or by task/goal requirements (–1)?

In the case of bricks without straw, the work is clearly organized by Egyptian slave drivers and Israelite foremen. The slave laborers expect that straw will be provided for them to make bricks. Pharaoh has the power to change the rules, and he does, insisting that the laborers gather their own straw. The same pattern is evident in an earlier period of history in the life of Joseph, who experienced drastic shifts in roles from slave to head of the chief officer's household, to prisoner, to head of all Egypt. As the head of Potiphar's house, he had overseer power and responsibilities, as a steward in the prison he had a subordinate administrative role, and as the second to Pharaoh he ruled over the system of tribute collection and redistribution.

The day laborers described by Jesus in his parable were available for any job offered. When the owner of the vineyard asked if they wanted to work, they didn't ask what kind of work, but eagerly accepted employment. When Jacob (Gen. 30) discerned the need to intervene to produce more speckled and spotted sheep, he placed peeled branches in all the watering troughs. This was not part of Jacob's job description, but rather something that he deemed necessary to achieve his particular objective as the custodian of Laban's flocks.

Is labor scheduled by standard/routine (+1) or by goal considerations (–1)?

In the case of the bricks without straw, the slave drivers held Israelite slaves to the same production schedule, in spite of the denial of straw. Somehow the Israelites had to fit the collection of straw into their daily plan. In contemporary western societies the use of the time clock, the requirement that employees punch in, and the prescription of break time and lunch time are evidences of scheduling by rule. People come to work at the scheduled time and leave at the scheduled time regardless of where they are in the work process. In a high grid social environment, the time dimension of work is prescribed by social conventions.

In the case of the day laborers, the owner invited them to begin work at the third, sixth, ninth, and eleventh hour. The owner recruited them whenever they were available and asked them to work until the end of the day. The text does not tell us if the owner felt a sense of urgency about a task to be finished. In a low grid environment people may define a very rigorous schedule in order to reach a goal. Conversely, they may extend a particular task over a much longer period of time than others would consider appropriate or practical. In the case study of Jacob, he placed the stripped branches in the watering trough when the females in the flocks were in heat. He chose a particular season in which he felt the labor would have its maximum impact. The urban Realtor schedules her work according to goal considerations. When a Realtor wishes to show property, she will schedule her day at a time when she believes customers will be available to see property. Realtors often work on Saturdays, Sundays, and evenings since these are the times when potential customers are most able to utilize their service. These times do not coincide with the general public standard in the United States, which schedules work Monday through Friday, from 8:00 A.M. to 5:00 P.M.

Is productivity gauged by time/product (+1) or by effort/goal achieved (–1)?

The demand for measured productivity for labor is not new to this century. The opening case in this chapter describes the despair of the Israelites in Egypt when Pharaoh instructed his foremen to withhold straw for making bricks, yet required the people to make the same number of bricks as before. The foremen pressed the people to find their own straw and to produce the same number of bricks in the same time. In today's factories, engineers study time and productivity and prescribe production quotas for assembly-line and machine-operating employees. An Eastman Kodak employee will be awarded a bonus if he produces up to 15 percent more on his stamping machine than the engineer has prescribed for a given time. If, however, he produces more than 15 percent, the engineers will evaluate their assessment of the job and increase the quantity of parts that a machine operator must produce to earn a satisfactory performance evaluation. This connection of time and product is part of the high grid social environment of labor.

In a low grid environment people have no fixed measure, but test effort expended over a period of time against satisfaction with their returns. In the parable of the day laborers, those who worked all day were unhappy that they were paid the same amount as those who came at the eleventh hour. They did not dispute the rate of pay, but the fact that the owner did not reward them any more highly than those who worked just one hour. In Jacob's case (Gen. 30), he benefited from his efforts to produce speckled and black sheep. His flocks expanded greatly while Laban's remained fairly static. Laban saw this and accused him of stealing his flocks. The Realtor in the modern American city will evaluate the amount of effort, the expenses of advertising, and the time that she invests in relationship to the quantity of income that is produced by sales. The person who is unsuccessful will likely either quit the business or seek to join force with another Realtor to maximize their effort.

Are workers motivated by role/reward (+1) or by self-defined interests (−1)?

In our society, the faculty member is promoted to higher ranks, the administrator is given greater responsibility, and the outstanding employee becomes a foreman or a supervisor in his or her particular area. The employee or worker is motivated by the anticipation of increasing role responsibility, and with that responsibility, greater economic reward. A hierarchical system defines roles and rewards effective service with both wages and a promotion in role, while at the same time punishing unsatisfactory work with pay reductions or layoffs. Making brick without straw was Pharaoh's way of punishing the Israelites for Moses' request for three days' leave to worship their God in the desert. Egyptians beat the Israelite foremen because their workers failed to meet the quota. Pharaoh rejected the frantic appeal of the foremen out of hand.

In a low grid environment people do not aspire to higher positions; there are none. Jacob had no career goal other than to increase his flocks. The Realtor intends to produce an income that satisfies her personal objectives. Each of them has the opportunity to work within the framework of his or her knowledge, resources, and particular tasks to achieve an objective. The motivation to work comes from an expectation that effort will lead to achievement of one's interests.

Are labor objectives authority-directed (+1) or self-directed (−1)?

The Israelites making bricks worked under the direction of Israelite foremen and Egyptian slave drivers; Pharaoh set the production quotas and the conditions of work. The Egyptians during the time of Joseph worked under his direction to store grain and, in famine years, to sell it back to those from whom it had been taken in taxes. This authority pattern is familiar to those who work in modern industrial and bureaucratic organizations. In all such organizations, supervisors or bosses oversee the work of subordinates. Supervisors organize and direct production in these high grid social contexts.

Low grid, by definition, allows great individual autonomy. Individuals are self-directed in their work activities and are in control of their energy, resources, and productive outcomes. It is possible to have self-directed labor in many different social settings. Jacob was clearly self-directed in his shepherding of Laban's flocks. The cottage weaver in eighteenth-century England, as illustrated by the novel *Silas Marner,* was self-directed in terms of the quantity of goods produced and the amount of time invested to produce those materials. The self-employed Realtor in an American city has the same freedom and self-direction.

Group: Labor Corporately Directed or Individually Directed?

In a strong group social environment individuals have separate work activities, but the group will call or even coerce members to participate in corporately organized production. The group organizes discussion about the viability of a labor project, plans the schedule and details of the work, and requires members to participate. Group elders or leaders assign tasks and responsibilities to various members or collectives within the group. By the very nature of its group focus, corporate labor involves extensive social interaction among the participants; people enjoy being together and often spend as much time in social interaction as they do in work. When the project is completed, the group celebrates its collective achievement and recognizes and rewards the individuals and collectives who have contributed.

A weak group social environment is not devoid of collective activity, but cooperation is focused upon specific individuals and activities rather than upon the organization of a group. The decision to work and the compelling drive to organize an activity group usually falls to individuals. The cohesion of an activity-focused group usually derives from its effective functioning together. Laborers become impatient when social interaction interferes with their personal interests and work activity, and they place little value on interaction around food or rituals of recognition. Their primary preoccupation is to carry out the necessary activities to accomplish the common goal. Once the goal has been achieved the reason for the cooperative no longer exists. This is why such groups dissolve and are rarely formed again in the same configuration. The rewards for participating in weak group cooperative activities are individual. Participants do so with the expectation of personal reward.

Is labor initiated/planned by group (+1) or by individuals acting alone (–1)?

The case of Nehemiah rebuilding the wall of Jerusalem (Neh. 2–5) illustrates the corporate initiating and planning of a public work project. The vision was clearly Nehemiah's, but he could not proceed without a group discussion involving the family leaders, nobles, priests, and officials of the city of Jerusalem. Nehemiah enlisted their support to recruit laborers; they in turn mobilized members of their extended families and kin groups to rebuild the walls. The decision as to when to work, where to work, and what work shall be done lies with the corporate leadership. Group decision making generally takes longer than individual decision making because of the requirements of group process.

The two cases that open the chapter illustrate individually directed work projects. The individual owner of the vineyard recruited day laborers for work on that particular day. He planned the project and employed as many laborers as he deemed useful. Pharaoh supervised a well-developed Egyptian bureaucracy with extensive corporate work projects. He incorporated the Israelites into the group as slaves and forced them to make bricks for the corporate bureaucracy. However, we see no evidence of Pharaoh consulting with other officials; he apparently acted individually, exercising his independent power as ruler of all Egypt.

Is work corporately organized cooperation (+1) or activity-focused cooperation (–1)?

Nehemiah used consensus leadership to plan and organize his work. He and the city leaders assigned sections of the wall and the gates to the heads of families living closest to that section, or to leaders of residential districts outside the city who brought their laborers in to do the work. Because of political pressures against them, they decided to work from dawn to dark and to divide their labor force into two groups, one to work and the other to stand guard (Neh. 4:21–23). When things were not going right (famine; complaints about extortionary interest rates), Nehemiah used heavy persuasion, but still waited for consensus among those who were leaders (Neh. 5:12–13).

The case of the day laborers is activity-focused. A task in the vineyard required more than the owner's usual labor force. The owner acted on his own imperative and delegated the supervision of the work to his foreman. The case of bricks without straw illustrates an independent decision to create hardship for the slaves. Pharaoh instructed the slave drivers to withhold straw and to hold the Hebrew foremen to the same quota of bricks. The bureaucratic structure subordinate to Pharaoh enforced these decisions, and the foremen appealed to Pharaoh after they were beaten.

Are interaction and work comingled (+1) or kept separate activities (–1)?

Nehemiah insisted that all the workers stay inside Jerusalem while they were working on the wall. Since they worked from dawn until dusk, and in groups ordered by neighborhood and kinship, people who were already well acquainted spent day and night together on this project. The division of the work force into two shifts, one on guard duty and the other working on the wall, also permitted people to alternate periods of rest and conversation with hard labor.

Perhaps Pharaoh accused the Israelites of being lazy because they enjoyed working together; whatever time people had for such interaction was absorbed by the new requirement to collect straw. The case of the day laborers tells nothing about the relationships among the laborers during the day. However, when they were paid at the end of the day, those who worked the whole day were aggrieved with the others, who worked fewer hours yet received the same pay; their disappointment reflects an individualist rather than a group expectation. This orientation is quite typical of industrial labor, in which employers pay by the hour, schedule coffee and lunch breaks, and warn workers that they are not to use work time for socializing. Schooling in western societies prepares children for the work place by following the same routine in the classroom; students may socialize at recess and lunch, but are often punished for talking during lessons or for failing to do schoolwork during assigned times. The school day gets longer as the child progresses in grade, until high school usually involves a child in an eight-hour or longer day.

Is labor integrated by eating and ritual symbolism (+1) or by functional utility (–1)?

Neither of the opening cases provides information on these questions. Pharaoh's decision to eliminate straw made Israelite work all business, if it had not been so before. Nehemiah's project was also a high-stress, high-commitment enterprise. However, eating together was apparently part of the program (Neh. 5:17–18), certainly for the leaders and probably for the workers as well. Nehemiah reports that leaders and helpers worked side by side, and they were so busy that they never took off their clothes.

Among the Yap Islanders, people mingle work, conversation, and chewing of betelnut; to work without long periods of conversation is inconceivable. When the work project is of high community value, the organizers provide food and drink for the laborers, and present these with appropriate ceremony.

The American notion of a ten-minute coffee break or a half-hour lunch is alien to Yapese minds. Work in industrial businesses and factories is governed more by the press of the tasks involved (checking out customers in a supermarket or operating a stamping machine) than by the desire of workers to engage with one another in conversation or eating fellowship. Many workers may be socially motivated, but the task does not allow unscheduled interaction.

Are rewards a group-focused payoff (+1) or an individual payoff (−1)?

The case of Nehemiah shows people working out of a strong sense of duty to God and to restoring their honor as a people. Because their collective honor was at stake, they worked without pay, some going into debt and others making major contributions to support the work. When the walls and gates were finished, Nehemiah installed gatekeepers, singers, and Levites to conduct worship and assembled all the people for registration by families. They then began to hold the traditional festivals of worship under the leadership of Ezra (Neh. 8).

In the case of the day laborers the owner paid each individual a day's wage, even though some worked only part of the day. When those who worked all day complained about inequity, the owner justified his payment in terms of the work agreement, a fair day's wage, which he paid to all. The case of bricks without straw is not resolved until the completion of the ten plagues, when Pharaoh releases the Hebrews altogether.

UNION Ltd.: Labor and Productivity
by Donna R. Downes

Utilizing the questions already posed, I have examined the labor relationships of western and African missionaries in UNION Ltd. The data under consideration include office organization and procedures, ministry assignments, and the setting of objectives and calendar for ministry. The space where interaction occurs most frequently is the office, and less frequently the homes of team members. Ministry assignments are carried out in the field and usually by individuals acting alone. Team members support one another, hold one another accountable, and substitute for one another in ministry activities when needed.

The Grid Dimension

The sum of scores show low grid labor values for Africans (–3.5) and westerners (–4.5) (see table 5.1). The UNION Ltd. team organizes labor by the goals and task requirements (–1) of their collective ministries. They set these goals in-country, building upon the giftedness and background of each member. Further, individuals expect other team members to teach in their subject areas for the sake of continuity of ministry when they are on furlough. Yet, Africans and westerners have a few differences that are worth noting.

First, while a team director is a necessity for administrative purposes, the director is first among equals. The westerners view the team director as an equal among equals, while Africans honor the role of director and respect his authority (+.5). David, an African and a former director, stated, "I really think the role of team director is important. He must be a spiritual leader. But he must also be willing to follow others and be just one vote in the decision making process."

A greater difference is evident in the practical objectives set by the team. The westerners determine their weekly schedule by team ministry goals (–1). While Africans commit to ministry goals (–.5), they are less compulsive about their schedules and accomplishments, ordering their time and labor by a standard routine (+.5). Because of their numerous social and extended family obligations, their time is divided among more people than is typical of expatriate missionaries. Western missionaries do not experience these family expectations and obligations.

Despite these differences, the team evaluates its productivity on the basis of goals achieved (–1) and the motivation to work comes from the team's self-defined interest (–1) in serving Christ and building his kingdom. Westerners feel some constituency pressure to achieve in the role of missionary (+.5), but that is not their primary motivation. All members are self-directed (–1) in achieving these labor objectives.

The Group Dimension

The sum of group scores for labor showed a marked difference between westerners (+1) and Africans (+4.5). This assessment is per-

Table 5.1
Labor in UNION Ltd.: Western v. African

High Grid	Low Grid		
Labor by Rule, Role	**Labor by Goal, Task**	**Westerners**	**Africans**
+1 Organized by rule, role assignment	−1 Organized by task/goal	0, −1	.5, −1
+1 Schedule by standard and routine	−1 Schedule by goal considerations	0, −1	.5, −.5
+1 Productivity = time and product rule	−1 Productivity = effort and goals achieved	0, −1	0, −1
+1 Motivation = role and reward	−1 Motivation = self-defined interest	.5, −1	0, −1
+1 Objectives are authority-directed	−1 Objectives are self-directed	0, −1	0, −1
Sum of Grid Variables:		**−4.5**	**−3.5**

Strong Group	Weak Group		
Corporately Directed	**Individually Directed**	**Westerners**	**Africans**
+1 Group-initiated, planned work projects	−1 Individually initiated, planned work projects	1, −.5	1, −.5
+1 Corporately organized cooperation	−1 Activity-focused cooperation	1, 0	1, 0
+1 Interaction/work comingled	−1 Interaction/work separated	0, −1	1, 0
+1 Integration of labor by symbol (food/ritual)	−1 Integration of labor by functional utility	.5, −1	1, 0
+1 Group-focused celebration and reward	−1 Individual-focused reward, payment	1, 0	1, 0
Sum of Group Variables:		**1.0**	**+4.5**

plexing since UNIWORLD prides itself on its team orientation. Westerners and Africans alike who wish to join UNIWORLD must be committed to the principle and practice of team and a high group orientation. Some of the value responses of the UNION Ltd. team are consistent with this orientation. Both Africans and westerners value team initiative to plan work projects (+1). The group works together to organize cooperative work (+1) and celebrates team accomplishments (+1).

But, there are several marked differences. First, westerners prefer separation of work and interaction (−1), while African members resist separation and assert that social interaction is "just as important" (+1) as work activities. Africans expect members to attend their family social affairs (weddings, funerals, graduations). When a westerner is unable to attend, formal "regrets" are a must or work relationships will suffer. Further, Africans see making relationships as important as accomplishing a written set of objectives. For example, the former African director reported his productivity in terms of the number of people contacted rather than the tasks accomplished.

Another difference occurs in the integration of symbolic ritual (and food) (+1) into work activities. The African leader saw any cause, however small, as something to celebrate, and he organized goat roasts, ceremonies, and awards for team accomplishments. The westerners see food and ritual as less important (+.5), even bothersome at times. The west-

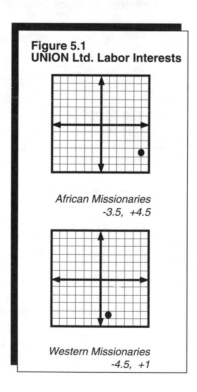

Figure 5.1
UNION Ltd. Labor Interests

African Missionaries
-3.5, +4.5

Western Missionaries
-4.5, +1

erners view task as more important than relationship and prefer labor integrated around functional utility (−1). Even their strong commitment to meet together for group prayer seems rooted in "strategy-effective" rather than "relationship-effective" values.

Conclusion

While both westerners and the Africans have embraced the egalitarian team game (fig. 5.1), it is clear that they do not play by the same rules. In fact, the group score for westerners shows a strong leaning toward the individualist cosmology. The Africans are solidly committed to the egalitarian game. By way of explanation, the strong group ideals of UNIWORLD fit well with African notions of extended family. The African director, David, praised UNIWORLD's family approach to ministry. In contrast, in spite of UNIWORLD's team value, westerners approach labor and productivity as an individualist game, which they have practiced for most of their schooling and work careers. While UNIWORLD team ideology attracts them to a ministry group, they are motivated strongly by personal interests and values that focus on task and individual calling.

Research Questions 5.1
Grid and Labor Interests

High Grid	Low Grid
+1 *Organized by rule, role assignment.* Do people organize their work in terms of clearly defined roles to which individuals are assigned (a job title and job description)? Can people outline a series of written or unwritten rules that govern the practice of a particular role? or	−1 *Organized by task /goal requirements.* Is work organized by the objective requirements of the task, and the laborers change their activities as the tasks change?
+1 *Schedule by standard/routine.* To what extent is the time of work determined by social rules? How is the routine of work established by calendar and daily schedule? or	−1 *Schedule by goal considerations.* To what extent is the time of work a product of environmental concerns, consideration of work objective, and disposition of the workers? How variable is the work routine in response to such considerations?
+1 *Productivity equals time and product rule.* To what extent is productivity linked directly to time limits or product quotas? How are these limits measured? or	−1 *Productivity equals effort and goals achieved.* To what extent do people measure productivity in terms of effort expended and goals achieved? How do they evaluate whether the products have been worth the expenditure?
+1 *Motivation equals role and reward.* To what extent is the worker motivated by promises of promotion in role and increased economic compensation or by threat of punitive action? or	−1 *Motivation equals self-defined interests.* Is the worker motivated primarily from personal interest, self-direction, or basic subsistence goals?
+1 *Objectives are authority-directed.* To what extent do institutional authorities direct labor activities, and people who do not work set objectives for those who do? or	−1 *Objectives are self-directed.* Are the expected outcomes of labor defined and the labor directed by those who do the work?

Research Questions 5.2
Group and Labor Interests

Strong Group	Weak Group
+1 *Group-initiated, planned work projects.* Are projects initiated by group consensus or majority decisions? Are individuals drafted to work in corporate work projects? Must individuals consult with group elders or leaders when they need the help of others for a domestic or public work project? or	−1 *Individually initiated, planned work projects.* Are work activity groups recruited by individuals drawing upon personal networks or institutional authority? Is the planning of domestic or public labor projects and recruitment of supporting laborers left to the persons initiating or supervising them?
+1 *Corporately organized cooperation.* Are cooperative work projects organized by majority or consensus leaders? Do they seek consensus on activities and schedule? Do they assign tasks and responsibilities according to group tradition and interests? or	−1 *Activity-focused cooperation.* Is cooperative work focused on an activity agenda? Is planning primarily in the hands of entrepreneurial individuals? Is the work contracted out to partners in such a way as to profit the cooperating parties?
+1 *Interaction/work comingled.* To what extent are relationships between people working together as important as the work activity? How is the activity organized to promote social interaction as well as the emphasis on work? or	−1 *Interaction/work separated.* To what extent do the parties emphasize work at the expense of social interaction? How is the activity organized to constrain and separate social interaction and promote the work activity above social interests?
+1 *Integration of labor by symbol (food/ritual).* Is cooperative work facilitated by social activities such as corporate eating and drinking, rituals to begin work, or other symbolic action as part of the work process? or	−1 *Integration of labor by functional utility.* Is cooperative work all business, in which people focus on task and cooperate with others only to the extent required by the technical demands of the work?
+1 *Group-focused celebration and reward.* Is celebration at the culmination of the project a corporate affair? Do people gain their reward primarily by fulfilling their duty to the group? Does the group distribute shares or benefits publicly from the labor? or	−1 *Individual-focused celebration and payoff.* Is celebration a private affair or an individual marking a project completion as a personal achievement? Are payoffs private, individual, and according to terms of agreement or contract?

Exchange Interests and Cultural Bias

Case of Esther and Mordecai

So the king and Haman went to dine with Queen Esther, and as they were drinking wine on that second day, the king again asked, "Queen Esther, what is your petition? It will be given you. What is your request? Even up to half the kingdom, it will be granted."

Then Queen Esther answered, "If I have found favor with you, O king, and if it pleases your majesty, grant me my life—this is my petition. And spare my people—this is my request. For I and my people have been sold for destruction and slaughter and annihilation. If we had merely been sold as male and female slaves, I would have kept quiet, because no such distress would justify disturbing the king."

King Xerxes asked Queen Esther, "Who is he? Where is the man who has dared to do such thing?"

Esther said, "The adversary and enemy is this vile Haman." (Esther 7:1–6)

Case of Leah and Rachel

During wheat harvest, Reuben went out into the fields and found some mandrake plants, which he brought to his mother Leah. Rachel said to Leah, "Please give me some of your son's mandrakes."

But she said to her, "Wasn't it enough that you took away my husband? Will you take my son's mandrakes too?"

"Very well," Rachel said, "he can sleep with you tonight in return for your son's mandrakes."

So when Jacob came in from the fields that evening, Leah went out to meet him. "You must sleep with me," she said. "I have hired you with my son's mandrakes." So he slept with her that night. (Gen. 30:14–16)

Reciprocity, Redistribution, and Market Exchange

Anthropologists look at the issues of exchange in society from the perspective of the concepts of reciprocity, redistribution, and market exchange. Marshall Sahlins (1972) has clarified the concepts of balanced, generalized, and negative reciprocity as they are played out in subsistence economies. *Balanced reciprocity* refers to the kind of exchange in which individuals keep count of the transactions in relationship to one another, and a careful sense of debt and obligation is recognized by both parties to the transaction. *Generalized reciprocity* is the method of exchange in which people engage in a continuous series of transactions for which no particular balance sheet is kept. This reciprocity is somewhat open-ended and the important dimension of exchange is the continuous expectation of sharing. *Negative reciprocity* refers to a pattern of exchange in which one person loses and the other person gains through the transaction. This type of exchange is characterized by a differential of power in which one individual in the transaction utilizes that power for personal gain.

Collection and redistribution is another important social process for exchange. A centralized leader initiates the collection of goods or calls for people to gather for collective labor. The central leader coordinates the collection of food or other goods produced by members of the society and then organizes the redistribution of goods in ways that are acceptable to the members. Oftentimes redistribution is in the form of public feasts or public ceremony in which people consume the food contributed. On other occasions the distribution may be to specified individuals within the social setting who have rights to certain portions of the goods.

Anthropologists use the concept of market exchange to classify those activities in which individuals either barter or use money to conduct economic transactions in a public marketplace. When individuals produce a surplus of food or other material goods, market exchange provides a means of circulating surplus to others who need it. This pattern of exchange usually involves regional distribution of materials and middlemen who act as merchants or brokers for the people who produce in that region.

Anthropologists have linked these types of exchange to a typology of societies into band, tribe, chiefdom, and state. They associate generalized reciprocity with band-level, hunting and gathering societies, and balanced reciprocity with tribal societies that have some degree of centralized control and agricultural production. Collection and redistribution and market societies produce agricultural surplus, which leads to political integration, either as chiefdoms or as peasant societies and primitive states.

While this system of classification in the anthropological literature is useful for understanding broad political and economic differences in society and culture, it does not provide a systematic understanding of cultural differences, nor of the social games and the value orientations derived from social structure. We shall use grid and group analysis to differentiate between different types of exchange games employed at all levels of economic and political integration.

Grid: Superior/Inferior, Prescribed or Instrumental, Negotiated?

The general characteristic of high grid exchange relationships is the prevalence of superior/inferior relationship. The social hierarchy pervades the social environment, and nearly every relationship involves some dimension of high and low exchange. Reciprocity and redistribution take on distinctive features in the high grid social environment. The high/low structure produces relationships of balanced complementarity, so that the low contribute labor, respect, and political support, and the high reciprocate with material goods and other benefits of patronage. Tribute and taxation are the common forms of collection, and rulers redistribute selectively to subordinates or to projects for the "public good," which usually reinforce the power and privilege of the hierarchy. Even market relationships are regulated in the high grid environment, with bureaucrats controlling prices, setting trade boundaries and tariffs, regulating or establishing monopolies, and requiring license to the marketplace. The structuring of relationships is prescribed in the total framework of the social structure.

Low grid social environments are characterized by an openness and flexibility of structure. Individuals negotiate reciprocal relationships, subject to renegotiation as circumstances and interests change. Such relationships may range from carefully negotiated balanced exchange partnerships to generalized, open credit, open trust. Entrepreneurs must attract investors rather than rely on the high grid mechanisms of taxation or tribute. Collection of goods and capital can be sustained only by promise of return on the investment, so that entrepreneurs may garner the support of others, but at the cost of specific commitments for returns. Redistribution occurs in the form of shares of profit or other negotiated repayment to the investor. Market exchange is open and unregulated; people trade, buy, and sell, seeking the price and profit that the market will sustain at any given time.

The essence of low grid is freedom for individuals to choose the kinds and quantity of relationships, and to negotiate the substance exchanged in each. People seek relationships that have some economic or social contribution to make to their personal or family interests—relationships of instrumental value. They evaluate these relationships over time and extend and strengthen those deemed beneficial and withdraw from those that cost more or contribute little to their personal interest.

The following questions provide diagnostic criteria that one may apply to the analysis of exchange activities.

Are exchange relationships superior/inferior (+1) or instrumental (−1) in character?

In the case study of Esther that opens the chapter, relationships between all the participants are relationships between superior and inferior. Esther as queen is inferior to the king; as adopted daughter she is inferior to Mordecai; and as queen she is superior to Haman, the king's official. Esther began the exchange by asking if the king and Haman would come to a dinner she had prepared for them. The king recognized that Esther wanted something more, but agreed to accept her invitation to dinner and to bring Haman as his guest. Haman was, of course, ecstatic to be invited to dinner with the king and the queen, seeing an opportunity to enhance his prestige and honor in the kingdom. Throughout the Book of Esther, Haman sought to enhance his personal prestige and to increase his power as the most intimate official of the king.

The second case study, of Leah and Rachel, illustrates quite a different set of relationships. Rachel is the wife of Jacob, but shows none of the deference that Esther does toward her husband. Rachel complained openly to him that she had no children and demanded that he do something about it. Although Leah is the elder of the two sisters her age does not seem to give her any advantage in their relationship. Rachel negotiated with Jacob to give her a child through her maidservant; Leah countered in the competition with the same strategy. The exchanges that occurred between them were negotiated exchanges, with each individual attempting to gain the advantage for her or his interest in opposition to the one with whom she or he was competing.

Is asking humiliating (+1) or is asking negotiating (−1)?

In a superior/inferior relationship, to ask for something is to confess that one has a lack that someone who is higher can fulfill. Therefore, the act of asking is to state publicly that one is inferior to the person hearing the request.

When Mordecai asked Esther to plead on behalf of her people to the king, she was extremely reluctant to do so. She told Mordecai that she had not been invited into the king's presence for nearly a month and to enter into his presence without invitation could mean death. If the king was in a good mood, he might extend his scepter to her, rather than demand her execution. Afraid for her own safety, Esther resisted Mordecai's request. In the portion of the text included at the opening of the chapter, Esther takes a humble posture before the king, showing deference and honor toward him.

In the case of Leah and Rachel, they show no humility in the exchanges reported in this incident. Each person takes a negotiating posture. Rachel demanded that her husband give her children, by her handmaiden if she could not bear a child herself. Jacob agreed and Rachel gained two children by her maiden, Bilhah. Rachel then negotiated for mandrakes that Leah's son Reuben had found in the desert. Leah counterbargained for access to her husband again. Asking and giving is a matter of bargaining among them; they are competitors.

Is giving structured by duty of role (+1) or by competition for profit (–1)?

An earlier incident in the story of Esther, Mordecai, and King Xerxes illustrated the importance of duty in structuring the giving relationship. The king had difficulty sleeping after the first evening banquet with Esther. He asked for one of his servants to bring in the chronicles of his kingdom. In reading through the chronicles he discovered that Mordecai had performed an invaluable service to him by exposing two gatekeepers who were plotting his assassination. The king called in his servant and asked if Mordecai had been repaid or honored for this deed of service to the king. When he discovered that he had done nothing the king was immediately pricked in conscience and called in Haman to ask how he should repay someone who had given outstanding service to him. Apparently the king was motivated by a sense of law, duty, and honor in his relationship to his people. Throughout the Book of Esther these themes are repeated. In the portion of the story recorded at the opening of this chapter, the king also demonstrates a sense of duty to his queen, Esther. He is deeply angered that Haman should plot against his queen and her people, and when he finds Haman violating the rules of propriety with regard to his wife, Haman's death is certain. King Xerxes acts consistently within his character as a man of law and justice.

For Rachel, Leah, and Jacob, the issue of law and justice never entered their discussions. Each sister sought honor through the children that she bore for her husband. Leah won in this competition, having many children and giving Jacob children by her handmaiden, Zilpah. Rachel, even though she was loved by her husband, became increasingly distraught until she had children who brought honor to her name. Rachel gave her handmaiden to Jacob to obtain a child in her name. Leah instructed her son Reuben to give Rachel the mandrakes in return for sexual access to her husband. Giving between these two women was motivated by personal advantage and profit that they desired from the relationship.

Do debtors repay with service or honor (+1) or in kind with interest (–1)?

King Xerxes repaid Mordecai for exposing the traitors by dressing him in a royal robe and giving him one of the king's horses with the king's insignia on its forehead. Then Haman led him through the city declaring the king's honor before the public. In return for loyalty and information, the king gave Mordecai public recognition and honor. He repaid his debt with a reward of a different kind than the service rendered.

Rachel asked Leah for mandrakes, which they believed to be a fertility drug. Rachel hoped that by eating the mandrakes she might become fertile and bear children. Leah, knowing Rachel's objective, demanded access to her husband again. They agreed to the exchange, and each received what she desired. Both became pregnant and bore a child to Jacob. While it is difficult to calculate the value of these exchanges, Leah gained as much if not more than her sister from the mandrakes.

Is exchange value prescribed (+1) or negotiated (–1)?

While the specific exchanges that occurred between Esther and Xerxes and between Xerxes and Mordecai were unique, the laws of the Medes and the Persians prescribed all of the activities surrounding these exchanges. Xerxes clearly felt it his duty to reward Mordecai for his significant service. Understanding that he had been deceived by Haman, Xerxes acted to empower Esther and her people to resist the decree allowing Persians to execute Jews, authorizing the Jewish people to fight with all of their might against their enemies on the appointed day (Esther 8:8–13). Haman was a doomed man; the king had no choice other than to execute him because of his reprehensible actions toward the queen. Hung on the gallows that he had erected to execute Mordecai, Haman received a fitting reward for his betrayal of the king's interest.

The case of Rachel and Leah is remarkable by the extent of negotiation that passes among the participants. Rachel's despair at having no children led her to offer her servant girl to her husband to bear children on her behalf. Rachel hoped through her servant girl to gain honor and to remove the stigma of her barrenness. She gave up what had become her exclusive right to her husband in return for the hope of having children. Apparently she used Jacob's love for her to keep him from normal marriage relationships with Leah. However, she relinquished this in return for the mandrakes and the hope of having children of her own. She renegotiated the value of her rights to her husband on at least two occasions. Both Leah and Rachel gave up their exclusive sexual rights as wives to their handmaidens because of their competitive interest in outdoing one another through the bearing of children.

Group: Corporately Regulated or Individually Regulated?

In a strong group social environment the distinction between outsider and insider is crucial for the regulation of economic exchanges. When members of a group engage in exchanges with one another, the particular codes of group obligation and consideration hold members accountable to one another. Generally, sharing and generosity are highly valued among members of a group, and the group defines specific expectations for such exchange among members.

Exchanges with outsiders are regulated in significantly different ways. When a member of a group engages in a transaction with an outsider that has no significant social implications for the group, the individual is generally free to negotiate an exchange that is in one's interest. However, when an exchange with an outsider incurs obligations of one's group and is considered to represent the membership of the group to the membership of a competing group, then significant regulation of those exchanges occurs.

The definition of outsider may also vary or may take complex multiple forms. In a social context where clans or villages have strong identities, other clans and other villages are competitors with whom one may incur group debt. For example, Aukaners in Surinam consider the interest of their clan and village, as well as their personal interest, when relating to members of other clans and villages. But, when they meet government officials, members of other ethnic groups, such as Hindustani, Javanese, or Carib Indians, they are free to negotiate openly.

In a weak group social environment, people make no distinction between insiders and outsiders since group is an insignificant variable.

Exchanges with others occur on an individual basis and are regulated by the considerations of individual interest. While people form relationships of interdependence and occasional activity groups, those groups are short lived, and as such, members gain little collective power to coerce others to conform to a group norm.

Do members calculate social gain/debt (+1) or economic gain/cost (−1)?

In the case study of Esther the king refers to the law of the Medes and the Persians on several occasions. King Xerxes' membership within the royal family and lineage of the Medes and the Persians bound him to a long history and custom of group law. When Xerxes discovered that he had approved the law to exterminate all the Jewish people he was distraught but could do nothing to change it. To reverse his decision would undermine his authority and the support of the people whom he served as king. However, Xerxes also recognized Esther's commitment and loyalty to her own people and his great debt to Mordecai who had served him so well in the court. By authorizing the Jews as a people to defend themselves against others who sought to destroy them, Xerxes highlighted the group nature of the conflict between Mordecai and Haman.

The case of Leah and Rachel shows a much greater concern with personal gain and loss than with collective gain or loss. Although they were members of one family, they engaged in intense competitive relationships with one another. The unity of family was a lower value than the respective honor of each. While honor is not an economic gain or loss, Leah contributed mandrakes to Rachel to further her personal interest. The next chapter in the Book of Genesis shows Jacob negotiating in a similar fashion with Laban, his father-in-law, with regard to specific material interest. Jacob told Laban that he was tired of being exploited, and wanted to take his family and strike out on his own. Laban bargained with Jacob, pleading with him to stay, divining that Jacob was the source of his great prosperity. Economic gain was the central focus of their discussion and Jacob agreed to stay longer in return for a greater share of Laban's flocks.

Do leaders minimize group debt (+1) or maximize personal debt (−1)?

The case study of Esther focuses on the interpersonal rivalries of Mordecai and Haman. Haman's hatred stemmed from Mordecai's identity as a Jew, and his refusal to bow to Haman. Haman apparently had the support of others in his opposition to the Jews and used his advantaged position with the king to pass the edict against them. Haman plotted carefully to eliminate Mordecai and the Jews without jeopardizing his own or his family's interests. At the encouragement of his family and friends he erected a gallows on which to hang Mordecai. When he came to the king to ask for permission, he received the stunning instructions to lead Mordecai through the streets proclaiming honor and the king's deepest appreciation for Mordecai's service. At this point Haman's family and friends recognized that he and they were in jeopardy with the king. Haman's family and friends allowed Haman to be sacrificed on his own gallows, and in spite of their opposition to the Jews, retreated from this agenda that Haman had inspired.

Rachel's behavior was much less cautious than that of Haman and Esther. She used her most valued relationship, that with her husband, Jacob, to advance her personal interest in competition with her sister, Leah. Jacob did the same in his relationship with his own family and with Rachel's family. Offering a hot meal to his famished brother in exchange for his birthright and then cheating the same brother out of his father's blessing were part of Jacob's strategy to get ahead. He indebted himself to labor fourteen years for his father-in-law, Laban, to obtain Rachel as his wife. Laban, who knew that his prosperity was due to Jacob's presence, relinquished all the spotted animals in his flocks, just to keep Jacob around for a longer period of time. Exercising personal debt to get ahead came easily to these people.

Is exchange public and symbolic (+1) or is exchange private and material (−1)?

Each of the significant transactions of the case study of Esther were conducted in a public arena. Xerxes rewarded Mordecai publicly for his service, granting to him the king's robe, the king's horse, and a parade through the streets, declaring the king's indebtedness to him. Haman was hanged publicly for his betrayal of the king's interest, and Esther was granted her request publicly by the formal declaration of a law of the Medes and Persians authorizing the Jews to resist all those who would attempt to kill them.

In contrast, the exchanges between Rachel and Jacob, Rachel and Leah, and Jacob and Laban were apparently personal and private exchanges. We do not read of any formal ceremony in which Rachel gave Bilhah to Jacob, as was the case when Jacob married Rachel and Leah. This was a private transaction in which Jacob had marital relations with Bilhah. Likewise, the exchange of the mandrakes and the restoration of marital relationships for Leah were personal and private matters. Laban also apparently negotiated with Jacob in private with regard to his continuing service to Laban as supervisor of his livestock.

Are transactions negotiated privately for parity (+1) or openly for profit (−1)?

In spite of the fact that the major transactions between the participants in the case of Esther were announced publicly, they conducted negotiations leading to the exchanges in private. Esther invited the king and Haman to dinner on two separate occasions to discuss these matters with them. Haman arranged for the decree to eliminate the Jews through a private conversation with King Xerxes. The king decided upon a particular reward for Mordecai through a private conversation with Haman. Mordecai used the position that Esther had as queen to gain equal treatment for the Jewish people in the kingdom. The contest between Haman and Mordecai became public only at its conclusion. All of the strategic moves were conducted privately and secretly so that even the king was not aware of the intrigues.

Since the exchanges between Rachel and Leah, and Jacob and Laban, were individual exchanges, they had no group interests to protect. Each bargained openly with the other, seeking to gain advantages and to serve their personal interests inasmuch as was possible.

Is sharing and generosity highly valued (+1) or is self-interest expected (−1)?

Xerxes was disappointed with himself when he recognized that he had not rewarded Mordecai for his service. Even given Haman's selfish bent, he also recognized the importance of extending generous rewards. Perhaps a better case study to illustrate the high value for generosity is that of Nehemiah and his colleagues rebuilding the wall in Jerusalem. Nehemiah publicly reprimanded the leaders of the families and the city of Jerusalem for loaning to their fellow men with interest. After he rebuked them, he demanded that they loan to people as they had need and not claim their property as security or payment for these loans. Nehemiah had no problem with charging interest to outsiders, but he argued they should be helping and sharing with one another rather than getting rich at the expense of the less fortunate in the group.

In the dialogues between Jacob and Laban, Jacob and Esau, and Rachel and Leah, self-interest was expected. Each person was aware that the other sought an advantage. While they were members of one extended family and respected one another as kinsmen, their expectations and actions reject generosity in favor of personal gain or advantage.

UNION Ltd.: Exchange Interests
by Donna R. Downes

Utilizing the questions posed, I have examined the exchange interests of western and African missionaries in UNION Ltd. I have restricted my analysis to the organizational environment of the team, although all members participate in exchange relations with outsiders. All members negotiate prices of purchased items in the public market—from a head of lettuce to a postage stamp to an automobile. However, these same people expect that exchanges within the group follow values of fairness, generosity, parity, and attitudes of love and forgiveness.

The Grid Dimension

While the African team members (−2), like the westerners (−1.5), appear to operate with low grid values for exchange, there are some differences (see table 6.1). First, both reject the idea of inferior-superior relationships and base their exchanges on negotiation (instrumental relationship, −1), yet Africans seek parity with westerners in reference to pay and benefits packages and team assignments (+.5). The westerners seem equally concerned that housing, benefits, and insurance be the same for members.

Most internal exchanges, however, are negotiated individually. It is common for members to exchange gifts and to buy and sell property. For example, one member bought a set of children's books and tapes from another at a fair price, negotiated between them. Members exchange resources to meet the needs or wants of each family, without reference to social status. The exchange values were fully negotiable (−1) for all.

Westerners see asking as humiliating (+1) and somehow demeaning—even in times of sickness or loss (e.g., theft). Africans, sensitive about relying on westerners, have expressed reluctance to ask (+.5), yet they generally see asking as negotiating (−1). This difference has caused much misunderstanding on the team, particularly when Africans ask for items westerners deem impractical. The Africans are in effect negotiating, but their colleagues judge them as poor stewards and careless with the team's resources. For example, African team members suggested that a surplus of funds be spent either on increased ministry opportunities, or distributed to personal car accounts for repairs. The westerners balked, and

91

Table 6.1
Exchange in UNION Ltd.: Western v. African Missionaries

High Grid		Low Grid			
Superior/Inferior, Prescribed		Instrumental, Negotiated		Westerners	Africans
+1	Superior/inferior relationships	−1	Instrumental relationship	0, −1	.5, −1
+1	Asking is humiliating	−1	Asking is negotiating	1, 0	.5, −1
+1	Giving is structured by duty of role	−1	Giving is structured for profit	1, −.5	.5, −1
+1	Repaying includes service, respect, kind	−1	Repaying in kind, with interest	0, −1	1, −.5
+1	Exchange value is prescribed	−1	Exchange value is negotiated	0, −1	0, −1
	Sum of Grid Variables:			**−1.5**	**−2.0**

Strong Group		Weak Group			
Corporately Regulated		Individually Regulated		Westerners	Africans
+1	Calculate social gain/debt	−1	Calculate economic gain/cost	.5, −.5	1, 0
+1	Minimize group debt	−1	Maximize personal debt	1, 0	1, −1
+1	Exchange is public, symbolic	−1	Exchange is private, material	.5, −.5	1, 0
+1	Negotiate privately for parity	−1	Negotiate openly for profit	1, 0	1, 0
+1	Sharing/generosity highly valued	−1	Self-interest is expected	1, 0	1, 0
	Sum of Group Variables:			**+3.0**	**+4.0**

proposed saving for future unknown contingencies. Each viewed the other's motives with mistrust.

Giving creates another area of team difference. Westerners deem giving a biblical duty (+1). Africans acknowledge duty (+.5), but also calculate future political or social profit (−1). Africans remind the team of the social status it will receive as a result of their giving, while the westerners play down such instrumental reasons, even though they use them (−.5). For example, an African leader achieved a favorable decision for the team by praying with a government official and visiting his wife in the hospital. The westerners on the team were a bit embarrassed by the means, but thrilled at the results. The Africans were proud of their achievement.

The Group Dimension

The sum of scores for group values shows close similarity of Africans (+4) and westerners (+3) (see table 6.1). Both seek to minimize group debt (+1) and to keep the group's reputation in good social standing. They negotiate most intragroup exchanges privately for parity (+1), so that no one member gains status over another. All place high value on sharing (+1) with one another and with outsiders. All reject negotiations with team members for personal profit or self-interest. A former team member from Ethiopia bargained with teammates as he would with anyone in the open market; other teammates felt he was defrauding them. This man eventually joined another mission because he could not conform to group expectations for exchange and generosity.

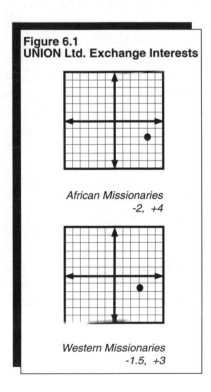

**Figure 6.1
UNION Ltd. Exchange Interests**

*African Missionaries
-2, +4*

*Western Missionaries
-1.5, +3*

Despite these similarities, African team members (+1) are more likely than westerners (+.5) to calculate social gain or loss as a result of giving. The westerners view the team's financial negotiations with the national churches as strictly monetary (−.5) or exchanges in kind for which they seek parity. By way of illustration, the team funds its own transportation, provides materials and teachers, and pays for the meeting room for a pastors' conference. They in turn expect pastors to fund their own transportation and to arrange and pay for their living expenses and food. While westerners see such arrangements as business agreements, the Africans treat them as issues of social status. The more the national church can provide, the more power it has in making decisions about the conference.

A second area of difference is the symbolism involving exchange agreements. African team members publicize the results of exchanges (+1) to raise the team's status and reputation in the eyes of the local church. Embarrassed by such agreements, westerners (+.5) keep exchanges private (−.5) lest someone take advantage of them.

Africans easily maximize personal debt (−1) while the westerners (0) avoid it. The two African team members have loan indebtedness to the team of over five thousand dollars U.S. for the purchase of property and for family hospital expenses. Both loans conferred higher status to these men within their social spheres of influence. Westerners, by contrast, rarely keep more than one hundred dollars in debt to the team and are not understanding of the Africans' willingness to incur high debt.

Conclusions

Africans and westerners both play the egalitarian game in reference to their economic exchanges within the team (fig. 6.1). While some differences do exist, they stem in large part from the fact that the Africans must play several social games concurrently or risk loss of social status. Westerners also must be able to operate well in other social environments outside of UNION Ltd., but the national society allows leeway for cultural differences and mistakes. They can, therefore, afford to operate more in accordance with UNION Ltd.'s organizational culture, while African team members have much more at stake in every negotiation by virtue of their identity as Africans.

Research Questions 6.1
Grid and Exchange Interests

High Grid	Low Grid
+1 *Superior/inferior relationships.* To what extent is the social structure characterized by prescribed superior/inferior relationships between which exchange of goods and services transpire? or	−1 *Instrumental relationships.* To what extent are the relationships of exchange left to the negotiation of individuals and/or to instrumental ties such as middlemen, brokers, or trading partners?
+1 *Asking is humiliating.* To what extent is asking for material goods or services a humiliating experience for a person in this social environment? Does the act of asking for goods or services signal a role of humility and vulnerability? or	−1 *Asking is negotiating.* To what extent is the potential giver an equal competitor, and is the act of asking a negotiable demand? Does the act of asking for goods or services signal the opening of the process of negotiation?
+1 *Giving is structured by duty of role.* Is giving structured around duty attributed to one's position? Is giving a strategy used to achieve status or to gain favor? Does the denial of a request diminish the stature of the giver in the eyes of the public? or	−1 *Giving is structured by competition for profit.* Is the structure of giving framed around competition and the potential for profit in some future exchange? What material, social, or political advantage might the giver obtain at a future time?
+1 *Repaying in service, respect, different kind.* To what extent does payment include service, respect, prestige, or gifts of a different kind from that received? or	−1 *Repaying in kind with interest.* Do participants expect payment of similar or equivalent material value? Must debt obligations be repaid with interest?
+1 *Exchange value is prescribed.* To what extent is the value of goods or services prescribed in the social structure? or	−1 *Exchange value is negotiated.* Are the values of commodities open to negotiation?

Research Questions 6.2
Group and Exchange Interests

Strong Group	Weak Group
+1 *Calculate social gain/debt.* Do group members calculate the social gain or debt when engaging in transactions with outsiders? Are there different kinds of outsiders? If so, how do these differences affect economic exchanges? or	*−1* *Calculate economic gain/cost.* To what extent is asking, giving, and repayment restricted to material considerations of gain and loss? Do participants minimize the social factors in economic exchange?
+1 *Minimize group debt.* Are group leaders cautious about putting members in debt to outsiders? Are they careful to manage indebtedness and have plans to erase debt in a timely manner? or	*−1* *Maximize personal debt.* To what extent are individuals willing to extend their personal debt to the maximum possible as part of their economic exchanges?
+1 *Exchange is public, symbolic.* To what extent is intergroup exchange a public activity and to what extent does it confer symbolic meaning and significance upon the participants? or	*−1* *Exchange is private, material.* Do individuals generally conduct their business on a one-to-one private basis? Is ceremony considered a nuisance and an impediment to good business?
+1 *Negotiate privately for parity.* Are public transactions negotiated privately so that the competing groups exchange in parity with one another? or	*−1* *Negotiate openly for profit.* Do individuals negotiate openly the cost of goods, loans, or the value of an item to be exchanged?
+1 *Sharing/generosity highly valued.* Is sharing and generosity highly valued both for exchanges with members of one's group and with outsiders? To what extent is the concept of generosity extended to other ethnic groups and foreigners? or	*−1* *Self-interest is expected.* To what extent do participants in an economic exchange expect self-interest on the part of the participating parties?

Family Authority and Cultural Bias

Case of David

Now Jesse said to his son David, "Take this ephah of roasted grain and these ten loaves of bread for your brothers and hurry to their camp. Take along these ten cheeses to the commander of their unit. See how your brothers are and bring back some assurance from them. They are with Saul and all the men of Israel in the Valley of Elah, fighting against the Philistines."

Early in the morning David left the flock with a shepherd, loaded up and set out, as Jesse had directed. He reached the camp as the army was going out to its battle positions, shouting the war cry. . . . David left his things with the keeper of supplies, ran to the battle lines and greeted his brothers. . . .

David asked the men standing near him, "What will be done for the man who kills this Philistine and removes this disgrace from Israel? Who is this uncircumcised Philistine that he should defy the armies of the living God?" . . .

When Eliab, David's oldest brother, heard him speaking with the men, he burned with anger at him and asked, "Why have you come down here? And with whom did you leave those few sheep in the desert? I know how conceited you are and how wicked your heart is; you came down only to watch the battle." (1 Sam. 17:17–28)

Case of Dinah and Shechem

Now Dinah, the daughter Leah had borne to Jacob, went out to visit the women of the land. When Shechem son of

97

Hamor the Hivite, the ruler of that area, saw her, he took her and violated her. His heart was drawn to Dinah daughter of Jacob, and he loved the girl and spoke tenderly to her. And Shechem said to his father Hamor, "Get me this girl as my wife."

When Jacob heard that his daughter Dinah had been defiled, his sons were in the fields with his livestock; so he kept quiet about it until they came home. . . . Now Jacob's sons had come in from the fields as soon as they heard what had happened. They were filled with grief and fury. . . .

But Hamor said to them, "My son Shechem has his heart set on your daughter. Please give her to him as his wife. . . ." Jacob's sons replied . . . "We will give our consent to you on one condition only: that you become like us by circumcising all your males." . . .

All the men who went out of the city gate agreed with Hamor and his son Shechem, and every male in the city was circumcised.

Three days later, while all of them were still in pain, two of Jacob's sons, Simeon and Levi, Dinah's brothers, took their swords and attacked the unsuspecting city, killing every male. . . .

Then Jacob said to Simeon and Levi, "You have brought trouble on me by making me a stench to the Canaanites and Perizzites, the people living in this land. We are few in number, and if they join forces against me and attack me, I and my household will be destroyed." (Gen. 34)

Households as Domestic Groups

In many societies, household and family are synonymous and the theme of kinship is as important as the notion of economic cooperation and support. People define appropriate sex and age roles for the division of labor, establish expectations and patterns for economic cooperation, and organize kinship relationships and activities for the socialization of a new generation within households. Household members make significant decisions such as whom to marry, where to build a house, how to support the education of children, and whether to cooperate with others. People in households work together for cooking, eating, entertaining, and recreation, and they share common space, and shelter, and financial resources.

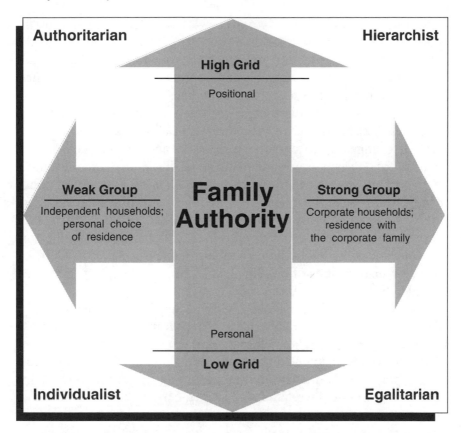

While households are present everywhere, scholars have discovered that these domestic groups vary significantly from society to society and even within a particular society. Criteria for determining household membership may range over a broad level of activities including co-residence, cooperative work, shared meals, and financial or other reciprocal exchanges among members. In western societies the concept of household typically signifies a place where people live together under a common roof. This definition fails in other areas of the world, particularly in the tropics, where "living inside" is strange behavior. Yet household membership is frequently synonymous with co-residence of some kind— where members share a residential compound or a common cooking hearth together. Cultural preferences for co-residence may be modified by economic necessity and the particular life careers of individual members; it is possible for family members to cooperate effectively without co-residing over extended periods of time.

Richard Wilk and Robert Netting (1984) have attempted to clarify the problem of defining households by focusing on what households do. They propose that households are organized around activities that include production, distribution, transmission, reproduction, and co-residence. Production includes housekeeping and domestic labor as well as farming, hunting, fishing, herding, wage work, and commercial activities possible in the broad range of world cultures. Household distribution focuses on the exchanges that occur among members and between households. Members of households generally pool some, if not all, of their resources to support the diverse needs of members of all ages. They differ significantly, however, in the degree to which they control resources corporately or as autonomous individual participants. The transmission or inheritance of property is often controlled by or within the membership of a domestic group. Household members frequently make the decisions regarding distributions of buildings, land, personal property, and other considerations of inheritance.

Households are also organized with the specific objective of social reproduction—the bearing of young, and the training of those young to become fully competent adult members of the society. The broad scope of activities subsumed under social reproduction include marriage, customary practices around childbirth and naming, child training and discipline regarding social relationships, and the transmission of adult economic roles and responsibilities. Children learn in the household the basic social and political skills for survival in the larger social world. They also learn strategies and customary practice for coping with illness and death. Because of this very broad social agenda, households are defensive structures, organized to reproduce themselves, to serve the interests of members, and to defend themselves from encroachments of outsiders.

The factors of grid and group are as evident in domestic life as they are in larger-scale economic and social relations. Through grid/group analysis we may explain how the structure of domestic groups varies between cultures and even in the same culture, and we may identify which of the five social game prototypes provides the basis for household activities.

For example, the eating practices of urban and rural American households reflect distinctive social conditions. In urban America, people may share a common house but have very diverse economic activities upon which members depend for income and subsistence. Rather than share the produce of their common efforts, they pool financial resources and organize themselves in a division of labor to provide for mutual subsistence needs. In some households those activities may be highly individualistic; in others, a division of labor may coordinate activities for the collective whole. In an urban household where parents, son, and daughter are all adults and employed independently, it is often the case that each member plans his or her meals and eating activities. Only on rare occasions do they eat together. The urban pattern is a variant of the individualist game in which individuals work in separate economic enterprises and practice a highly individualized eating and cooking pattern.

In rural households, members of the family may work as a team to manage the farm. One woman may be in charge of the cooking and all the members of the household may eat collectively at a mutually agreed time. The rural pattern is a variant of the hierarchist game in which one person is in charge of the kitchen and people have common meal times. Members of the household act together as a group for productive work on the farm.

Caution is essential in the investigation of domestic households. Parents in every society differ in how they rear their children and govern their particular households. For example, a student research team in my class studying a Korean church in Southern California discovered that some member families were strongly authoritarian, which might be considered traditional Korean, while others were distinctively egalitarian in their structure and value orientation. One might presume that the egalitarian families were responding to pressure for change in America, but that may or may not be so. In the case of that particular church, some of the egalitarian families were recent immigrants from Korea, suggesting that they brought their egalitarian perspective with them. We must be careful to not reduce the variability of human life and behavior to a stereotypic presentation of a society and culture.

Domestic structures and values will be carried by people from their households into their relationships in the larger society, and if those values are not consonant with the social games of others, the differences will create tension and conflict. The Korean church is a case in point. Elders in the church had distinctively different domestic structures and values. When they had to address issues of leadership and decision making in the church, those from authoritarian families proposed authoritarian procedures and solutions; those from egalitarian families objected to this course and sought broader participation in decision making. As

101

a consequence the social environment of the church exhibited tensions and conflicts, reflecting the divergent family values of its members.

Research on the cultural bias of households is crucial to understanding the tensions and dynamics of personal interaction that occur in other social environments. Men who work in a fire station may come from very different domestic environments that cannot help but enter into their relationships with fellow workers. Likewise, missionaries in an organization such as UNION Ltd. will come from different domestic backgrounds and thus carry different personal values. It is crucial to remember that a family is a defensive organization whose objective is to nurture young and to perpetuate the biological, social, and cultural way of life of its adult members.

Grid: Positional v. Personal Households

Mary Douglas (1970, 24–27) outlines Basil Bernstein's distinction between positional and personal family role systems in society. This distinction is based upon an analysis of the nature of control in the family structure. In the positional family structure, control is exercised through the definition of social roles in the family and the structuring of obligations and interaction through those role relationships. Parents correct and control their children by reference to social rules and relationships. A child learns that he or she must speak to a father in one way and to a younger brother or sister in a different way. A child is told "act your age," "be a man," "girls don't climb trees." Parents define appropriate behaviors for children in terms of role categories that structure patterned relationships.

The personal system of family control relies upon sensitizing the child to the feelings of others and encouraging the child to consider his own feelings. A child is identified by name and by personal characteristics rather than by role. The child is directed on the basis of his or her unique individuality and gifts. A girl may be encouraged to play baseball and a boy may be encouraged to become a pianist, or one twin (Jacob) may be encouraged to cook and work around the camp and the other (Esau) may be encouraged to hunt and work in the fields. The parents do not attempt to redirect these interests to patterned roles, but rather encourage children to develop according to their inclinations. Parents express their personal grief or joy at the action of a child rather than calling upon an external social force.

The *positional* role system in households is characteristic of high grid social environments, while the *personal* role system is characteristic of low grid social environments. In positional high grid households, parents have a greater degree of authority over children and grandchildren because of their priority as the senior members in the domestic group. Parents take a directive role in the affairs of members, calling members to joint labor activities and to contribute resources for projects of high family priority. Children are subordinate and are expected to serve their elders. Household members are differentiated on the basis of their relative age, and senior members have authority over junior members within the group. The distinction of male and female is also important and domestic labor is usually divided and differentiated on the basis of male-female and elder-younger distinctions.

In personal low grid households parents take a motivating role. Individual autonomy is valued more than subordination to authority, and activities are structured around autonomous relationships. Children are co-laborers, and parents appeal to them to assist in household endeavors, using example and expressions of relationship, need, and rewards to motivate them. Such domestic groups tend toward egalitarian roles and relationships in the family structure, and siblings see one another as co-equals. Parental authority and respect are present, yet the family activities follow from the interest and motivations of each participant.

The following questions provide the diagnostic criteria from which to determine the extent to which authority is located in specific roles or individuals and the criteria by which control is sustained in a household. The cases of David and Dinah provide illustrations of different types of family in Scripture.

Do parents take a directive role (+1) or a motivating role (–1)?

In the case study of David we find two authority figures acting in relationship to David—his father, Jesse, and his brother Eliab. In the dialogue recorded from each of these men, the tone of interaction with David is one of directive authority. Jesse gives David some clear instructions that he is expected to follow, and David does in fact follow them. Eliab, his oldest brother, does not give instructions as Jesse did, but his questions to David are pointed and Eliab charges him with shirking his duty (leaving those few sheep in the desert) and with conceit, wickedness, and frivolity. If we can deduce from this information the character of relationships in Jesse's household, we should conclude that authority is a matter of rule and right behavior (+1). David certainly acts appropriately in relationship to his father, but Eliab is not convinced that David's behavior is appropriate.

The role of father in relationship to sons appears to be different in the case study of Dinah and Shechem. The text tells us that when Jacob heard about the defilement of his daughter, his sons were away in the fields and he kept quiet until they returned. Reading throughout this case we find the sons having as much to say about the matter with Shechem as does the father. It is Jacob's sons who demand that the men of Shechem be circumcised. From the data in this case it appears that all of the adult men in Jacob's household had the right to participate in household decisions. In fact, Jacob's hesitation to say anything about the subject until his sons returned indicates the importance of consulting with them before he responded on the matter of Dinah's defilement. The case of Dinah and Shechem illustrates that personal egalitarian mode of parental leadership (−1). Jacob, having little power over his sons, was unable to restrain a course of action that was repulsive to him.

Do children have subordinate roles (+1) or do they act as co-laborers (−1)?

The case studies of David and Dinah and Shechem show two distinctive patterns of parent-child relationships. It is clear that David's relationship to his father and to his older brother is subordinate. David is expected to do what his father instructs him to do, and he responds in obedience. Eliab apparently expects David to respond in subordination to him as well, and David does not defy him, but questions the legitimacy of his complaint.

The children in the case of Dinah and Shechem are co-laborers rather than subordinates to their father, Jacob. It is obvious that Jacob is an elderly man and his adult sons are the primary laborers in the household. Jacob treats his sons as significant adult parties who must be consulted toward a resolution of the dispute. In other texts in Genesis, Jacob acts in the same manner with his sons. For example, in Genesis 43 Jacob debates with his sons the issue of sending Benjamin with them into Egypt to buy food. He finally concedes to Judah's demands and assurances and agrees to let Benjamin go with him (−1).

Does elder have authority over younger (+1) or are siblings co-equals (−1)?

The data in our two cases are rather skimpy on relationships of elder and younger siblings. However, in the relationship between Eliab and David, Eliab assumes authority over his younger brother. At an earlier time when Samuel comes to Jesse and asks him to present his sons, Jesse presents them in order of their age, elder to younger. These texts suggest that relative age is important (+1) in establishing hierarchy of authority, and Eliab's response to David is consistent with that analysis.

In the case of Dinah and Shechem, Simeon and Levi are the second and third sons of Jacob. They are the ones who take it upon themselves to avenge the rape of their sister. In the later incident when Jacob's sons sell their brother Joseph into Egypt, it is Judah, the fourth son, who instigates this decision and enlists the support of his brothers. It is Judah again who intervenes on behalf of his brothers with Jacob with regard to the decision to take Benjamin into Egypt. These incidents suggest that age distinctions in Jacob's family were unimportant (−1). Brothers were apparently relative equals and those with particular interests or particular gifts for leadership rise to lead the others in specific situations.

Is appropriate behavior prescribed (+1) or unstructured and person-directed (−1)?

The case of David suggests that the role of tending their father's sheep fell to younger boys who had not yet assumed adult roles. It is reported that David was the youngest and he was the one who had the responsibility of tending his father's sheep. The three eldest sons had left home to join Saul and the army of Israel. We may expect that each of the elder sons at sometime in his life had the responsibility of tending sheep, and continued that until they reached an age when they were ready to move into broader adult responsibilities (+1). Eliab's comment to David implies that David is not fulfilling his proper role. Instead of watching his sheep in the desert, David has come down to watch the battle and make his impertinent comments. This particular text tells us nothing about the relationship between male and female in domestic units, yet David's interaction with Abigail at a later point in his life suggests a clear division of labor between men and women in Israelite households. Abigail was noteworthy in that she stepped out of role to intervene on behalf of her husband and his family when her husband, Nabal, proved to be stupid and incompetent. Of all other women in David's life, none assumed the kind of role that Abigail did in that situation.

The case study of Dinah and Shechem presents a much less structured situation. While Jacob and Hamor are the heads of the two families in question, it is really their sons who play a major role in the development of solution to this conflict. The strong passion that Simeon and Levi have about the defilement of their sister becomes the primary force in the culmination of this conflict. Jacob makes it clear that their actions were not in accordance with his will or with his words with Hamor (–1).

Do parents correct and control children by reference to rules, roles, or self (+1) or by reference to grief, joy, or others (–1)?

In the case of David, Eliab attempts to control him through references to appropriate and inappropriate role behavior (+1). In particular Eliab charges David with neglecting his sheep to come out to be a spectator at a life-and-death conflict with the Philistines. Jacob's complaint to Simeon and Levi stands in marked contrast to Eliab's complaint against David. Jacob does not complain about these men violating an appropriate role of a son. Rather he says, "You have brought trouble on me by making me a stench to the Canaanites and Perizzites." Jacob expresses his hurt and his fear that their actions place his whole household in jeopardy. Simeon and Levi defend themselves in similar terms: focusing on how Shechem had treated their sister. Both Jacob and his sons define appropriate behaviors in terms of the positive and negative effects that those behaviors have on others (–1).

Group: Residence and Independent
v. Corporate Households

The decisions that people make with regard to residence and household composition tell us much about their strength of commitment to group. What are the criteria upon which a young couple determines residence at marriage and what options are open to them at later phases of their domestic life? What are the criteria upon which people base decisions for changes in residence and for separation from or association with other members of their society?

Anthropologists have found many societies in which members encourage, commend, or even prescribe the co-residence of married children with their parents or married siblings. These residential preferences produce multigenerational (vertical) households (parents, married children, grandchildren) that give high priority to group interests. The kinship relationship of strongest focus in these households is either the parent/child or the sibling relationship. Bigenerational (horizontal) households (parents/children) do occur in these societies, but they are either a phase of the development of a corporate family or an exception based upon unusual needs, preferences, or conflicts.

In multigenerational households the group, rather than the individual, makes decisions about marriage. Parents or elder siblings arrange marriages, or the couple must at least consult with and gain their approval. Usually one of the marrying partners joins the family of his or her spouse as a new member. Where marriage requires bridewealth or dowry, or when births involve economic exchanges between the families, family members pool their capital, income, and labor. The most common activities for pooling include marriages, funerals, naming ceremonies, education of children, and projects (clearing fields, building houses) that require collective labor.

In multigenerational families the patterns of residence following marriage vary in terms of kinship preferences. In the patrilineal society of Yap in Micronesia young men marry and bring their wives home to the estate group of their father. Since Yapese sons depend upon their fathers for land and inheritance, they nearly always reside *patrilocally*. In the matrilineal societies of the Hopi and Navajo in Arizona, daughters remain with their mothers and new husbands live with their wives in *matrilocal* households. Among the Hopi farmers individuals often marry within the same pueblo, so parents are nearby. With the Navajo sheepherders, men scatter over much wider ranging territory as marriage takes them to the camps of their new brides. Both Navajo and Hopi, however, emphasize corporate-focused residence as members of the domestic groups live and work together for common economic, social, and religious interests.

Among bilateral domestic groups, the act of choice of residence establishes one's affiliation with a group. This pattern is described for the Gilbert Islanders and for other bilateral or cognatic societies such as the Polynesians of Hawaii, Tonga, and Samoa. Individual members in these societies are faced with choices of residence at marriage. Married couples live with either set of parents, where they become heirs to that estate and part of the corporate family group.

In weak group social environments, people form independent households primarily around the husband/wife relationship. Individuals arrange their own marriages, consulting with kinsmen to the extent necessary to achieve needed family support. The ritual of marriage marks the beginning of the separation of each individual from his or her natal household and the establishment of a new domestic unit. Households are predominantly bigenerational (parents and children), and multigenerational households are a concession to the needs of individuals rather than a preference for corporate rights and interests. Individuals control their own capital, income, and labor, although a husband and wife may pool their resources for their common interests.

For independent households the choice of residence after marriage is a matter of personal rather than corporate interest. Separation may occur immediately or may follow temporary residence with one set of parents for a limited time. In a society of patrilineal emphasis a couple may reside at the place of the husband (*virilocal*) without a necessary connection to a larger corporate group. In a society emphasizing matrilineal ties, residence in the place of the wife (*uxorilocal*) need not confer any corporate obligation or affiliation. Further, such arrangements may be temporary. For example, among the Deni in Brazil a couple reside at marriage with the bride's parents. For two or three years the father-in-law exercises control over his daughter, since she is usually very young (12–15 years), but the marriage does not result in a corporate group or long-term corporate interest. After the couple have their own children, they may continue to reside near the woman's parents, they may move near the man's brothers, or they may take up residence in a different village altogether. Residence choice is based primarily upon the couple's interests and the relationships they have with others. Corporate interests are absent and therefore play no role in decisions of domestic residence.

Individual choice of residence at marriage and in later life is typical of urban industrial social relationships. In the bilateral European and American societies, urban people form highly individualistic and mobile households, whereas rural families with limited resources allocate the family farm to one or two children and send the others off to establish new self-sufficient households.

The fieldworker must ascertain if the survival of the domestic unit as a group has higher priority than the rights of individuals within the unit to establish their own independent relationships. The diagnostic questions that follow prompt the fieldworker to observe patterns of residence and to discover the weak or strong group factors that characterize the organization and authority of domestic groups.

Are households made up of three or more generations (+1) or only two generations (–1)?

The life history of Jacob provides an interesting case study in the generational development of a family. When Jacob leaves his parents' home and flees to join Laban, his mother's brother in Padan Aram, he joins Laban's multigenerational household. After years of work for Laban, Jacob marries Laban's two daughters and continues to live with Laban for twenty or more years. However, as Jacob's children near adulthood, he insists on breaking his relationship with Laban and departing to return to his homeland. For a brief time, Jacob establishes a bigenerational, independent household. However, he has twelve sons by his two wives and their two handmaidens. These sons soon marry and establish families of their own. Yet at the time that Joseph is sold down into Egypt these adult sons continue to work together shepherding their own and their father's flocks and supporting this large extended family household. From these data we may conclude that Jacob has spent most of his life as part of a multigenerational extended family group. Approximately half of that was spent in the corporate family of Laban, his father-in-law, and the other half he served as the head of a large extended family made up of his sons and their spouses and children (+1).

Are core relationships those of parents/children (+1) or husband/wife (–1)?

In the case studies both of David and of Dinah, the primary relationship discussed in the text is that of father and sons. The case study of Dinah is particularly interesting because at no point are we given any indication of Dinah's feelings. Her brothers do not consider whether she wishes or does not wish to be married to Shechem, and she is apparently not consulted either in terms of the marriage or in terms of the revenge wreaked by Simeon and Levi upon Shechem. Jacob also apparently does not consult with Leah, Dinah's mother. Focal bonds in Jacob's household are the bonds between father and sons (+1).

In the case study of David, father-and-son relationship is again the one in focus. Jesse's wife is never mentioned. In other accounts David's wives are mentioned, but only to the extent that they play a role in his relationships with their father or their husband. The only exception to this is Bathsheba, who plays a crucial role in gaining for her son, Solomon, the right to succeed David on the throne of Israel (+1).

Do members pool capital, income, or labor (+1) or do individuals control (–1)?

David's assignment from his father, Jesse, is to take roasted grain and ten loaves of bread for his brothers who are serving in the army of Israel. Jesse also sends along ten cheeses to be given to the commander of their unit. Even though Eliab, Abinadah, and Shammah are adults, probably already married and having established their own households, Jesse continues to provide economic support for them. While the text says nothing about the families of these three sons, in all likelihood Jesse is over-

Table 7.1
Comparison of Domestic Authority of Jacob, Shechem, and David

High Grid	Low Grid			
Positional/ Authoritarian	Personal/Egalitarian	Jacob	Shechem	David
+1 Parents take directive role	−1 Parents take motivating relationship	0, −1	1, 0	1, 0
+1 Children have subordinate roles	−1 Children are co-laborers	0, −1	1, 0	1, 0
+1 Elder siblings have authority over younger	−1 Siblings are co-equals	0, −1	0, 0	1, 0
+1 Appropriate behavior structured, prescribed	−1 Relations unstructured, person-directed	0, −1	1, 0	1, 0
+1 Control by reference to rules, roles, self	−1 Control by reference to grief, joy, others	0, −1	1, 0	1, 0
Sum of Grid Variables:		**−5.0**	**+4.0**	**+5.0**

Strong Group	Weak Group			
Corporate Domestic Units	Independent Domestic Units	Jacob	Shechem	David
+1 Multigenerational (3, 4 generations)	−1 Bigenerational (1, 2 generations)	1, 0	1, 0	1, 0
+1 Parent/child or sibling dyad in focus	−1 Husband/wife dyad in focus	1, 0	1, 0	1, 0
+1 Pooling of capital, income, labor	−1 Individual control of capital, income, labor	1, 0	1, 0	1, 0
+1 Co-residence with group members	−1 Residence by personal choice	1, 0	1, 0	1, 0
+1 Marriage a group agenda; bridewealth or dowry	−1 Marriage an individual agenda; ritual of separation	1, 0	1, 0	1, 0
Sum of Group Variables:		**+5.0**	**+5.0**	**+5.0**

seeing their welfare and providing for the wives and children of his sons while they are off at war (+1).

In the case of Dinah and Shechem, it is Simeon and Levi who attack and kill the unsuspecting men of Shechem. However, apparently all the sons of Jacob loot the city and seize the flocks, herds, donkeys, wealth, and women and children as plunder from this town. Later in Genesis, in the story of Joseph, we find Jacob's sons again pooling their resources to buy grain in Egypt and traveling again into Egypt to obtain food during this perilous time. Jacob and his sons continue to act as a corporate domestic unit even after some of his sons are middle-aged men (+1).

Is residence prescribed by rules and custom (+1) or by personal choice (–1)?

Neither the case study of David nor the case study of Shechem and Dinah provides information for us on the rules of residence practiced in Jacob's or in David's families. We do know from previous study of Jacob's family relationships that Jacob was uncomfortable remaining in the household of his father-in-law, Laban. After an extended period of residing there, Jacob insisted upon leaving and establishing his own independent domestic group. When he did break away from the household of Laban he returned to the land of his father, Isaac, and his brother, Esau. From these data we may conclude that the preferred pattern of residence was that men remain on the land and in the vicinity of their fathers while women leave their families and join the family of their husbands (+1). This was indeed the case when Rebekah married Jacob's father, Isaac, and left her home and came to live with Isaac. As we follow the life of Jacob we find that his sons continue to remain with him until his death. We know nothing of the residence of his daughters upon their marriage. The same pattern is apparently practiced by Jesse and David. Evidence to support this may be found in the Book of Ruth, where Ruth chooses to leave her family in Moab and to return with her mother-in-law, Naomi, to their ancestral residence in Bethlehem (+1).

Is marriage a group agenda—bridewealth or dowry (+1) or an individual agenda— ritual of separation (–1)?

Shechem and Hamor, his father, in their eagerness to gain Dinah as Shechem's wife, invite Jacob and his sons to settle in their land and to intermarry with them and their families. Shechem and Hamor tell their fellow townsmen that the land has plenty of room and that "we can marry their daughters and they can marry ours." In effect, Shechem and Hamor are proposing the exchange of daughters between the two extended family groups (+1). Jacob's sons agreed to this on the condition that the men of Shechem be circumcised. However, as the text shows, this was a deception that Simeon and Levi used to take revenge upon Shechem and the whole town.

Hamor attempted to arrange a marriage for his son, Shechem, with Jacob's daughter, Dinah. Rather than offer bridewealth or dowry, he offered land and a long-term prospect of exchanging daughters between the families as consideration for bridewealth. When Isaac married Rebekah more than two generations before, Abraham paid significant bridewealth to Rebekah's father to gain her release to become the wife of his son, Isaac. Jacob, in contrast, went as a refugee to the house of his father-in-law, Laban, and having nothing to offer for a daughter spent seven years of labor (bride service) to obtain the hand of Rachel. When Laban deceived him and gave him his oldest daughter, Leah, instead, Jacob agreed to work another seven years if Laban would only give him Rachel as his second wife. Bridewealth was certainly a primary consideration for marriage in Jacob's household, and that consideration carried through to Jacob's descendants in the households of Jesse and David (+1). We read in 1 Samuel 18:24 that Saul asked David for a hundred Philistines' foreskins as a bride price for his daughter Michal. In all of these cases the daughters become members of the household of the husbands they marry. The bride price is compensation to the father and the family of the bride, as they lose her as a contributing member of their domestic group.

Structural Variation in Domestic Groups

In the preceding discussion we have explored some of the variation that grid and group factors produce in the structure of households and

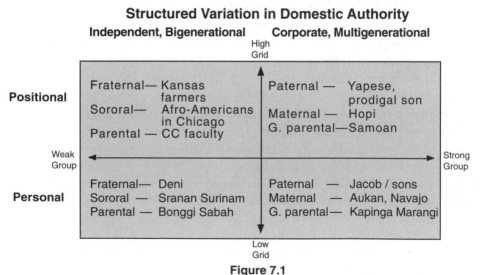

Figure 7.1

112

family groups. A more complete picture of this variation is illustrated in figure 7.1. The figure sorts by the positional and personal family types (high and low grid) and by the bigenerational and multigenerational residence patterns (weak group and strong group). Each frame then sorts family types and illustrating cases with reference to their emphasis on male (fraternal, paternal), female (sororal, maternal), or joint (parental, grandparental) kinship ties. Four of the cases cited have been described in detail in *Transforming Culture* (Lingenfelter 1992). Others have already been discussed briefly.

The prototype game that people employ in their households may not reflect the games played in the wider society. A common error in research in complex urban settings is to interview individuals about their personal and domestic values and to presume that these values apply to a wider social environment, when in fact they do not. Keeping this in focus, the following case study puts these criteria to good use in describing and analyzing the family values and practices of American and African missionaries.

UNION Ltd.: Authority and Family
by Donna R. Downes

While UNIWORLD International encourages a strong group orientation for its field teams in almost every aspect of ministry life, the group orientation does not apply to family. Individual families operate fully within their own authority structures and family autonomy is stressed during missionary training in the United States. The team's western and African family structures are described as they operate on a daily basis both inside and outside the organization, and particular attention is given to their influence on team relationships.

The Grid Dimension

The sum of grid scores shows pronounced differences between westerners (−1.5) and Africans (+4). Western parents take a motivating role (−1) with their children. Western children are given a fairly high profile in family decision making about furlough times, schooling, location and style of housing, and household activities. However, in keeping with a belief in biblical authority, westerners blend a directive role (+.5) into

113

Table 7.2
Domestic Authority in UNION Ltd.: Western v. African Missionaries

High Grid		Low Grid			
Positional/ Authoritarian		Personal/ Egalitarian		Westerners	Africans
+1 Parents take a directive role		−1 Parents take motivating role		.5, −1	1, 0
+1 Children have subordinate roles		−1 Children are co-laborers		0, −1	1, −.5
+1 Elder siblings have authority over younger		−1 Siblings are co-equals		.5, −.5	1, 0
+1 Appropriate behavior structure/prescribed		−1 Relations unstructured, person-directed		.5, −.5	1, 0
+1 Control by reference to rules, roles, self		−1 Control by reference to grief, joy, others		.5, −.5	1, −.5
Sum of Grid Variables:				**−1.5**	**+4.0**

Strong Group		Weak Group			
Corporate Domestic Units		Independent Domestic Units		Westerners	Africans
+1 Multigenerational (3, 4 generations)		−1 Bigenerational (1, 2 generations)		0, −1	.5, −1
+1 Parent/child or sibling dyad in focus		−1 Husband/wife dyad in focus		0, −1	0, −1
+1 Pooling of capital, income, labor		−1 Individual control of capital, income, labor		0, −1	1, 0
+1 Co-residence with group members		−1 Residence by personal choice		0, −1	0, −1
+1 Marriage a group agenda; bridewealth/dowry		−1 Marriage an individual agenda/ritual of separation		0, −1	1, 0
Sum of Group Variables:				**−5.0**	**−0.5**

their relationships, especially in the children's earlier years. Children are co-laborers (−1), assisting with household responsibilities, and older children occasionally accompany their fathers to help in conferences. While siblings generally have equal status (−.5) to one another and equal

114

vote on most matters, parents give greater authority, responsibility, and privilege to older (+.5) children as they mature. Some westerners blur male and female family roles and division of labor when they operate within their own cultural settings or are unobserved at home (−.5). Others have adopted what they construe to be biblical family role models that differentiate between male/female authority and activity (+.5).

In the matter of discipline westerners monitor the behavior of their children in reference to grief and joy (−.5). Conscious of the rules and roles (+.5) evident in the African cultural setting, western parents may adapt to the higher grid African expectations. At times westerners complain that they have unnaturally disciplined their children to sit quietly through several hours of an African church service or to refrain from interrupting adult conversations. African team members find western children undisciplined, noisy, and rude. The westerners sometimes view African children as abnormally subdued and underactive. The pressure on westerners to conform their domestic authority structures to their African environment pushes them up grid.

Africans also experience conflicting values in their team relations. African parents definitely direct (+1) the lives of their children. Parents share authority in their family only with adult members of their extended family. They do not ask for their children's opinions, and consider such a practice strange. Children have subordinate roles (+1) in which they do assigned tasks in the house by gender: young girls assist by serving tea, sewing, and taking care of siblings. Because all team members have maids to do housework, and the children attend school, Africans by necessity limit their children's co-labor role (−.5) to retain their status above that of maids.

African parents give elder siblings authority (+1) over the younger, except in male/female role relationships. One African father was a bit embarrassed by all the attention his older daughter received for her progress in school, and felt the younger son should get more attention: "It's just not good for a girl to be put in a position over her brother." Although the standards of the urban African team members differ slightly from those of their rural family counterparts, they also prescribe appropriate behavior (+1). For example, the African wives do not work in the team office; that is the husband's identity. While the men tolerate the influence of western wives in the team's ministry, they do not encourage a visible role for their own wives. In public settings African couples normally sit apart, and wives rarely speak in the presence of their husbands. Finally, Africans make frequent reference to social rules and role (+1), while finding themselves caught in tension with the westerners on the team who reference feelings rather than roles. They seek to please other team members (−.5) within the context of the social expectations of their own family values.

The Group Dimension

The sums of group scores also show remarkable differences between westerners (−5.0) and Africans (−.5). Westerners form bigenerational (−1) independent family units. They organize families around the husband/wife dyad (−1), and select residence by personal choice (−1). Couples arrange their own marriages (−1), and they retain control of their capital and labor (−1). These westerners resist all of the strong group variables.

The African picture is much more complex. While their sum (−.5) edges into the weak group quadrant, I am convinced that African members would rate considerably higher in their group orientation if the following were not true:

1. All members must live in the city. This separates Africans from their farm, extended family, and rural social environment, insulating them from the strong group obligations of rural society.
2. African members have lived in the west for more than six years, a fact that has influenced their family ideas and values.
3. Africans cite the influence of Christian values for partnership in marriage, which they elevate over rulership and obligation.

The two African families on the team live as bigenerational (−1), husband/wife dyadic units (−1), and they chose their urban residence by personal preference (−1). One family has either a maternal or a paternal grandparent (+.5) staying in their house, and they visit weekly their rural extended family. Both African families pool capital and income (+1) with other relatives, upgrading family-held properties and assisting nephews, nieces, and in-laws in school. According to one, "They took care of us; now we must take care of them. If we don't, neighbors and friends will look down on us. We would be a shame to our family." Finally, marriage is definitely a group project (+1). According to one couple—both educated in the west—bridewealth is essential: "If I hadn't paid brideprice, my wife and her family would think I wasn't committed to her and this marriage. Even in Christian circles the brideprice is still a sign of honor and respect to the bride and her family."

Conclusions

The family games for westerners and Africans are striking in their differences (fig. 7.2). Westerners show clear commitments to the individualist game, but do make some concessions to the authoritarian expectations of their African colleagues. For Africans the concessions to membership on the team and perhaps the influence of living in America have pulled them from a hierarchist family tradition into the authoritarian game. Yet, African and westerner remain far apart in their domestic values and expectations. The mission provides no assistance or guidance in this area of team life, deeming family as off-limits to mission policy and influence. The team then lacks direction to cope with an area of continuing potential for conflict.

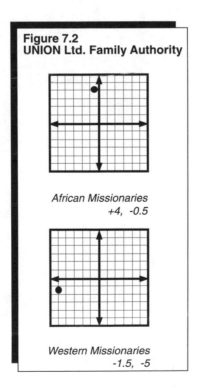

Figure 7.2
UNION Ltd. Family Authority

African Missionaries
+4, -0.5

Western Missionaries
-1.5, -5

117

For example, when one western woman requested a more visible role in UNION Ltd.'s ministry, her African teammate denied her request, saying her visibility would "lessen the status of the organization" in the eyes of the local culture. Over several years his views softened as he noted other Christian organizations allowing women in leadership roles. The two western women who wanted more visible roles succeeded after major internal battles.

African team families also struggle with the expectations of their rural extended families. Caught between the demands of extended family members and of ministry, they satisfy no one. Westerners resent the time taken from the mission work and wonder why Africans can't live more independently from their families. This problem, among others, led UNI-WORLD International to enforce an unpopular organizational policy of assigning nonwestern missionaries to countries other than their own to minimize social obligations. These different family games have affected not only UNION Ltd.'s operations, but the international organization's policies as well.

Research Questions 7.1
Grid and Domestic Authority

High Grid	Low Grid
+1 *Parents take directive role.* Is authority in the household designated to senior individuals, and is it a matter of rule and right to which members conform? or	−1 *Parents take motivating role.* Are household decisions re: resources, space, organization of household activities shared? Do parents motivate children to participate?
+1 *Children have subordinate roles.* Are children to be seen and not heard? Do parents give the word and children run to obey? Are children's roles subject to authority of adults and structured so as to define specific responsibilities and duties? or	−1 *Children are co-laborers.* Are children invited early to participate in adult labor and activities of the household? Are children encouraged to work alongside of adults as co-laborers? Do adults of differing generations, residing in the same household, relate as peers?
+1 *Elder siblings have authority over younger.* Is relative age an important factor in the hierarchy of authority in the domestic group? Do elder siblings have authority over younger for economic and social activities? or	−1 *Siblings are co-equals.* Are age distinctions among siblings insignificant, particularly as children approach adulthood? Are siblings co-equal in their authority and responsibility for domestic activities?
+1 *Appropriate behavior is structured, prescribed.* Is the male/female division of labor strictly defined? Are domestic roles structured in terms of authority and expected behaviors? and are persons channeled into roles regardless of abilities or interests? or	−1 *Relations are unstructured, person-directed.* Do household members exchange or vary responsibilities for labor, food production, and authority? Are relations unstructured, so that persons with specific interests and abilities may perform roles according to their interests?
+1 *Control by reference to rules, roles, self.* Do parents correct children by reference to social rules and relationships and define appropriate behavior in terms of social roles? Do people learn to conform by measuring self against a socially defined, standard role? or	−1 *Control by reference to grief, joy, others.* Do parents correct by reference to how pleased, hurt, happy, or angry they are, and define appropriate behaviors in terms of positive or negative affect on others? Do people learn to conform by person-oriented appeals and ethical sensibilities?

Research Questions 7.2
Group and Domestic Authority

Strong Group	Weak Group
+1 *Multigenerational (3, 4 generations)*. Are three- or four-generation families valued by members of the society? Are newlyweds urged or required to live with parents? Do multigenerational families persist until the death of the senior generation or do other factors cause them to divide? or	−1 *Bigenerational (1, 2 generations)*. Do people prefer independent nuclear family households? Are three-generation households formed only under socially exceptional circumstances? How and when do couples assume independent authority and separate from their natal households?
+1 *Parent/child or sibling dyad in focus*. Do parents and children, or siblings, make household decisions? Are the strongest bonds in the household between parents and children, or between siblings, so that in situations of conflict children or siblings side with kin rather than their spouse? or	−1 *Husband/wife dyad in focus*. Do husband and wife make economic and social decisions on domestic matters, with the input of parents and siblings peripheral? Are the strongest bonds in the household between husband and wife so that in situations of conflict the couple stick together against the contrary interests of parents or siblings?
+1 *Pooling of capital, income, labor*. Do household members regularly share capital, income, and perform collective labor? Do members of the household turn to an extended family group for mutual economic support? or	−1 *Individual control of capital, income, labor*. Are household members expected to meet their needs independently of other kin? Are they reluctant to call upon kinsmen for labor or financial support in times of crisis?
+1 *Co-residence with group members*. Is residence prescribed by custom or rules? Do couples share common residence with rights of membership and obligation to participate in group activities? or	−1 *Residence by personal choice*. Is residence a matter of personal choice for the couple marrying? Does the pattern of choices reflect the interest of individuals or the pressure of ties of kinship and group?
+1 *Marriage a group agenda; bridewealth or dowry*. Are marriages arranged by or subject to group approval, and planned by the heads of families? Is bridewealth or dowry a consideration? Is marriage a rite of membership bringing the spouse into a group? or	−1 *Marriage an individual agenda; ritual of separation*. Are marriages contracted by the couple and planned in accord with their interests and wishes? Does marriage constitute a rite of separation in which the couple leave their natal domestic groups to form a household of their own?

Community Authority and Cultural Bias

Case of Shechem

After Abimelech had governed Israel three years, God sent an evil spirit between Abimelech and the citizens of Shechem, who acted treacherously against Abimelech. . . .

Now Gaal son of Ebed moved with his brothers into Shechem, and its citizens put their confidence in him. After they had gone out into the fields and gathered the grapes and trodden them, they held a festival in the temple of their god. While they were eating and drinking, they cursed Abimelech. Then Gaal son of Ebed said, "Who is Abimelech, and who is Shechem, that we should be subject to him? Isn't he Jerub-Baal's son, and isn't Zebul his deputy? Serve the men of Hamor, Shechem's father! Why should we serve Abimelech? If only this people were under my command! Then I would get rid of him. I would say to Abimelech, 'Call out your whole army!'" (Judg. 9:22–23, 26–29)

Case of Ephesus

A silversmith named Demetrius, who made silver shrines of Artemis, brought in no little business for the craftsmen. He called them together . . . and said: "Men, you know we receive a good income from this business. And you see and hear how this fellow Paul has convinced and led astray large numbers of people here in Ephesus. . . . There is danger not only that our trade will lose its good name, but also that the temple . . .

121

will be discredited and the goddess . . . will be robbed of her divine majesty."

When they heard this, they were furious and began shouting: "Great is Artemis of the Ephesians!" Soon the whole city was in an uproar. . . .

The city clerk quieted the crowd and said: "Men of Ephesus, . . . you ought to be quiet and not do anything rash. You have brought these men here, though they have neither robbed temples nor blasphemed our goddess. If, then, Demetrius and his fellow craftsmen have a grievance against anybody, the courts are open and there are proconsuls. They can press charges. If there is anything further you want to bring up, it must be settled in a legal assembly. As it is, we are in danger of being charged with rioting because of today's events. In that case we would not be able to account for this commotion, since there is no reason for it." After he had said this, he dismissed the assembly. (Acts 19:24–41)

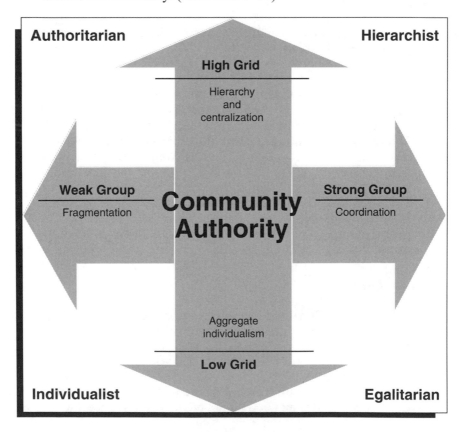

Authority and Community

Many scholars have examined the broad range of human societies with reference to authority and community and have elaborated models for comparison and analysis of these diverse peoples and systems. Among social anthropologists, Elman Service (1962) developed a typology of social organization that grouped peoples into bands, tribes, chiefdoms, and primitive states. This model has been very popular in the anthropological literature and is used in most introductory anthropology texts to discuss and compare the nature of communities and political systems cross-culturally. Morton Fried (1967) published a different developmental model of authority and stratification, proposing a typology of egalitarian, rank, stratified, and state societies. Fried's model emphasizes the differences in the way people control access to resources, defining four types of control. Service's model focuses on patterns of organization of family, kin, and community. Neither recognizes the patterning of authority that occurs within each of the levels they define, patterning after the game prototypes that I defined in chapter 2.

In the previous chapter we explored how authority and control may be high or low grid functions of generation, age, and sex in domestic groups. We examined the degree of cohesiveness or fragmentation in domestic groups by assessing how they share property, labor, and residence or assign these economic choices to individuals. In the study of community, the scale of authority becomes larger but the issues of power and control, and the five types of games, remain the same. To explore the grid variable in relationship to authority and community, we will examine the extent to which power is centralized (high grid) versus dispersed or aggregate (low grid). For the variable of group, we will explore the extent to which the community is coordinated and the members within the community have binding linkages with one another (strong group) or the extent to which it is fragmented and individuals have few linkages to bind them in collective activity (weak group).

Utilizing these theoretical concepts, I have developed the following diagnostic criteria to enable the fieldworker to research and analyze the grid and group dimensions of community authority in a social environment. To apply these concepts it is necessary to define carefully the center and boundaries of the social environment in question. The community authority in a Deni village will be strikingly different from the community authority of a Brazilian village two miles down river. The community authority of a private school will probably be somewhat different from that of a public school located in the same city. However, to research a school, one may not study just the teachers or a classroom. It is necessary to study the total environment, which for a public school extends to the central administration, the board of education, and the constituency that relies upon the school to educate its children. One cannot legitimately focus on the teachers or the nonteaching staff alone. They cannot exist in isolation; each is part of the larger social context of schooling.

Grid: Centralization v. Aggregation

Richard Adams (1975) provides an analysis of social power that facilitates an assessment of the degree of high or low grid in a particular social environment. Adams identifies four distinctive ways in which power can be distributed: independent power, granted power, allocated power, and delegated power.

One has *independent power* when one holds direct control over specific aspects of the natural environment, persons, or symbols. In feudal Europe, the lord of the manor exercised direct control over the land and the people who occupied it. His tenants' only recourse to excessive rents was to leave and take up tenancy on another manor. The feudal lord also controlled symbols to the extent that he employed a priest and through him exercised power over the religious life of the manor. The lord's independent power was constrained only by conflict and war with other lords who were his neighbors.

Unlike the feudal manor where only the lord had independent power, each Deni Indian in Brazil, man or woman, has independent power, although it is much more restricted in scope. The individual Deni may control any portion of the environment to which he or she extends his or her labor. Deni may also control persons who have agreed to live in a dependency relationship with them. However, individuals who are frustrated by that dependency may leave at will and attempt to sustain their livelihood through other relationships. The Deni shaman exercises direct control over knowledge and ritual, which gives him independent power over the spirit world.

Adams defines *granting power* as one person giving decision-making power to another. A wife may grant power to a husband, a younger brother may grant power to an older brother, or a weaker feudal lord may grant power to a stronger neighboring lord. In such relationships the person granted power may make decisions on behalf of the other.

When many individuals grant power to one of their peers, Adams refers to this as the *collective allocation of power.* This is typically done in congregationally organized American churches. People who attend such churches allocate power to a pastor who is the head of the congregation. These same people may also allocate power to a committee of their peers who act as leadership elders for the congregation. In either case, the people may withdraw that power by majority vote if the pastor or elders lose the support of the membership. Individuals within the membership grant power with their weekly contributions and their attendance at meetings. Any individual may withdraw that granted power by merely ceasing to attend or to contribute.

Missionaries who seek support from friends are requesting that those friends grant power to them over the funds contributed. Individual contributions to individual missionaries are a form of granted power. When a congregation agrees to put a missionary on its congregational budget, it has allocated power to that particular missionary. In this situation, the group has designated specific funds for the missionary and granted the missionary the right to make the decisions about how those funds should be used.

Finally, Adams refers to power given by one to many as *delegating power;* that is, the person who holds any other form of power—independent, granted, or allocated—may share that power with others. When power is delegated, the receiver is dependent upon the giver of that power. Sometimes the one delegating shares power with many, who may in turn compete with one another over shared access. For example, in a university, a president has ultimate authority and power over the budget. That power is delegated to the various vice presidents who supervise particular areas of the university. They in turn delegate to their deans and directors certain portions of the budget. Each of these subdivisions constitutes a competitive resource and cost center. In a typical university, managers who have received delegated power compete with others to obtain greater shares of the resources for their particular area. In all cases, those who have received power are dependent upon those who hold it.

A high grid social environment is one in which the differential allocation of power is great, and centralization is a critical feature of power relationships. In high grid social environments, all four types of power relationships are present. A very few individuals may hold independent power, but most power relationships are of the more complex forms—granted, allocated, or delegated power.

A low grid social environment, in contrast, is characterized by the greater presence of independent power and only limited granting or allocating of power to others within the community. Power relationships are decentralized and the importance of maintaining independent power is greater than the motivation for sharing power. Relationships tend to be aggregate, based upon proximity and utility, because of the high value of individual autonomy.

Is power organized in a hierarchy of units (+1) or in aggregate interest clusters (–1)?

Solomon, king of Israel, employed a three-tiered hierarchy of power, with the kingdom divided into twelve major districts through which officials supervised the tribal settlements. At the top were his chief officials designated in 1 Kings 4. Azariah, son of Nathan, was in charge of Solomon's twelve district governors, who served to collect tribute and bring supplies in support of Solomon and his court. The organization within each district is not described in the text, but probably included other subordinate power units to the district governors.

A contrasting case of aggregate clusters is found in New Guinea, where men form temporary alliances to sustain a conflict with another competing leader. Should conflict arise with a different leader from a different sector, the two individuals in conflict earlier may join to form an aggregate interest group. Alliances, then, may shift and change as the leader's interests and competition warrant.

Are decisions made by central authority (+1) or negotiated situationally by any interested parties (–1)?

In a high grid social environment, ultimate control lies with the independent power at the top of the hierarchy. Decision making occurs at various levels in the hierarchy as is appropriate to the demands of those exercising control. In the case of Solomon the collection of tribute from a particular district was left to the authority of the district officer, the agent of the central unit. The coordination of time and provisions required for Solomon were made by Azariah, son of Nathan, in charge of the district officers. The demands with regard to quantity of goods emanated from Solomon himself.

When decisions are negotiated situationally, people are not governed by rules or by precedent established from past decisions. The circumstances of the present and the power of those individuals whose interests are in competition with one another provide the major factors in decision making. In Aukan villages in Surinam, public decision making requires members in the whole village to participate in the discussion, and after long bargaining and debate, a decision is either negotiated or mediated through ritual and divination. In the latter case, people appeal to dead ancestors to make a decision that they are incapable of making for themselves. Among the Brazilian Deni, who are low grid and weak group, there are no ancestors who can assist. Deni either negotiate or separate. They have no one to call upon to arbitrate for them.

Do leaders delegate power (+1) or are they limited to aggregate support (−1)?

In a centralized system, a single leader at the top is unable to coordinate or direct all of the power decisions of the community or the state. As a consequence, power is distributed to subordinates within the power structure. Azariah, son of Nathan, was the recipient of delegated power to collect tribute and food supplies for Solomon. The officials named for each district were in turn delegated power by Azariah to collect in their region. This organizational structure has been reduplicated thousands of times over in high grid institutions throughout world history.

The New Guinea Big Man is a classic example of aggregate leadership power. The Big Man gains allies through the distribution of his own wealth to create reciprocal obligations for the receiver. Once the debt is paid, the leader loses his influence over the debtor. Big Men gain power by increasing the number of individuals indebted to them. In a strong group situation, the leader builds his power by generosity to the group rather than to the individuals. In both cases, however, power is sustained through ongoing reciprocity.

Do leaders exercise power independently (+1) or do members retain independent power (−1)?

Unlike people within the hierarchy, who are constrained by rules and pressures from above and below, the individuals at the top have relative autonomy and sometimes great independent power. The story of Rehoboam's (Solomon's son) decision to increase taxes in Israel (2 Chron. 10) is an illustration of this independent power. In spite of the wise council of elder officials he made his decision and suffered significant political consequences: rebellion and a divided kingdom.

In the low grid New Guinea situation, individuals built alliances to several Big Men in order to sustain a degree of independence from any of them. As long as individuals can balance the obligations to those to whom they are indebted, they retain social independence. In a strong group context, individuals lose power to the group but only in areas where group interest supersedes their individual autonomy. Aukan men, for example, who live for a time in the villages of their wives grant power to their wives' kinsmen on a reciprocal basis. They retain independent power in that community since they are not members of the kin group, nor are they forced to conform to its interests.

Do members grant power centrally (+1) or is power granted recip-rocally (–1)?

In a high grid social environment, the participants comply with the hierarchical structure and allocate power to those over them. A few individuals in such a social environment may resist or resent the power hierarchy, but most support the structure even though they may question the efficacy of individuals within it. As willing participants they agree to allocate power to leaders within the hierarchy and to support the norms of authority and relationship. The submission of the Ephesians to the clerk in the opening case illustrates this well.

In the low grid environment people prefer to manage power through reciprocal exchange. A Deni Indian hunter grants power over his kill to other individuals who will help him carry it home. He expects that an invitation will be extended to him to share in the same benefit at a future time. A real estate broker in an urban metropolitan center of the United States grants listing rights to other brokers with the understanding of reciprocity between them. This power granted may be withheld from those who refuse the reciprocal obligations. They deal with their leaders and other members of their community on the same terms.

Group: Fragmentation v. Coordination

To assess the strength of group in community, we must examine the nature of social bonds among individuals within that community and the strength or weakness of those linkages when they are subjected to pressures of conflicting interest. In a strong group social environment, the ties of individuals in groups are sustained in spite of the conflicting interests of individuals; individual interests are subordinate to the interests of the group. In a weak group social environment the reverse is true. The competing interests of individuals quickly fragment the links that bind the participants, and group unity dissolves.

In a weak group social environment communal authority and decision making are only weakly sustained, as is illustrated so well by the Deni case. The primary work of the Deni chief is to call feasts, which serve to celebrate good talk and to sustain ties between the members of the village. Yet the social facts are that any individual who is disenchanted with the leadership of the chief or with any one of his fellow villagers may choose not to participate, and the members of the community have no power to coerce that individual to conform. We observed several feasts in the late 1970s in which individuals, disgruntled with other members in the group, avoided the feast to the dismay of those participating. However, no forms of social sanction were available. The history of the villages shows a pattern of oscillating coordination and fragmentation; while we lived in the village, we observed the coordination phase, but approximately a year after our study the village broke into three sections, the fragmentation phase.

The contrasting strong group environment is sustained by social factors that create bonds and coordinate the activities of members of the group. In such a social environment, coordination becomes the value, toward the end of creating corporate unity and identity. American English teachers working in China in recent years have discovered that coordination of activities in the classroom is more important than creativity and academic freedom. American English teachers have experienced significant social pressure from their Chinese peers to conform to Chinese instructional methods and to coordinate their lesson plans and teaching with that already in practice by their Chinese colleagues. The interests of the individual teacher in this context are subject to the collective interests of the group. The linking of one's classroom activities with those of the other teachers is more important than the creative expression of one's unique teaching style and abilities.

Is there a heritage of common faith/beliefs (+1) or variant faith/beliefs (−1)?

Where the value of group is high, the unity of faith and doctrine becomes critical. Anabaptist Christian groups, such as Mennonites or Brethren, place great emphasis on their particular Anabaptist heritage. Individuals in these denominations may take pride in tracing their genealogy to one of the founding fathers, and the distinctive local groups gain strength from their reaffirmation of the doctrines and ordinances of the founders of their faith community. While the content of their faith is very different from that of the Aukaners in Surinam, they share an emphasis on ancestry and perpetuation of a belief system that is passed from one generation to the next.

The low grid social environment stands in marked contrast. Because of their individualism people find it extremely difficult to conceptualize the notion of faith community. They place value on diversity and scorn those who are constrained by common heritage. They delight in debunking the heritage of others and promoting an intellectual or social agnosticism. Unitarianism in the United States is a good illustration of a low grid religious organization. The Deni have a similar type of religious community, lacking common mythological themes and denying any particular core of religious values. Among the Deni there is no concept of sin, only of frustration at the behaviors of others that are annoying or interfering with one's own interest and activities.

Is unity affirmed by ritual/symbol (+1) or is structure brittle and isolating (−1)?

Powerful rituals reaffirm the unity and strength of groups. The form of baptism, three times forward, has become the symbol over which members in one Anabaptist denomination unite or divide. Some churches that have chosen to allow membership without rebaptism have been severely criticized by other churches that demand rebaptism for membership. The baptismal rite for some has become the cause celebre against which unity and commitment to truth are measured. Those local groups who admit members without this rebaptism have violated the faith code. Even though both groups of churches subscribe to the proper form of ritual, those who do not require it of all members are suspect and rejected by those who do. Aukaners in Surinam also affirm unity within the group by ritual and symbol. In the Aukan context, the rituals are usually rituals of cleansing and purification to which one must submit if one is to be reaffirmed as a loyal member.

Weak rituals and brittle structure delineate the weak group community. The fragmentation of crime families, such as the Mafia, is an illustration of brittle structure. The paramount interest among such a group is the self-interest of gain achieved through criminal activities. The structures of alliance formed to enhance social power are sustained only by the personal coercive power of leading individuals. When the leader is removed, the structure disintegrates as competing successors break into factional war against one another. The same phenomenon occurs in academic departments in major universities as the self-interest of faculty takes primacy over coordinated or collective activity. University departments are known for their factionalism and the isolation that individual faculty members experience in their academic work.

Are decisions by majority or consensus (+1) or by personal power (–1)?

Consensus decision making is the ideal in strong group situations. With consensus the members, at least publicly, all agree that this is the appropriate decision for that moment and that situation. Majority rule is less desirable, as can be seen in the conflict in the Anabaptist group mentioned. Even though the majority of delegates at their national conference affirmed the right of local groups to accept members without rebaptism, a minority refused to accept the decision, agitating first to rescind the majority decision and then withdrawing from the conference. In a strong group social context, members place a great deal of coercive force upon dissenters to bring them to a position of conformity. Rituals of divining and of purification serve this purpose among the Aukaners in Surinam. Among the Anabaptists, accusations of liberalism and denial of the truth of the Word of God are leveled at those who fail to conform.

A weak group social environment allows individuals or interest groups to seize power. Segmented, power-point decisions are those decisions made when individuals sense a superiority in power and are able to push a decision to achieve their personal objective. Such decisions are often coercive and fail to generate collective support. Abimelech, in the case opening the chapter, illustrates this well. The people of Shechem were divided, and Abimelech used their division, and outside power, to destroy the city.

Is support obligatory of members (+1) or conditioned by self-interest (–1)?

Strong group values inevitably press members to support leaders and the consensus decisions that follow their leadership. When people agree with one another, they form a consensus power bloc to support one another in opposition to outsiders or to members who fail to conform. Violation of such obligations of reciprocity breaks trust among the membership. When trust is broken the breach is nearly irreparable. The intensity of commitment members make to one another results in deep distrust and long-term alienation when these reciprocal expectations are thwarted. The history of the Anabaptist group is characterized by successive splitting and segmenting occurring nearly every fifty years. These divisions usually occur between the progressive and conservative congregations, and grow out of the failure of members to fulfill their reciprocal obligations of unity in the consensus group. A new authority is reformed as members agree to support one another with consensus doctrines, structures, and procedures.

In contrast, weak group values compel leaders to pursue personal loyalty from individuals. American advertising plays heavily upon the commitment of American people for self-fulfillment. "You owe it to yourself," "You only go around once; give it all the gusto you've got," are advertising slogans that illustrate the primacy of self over any other social obligations. The mere thought that a group should have prior demands over an individual is abhorrent to many Americans. The politician who desires political support must appeal to these individual interests. Deni village leaders face something of the same dilemma. Deni people will follow them only if they believe the chief is calling them to support something in their personal interest. The chief will invite people to participate in a day of feasting, which most people would find in their interest. However, if an individual has already decided to spend the day working on a special project, the chief has no power to coerce him to support the feast activities.

Do social links (kin, class) reinforce community authority (+1), or are social links a means to an end (–1)?

Where group is strong, community authority is reinforced by multiple social ties. For example, among the Anabaptists, members are not only committed to faith and practice, but also constitute a common social class and often intermarry so that kinship links bind together members of local congregations. Individuals in the group, then, are not only members but also kinsmen, and they participate in the same social economic class structure of the larger society. These cross-cutting ties create multiple linkages that bind together the members in a tight set of social relationships.

Where group is weak, community authority becomes the aggregate of conflicting interests and temporary alliances. Abimelech in the opening case uses conflicting interest to build his own power base. He forges alliances that are useful for his own agenda and advancement. In a more contemporary context, the stereotype of the social climber in American society grows out of such social relationships. The social climber uses connections of kin, social class, name dropping, and connections to forward his or her particular interest and career, yet feels little obligation to those persons or relationships apart from reciprocal interest or role obligations.

132

Shechem and Ephesus: Analysis and Comparison

The two case studies with which we opened the chapter provide distinctive illustrations of different patterns in the exercise of community authority (see table 8.1). Using the concepts and questions already presented, I will analyze each of these cases and compare them to see how community authority is operationalized in each of these settings. Since we are limited to the data that are presented in the particular text in Scripture, the conclusions drawn are tentative. However, the contrast between these two communities and the events of conflict that occur within them will become self-evident. I will begin with an analysis of grid.

The city of Shechem was apparently made up of extended family groups such as that described for Ruth and Boaz in the Book of Ruth. The text opens with Abimelech, son of Jerub-Baal, meeting with his mother's brothers and proposing to them that they should make him king. The people in Jerub-Baal's clan approached the other citizens of Shechem, and they agreed to this course of action. From this brief discussion we may conclude that Shechem was made up of various clan groups that were not united under single leadership, but constituted an aggregate of interest within the city (−1). The decision to make Abimelech king was a situational one (−1) in which Abimelech used his relationship with his mother's clan and their relationships with the other people of Shechem to put together an aggregate power base (−1).

By declaring Abimelech king of Shechem, the people established a hierarchy of power over their community (+.5). We read later that Zebul was Abimelech's deputy and served as governor of the city (+.5). By making Abimelech king, the people of Shechem allocated central power to him for a period of time (+.5).

After three years, however, the people in Shechem lost their enthusiasm for Abimelech and withdrew their support. Taking power into their own hands (−1), they began to ambush and rob anyone passing by their city. Gaal and his brothers moved into the city and convinced the people to grant power to them. Gaal argued that if the people would support him (−1) he would rid them of Abimelech and his onerous rule.

In summary, the social environment of Shechem was low grid (−3.5), in which people accepted the kingship of Abimelech for a time, but preferred to retain power in their own hands and to pursue their own advantage as situations warranted.

Table 8.1
Comparison of Community Authority for Schechem and Ephesus

High Grid	Low Grid		
Centralization (hierarchy, norm)	**Aggregation (individual interests)**	**Shechem**	**Ephesus**
+1 Hierarchy of power units	−1 Aggregate interest clusters	.5, −1	1, −.5
+1 Central unit decisions	−1 Decisions negotiated situationally	0, −1	1, 0
+1 Leader delegates power	−1 Leader's power is aggregate	.5, −1	1, −.5
+1 Leader exercises power independently	−1 Members retain independent power	0, −1	1, 0
+1 Members allocate power centrally	−1 Power granted only reciprocally	.5, −1	1, 0
Sum of Grid Variables:		**−3.5**	**+4.0**

Strong Group	Weak Group		
Coordination (group)	**Fragmentation (individual dyads)**	**Shechem**	**Ephesus**
+1 Heritage of common faith/beliefs	−1 Variant faith/beliefs	0, −1	1, −.5
+1 Affirmation of unity by ritual/symbol	−1 Brittle, isolating structure; identity relations	0, −1	1, 0
+1 Group decisions by majority or consensus	−1 Segmented, personal power decisions	0, −1	1, 0
+1 Obligation of reciprocity among members	−1 Support conditional upon interests	.5, −1	1, 0
+1 Social links reinforce authority (kin, class)	−1 Social links are means to ends	.5, −1	1, 0
Sum of Group Variables:		**−4.0**	**+4.5**

The city of Ephesus as depicted in the Book of Acts provides a striking contrast. The participants in this particular case all occupied distinctive roles. Demetrius, a silversmith, created significant business for fellow crafts-man in the city of Ephesus. Paul, a Jewish evangelist, and Gaius Aristarchus,

Paul's traveling companion, stayed with officials of the province who were friends of Paul. Alexander, who was apparently a Jew of some prominence and perhaps a silversmith as well, was called to testify. Finally, the city clerk addressed the crowd and mentions the courts and the proconsuls. From this list of participants it is easy to see that Ephesus had a much higher elaboration of status and role than that found in Shechem.

The text spells out with clarity the authority structure of the city. The city clerk was a member of the central power authority (+1), and the crowd quieted before him. He reminded the crowd that if they had a problem "the courts are open and there are proconsuls." These officials represented the central authority of the city (+1), and had been delegated the power (+1) to resolve charges of robbing or blaspheming. He then warned the crowd that further behavior of this kind might result in a charge of rioting, and this would bring the Roman authorities and perhaps the army to settle matters with a heavier hand (+1). The people responded to the authority of the city clerk (+1) and dispersed after he had dismissed them.

The social environment of the city of Ephesus was without question high grid. Only in the business sector do we see low grid forces significantly at work. Demetrius was able to mobilize the silversmiths in opposition to the apostle Paul. As such, he focused on the special interests of these craftsman, and they became a temporary power group (−.5). By arousing their discontent, and stimulating something of a riot, Demetrius used his aggregate power (−.5) to take action against Paul and his supporters. However, within a short period of time the power of the larger existing hierarchy reestablished control.

The people of Shechem and Ephesus also showed very different commitments in terms of group. In regard to their religious system, the people of Ephesus became greatly aroused in support of the "temple of the great Artemis" (+1). The success of Paul and his friends in converting people to Christianity provoked the riot described in Acts (−.5). The Christian faith was a divisive factor and this was unacceptable to Demetrius and his friends.

The people in Shechem, in contrast, were not moved by religious issues, but rather by political ones. Archaeologists have found the temple to Baal in the town close to the tower that apparently was burned by Abimelech. There was also a stronghold of the temple of El-Birith outside of the town on Mount Zalman. In all likelihood the people of Shechem worshiped Baal and the God of Israel and any other god they thought would be helpful to them (−1). The worship of the goddess

Artemis and the image in the temple in Ephesus were key symbols around which the people of Ephesus united (+1). In Shechem we found no uniting symbols, but rather competing kinship groups who can shift their allegiances and support at will (−1).

If we compare the decisions made in Shechem and in Ephesus we again find significant variation in process and group cohesion (see also fig. 8.1). In Ephesus the silversmiths and their laborers determined by consensus to riot. The action was rapid and quickly they gained support of much of the population of the city so that a huge assembly gathered. In like manner, after the sobering speech of the city clerk, there was a consensus to disperse (+1). The clerk appealed to their obligations as citizens of Ephesus and reminded them of the structures that were in place through which they could handle a difficult matter if they wished to do so (+1).

The dynamic of the decisions in Shechem were somewhat different. Because Abimelech was a son of Gideon, the recently deceased ruler of all Israel, he was able to convince his kinsman that he had the power to exalt them above their present status and to save them from domination by another of Gideon's sons who would not be their kinsman (−1). The argument they made to the other people in Shechem was that it was better to have a brother ruling them than to have someone from another family; that is, to support Abimelech was in their family interest (−1). While the other families in Shechem agreed to this for a time, within a period of three years new interests emerged and the people shifted their support to someone else who could further their particular designs (−1).

Factionalism characterized the social life of the town. For Abimelech and for the people of Shechem, their social links were primarily means to ends (−1). Abimelech used his family first to gain the support of the other citizens of Shechem and then to execute all of the other sons of Gideon to become ruler over all of Israel. Gaal used similar relationships to mobilize the citizens of Shechem against Abimelech. Abimelech turned against the people who had supported him (−1) and effectively destroyed Shechem and the neighboring city of Thebez, which apparently supported the Shechem rebellion. Zebul remained faithful to Abimelech; perhaps he was a member of his family (+.5). Abimelech apparently had other supporters who stayed with Zebul and were effective in driving Gaal and his brothers out of Shechem (+.5). The pervasive individualist social game was precisely what made it so difficult to rule over Israel. Matters could not be settled by ordinary political process; rather, people resorted to rebellion and warfare.

Ephesus, in contrast, demonstrated much higher group cohesion and a clear hierarchical structure. The social game of Ephesus was hierarchist. The dispute between Demetrius and Paul was settled in an orderly manner by public officials. These officials reestablished control over the crowd by the subtle threat of force and an appeal to the corporate institutional procedures well known to them.

UNION Ltd.: Community Authority
by Donna R. Downs

The mission team under investigation is composed of nine families who have as their mission the training of church leaders in East Africa. As such it is much smaller than the village at Shechem or the city of Ephesus. Yet, the diagnostic criteria utilized to analyze those towns are just as useful to understand community authority as practiced by this mission team. From our analysis of domestic authority, it is clear that the western and the African members bring different value expectations to

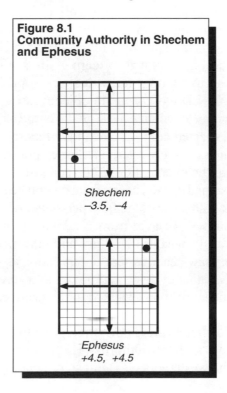

Figure 8.1
Community Authority in Shechem and Ephesus

Shechem
−3.5, −4

Ephesus
+4.5, +4.5

their ministry roles, which are derived from their prior family and community affiliations. This fact plays a key part in how they adapt to the mission philosophy of an egalitarian team.

The Grid Dimension

The strength of the westerners' low grid score (−4.5) highlights a quantitative, if not substantive, difference from their African colleagues (−1.5) (see table 8.2). The similarities in their outlook can be attributed to UNIWORLD team philosophy. The corporate culture of UNIWORLD attributes power to the aggregate interests (−1) of the team. The field team director has aggregate power (−1), limited by the consensus decision-making procedure and group objectives set by the team. Though technically the field leader cannot be fired, a majority of team members may influence international leaders to transfer or remove a director. Because the team sets ministry goals by consensus, members engage in considerable negotiation and dialogue (−1), and the leader serves to facilitate the process. Once team goals are set, members exercise independent power over field ministry (−1), individually setting their work tasks and schedules.

The team director and members grant power reciprocally (−1) to one another. Although he is responsible for reporting to UNIWORLD headquarters on the accomplishment of team goals, the team director may not act as an authority to judge individual accomplishment.

While UNIWORLD has corporate objectives for ministry, the field teams have autonomy to redefine these goals for the local context. African team members expected corporate headquarters to exercise more centralized power than did the westerners. For example, the African director, David, sought the intervention of the centralized hierarchy (+.5) on his behalf. He assumed that decisions from central headquarters (+.5) carried more weight than those of the field personnel with whom he worked daily. When promises to David from headquarters were never kept, he felt the team unfairly made its own rules and informed headquarters.

The westerners saw headquarters' intervention as unneeded or intrusive and rated the value of delegated power as a zero. Africans in contrast attribute independent power (+.5) to the team leader, derived from his position as delegated leader (+.5) of the team. The ethos of UNIWORLD is that members grant power reciprocally, but Africans tended to allocate power to a central authority (+.5) like headquarters, or a team director, while the westerners (+.5) did so reluctantly.

The Group Dimension

Given the team philosophy of UNION Ltd., we expect members to show a common value for group authority, yet the Africans prove more highly group oriented (+4) than the westerners (+1.5). Ideally, all members come to UNIWORLD with a commitment to common faith and the corporate ministry goals (+1). Although each team member interprets the objectives of UNIWORLD a little differently, the overall corporate vision ostensibly binds all staff and field teams together. Further, all major ministry decisions are ideally made by a consensus (+1) of the members.

The first difference occurs in how westerners and Africans affirm authority and identity within the group. Africans place high value on ritual and symbolic unity (+1) as expressed in laudatory introductions, frequent goat roasts, and ceremonies. The westerners shy away from these public rituals and expressions of group solidarity and achievement. According to one western teammate, "We're here because we have a task to do, not to identify with a team." While the westerners do attend these events (+.5), they do not value them, preferring a restricted identity (−.5) with the group.

Africans believe in reciprocal obligations (+1) such as trust, bonds of unity, and fidelity to friendships, but westerners support the team as much for personal interests (−.5) as they do because of team bonds (+.5). When an African teammate calls upon a westerner to support him in a conflict, he expects loyalty and solidarity. If the westerner refuses, he is viewed as a traitor. While westerners see reciprocity as important, they also tend to allow for individual differences and freedom to go one's own way and voice one's own opinion when necessary. Africans may also be conditional in their support, seeking personal interests (−.5), but they do so silently, avoiding the task or the decision with which they disagree.

Africans and westerners also differ in approach to social links within and outside the team. Africans place high value on their identity as team and staff member of an international mission agency, which elevates their prestige and authority (+1) and their economic status. Westerners (+.5) tend to play down organizational identity, minimizing the obligations of the social links within and outside the team and employing them primarily to enhance personal or ministry goals (−1). While Africans occasionally use such links to meet personal goals (−.5), they have greater awareness of the power and status such links provide outside of UNION Ltd.

Table 8.2
Community Authority in UNION Ltd.: Western v. African Missionaries

High Grid		Low Grid			
Centralization (hierarchy, norm)		**Aggregation (individual interests)**		**Westerners**	**Africans**
+1	Hierarchy of power units	−1	Aggregate interest clusters	0, −1	.5, −1
+1	Central unit decisions	−1	Decisions negotiated situationally	0, −1	.5, −1
+1	Leader delegates power	−1	Leader's power is aggregate	0, −1	.5, −1
+1	Leader exercises power independently	−1	Members retain independent power	0, −1	.5, −1
+1	Members allocate power centrally	−1	Power granted only reciprocally	.5, −1	1, −.5
Sum of Grid Variables:				**−4.5**	**−1.5**

Strong Group		Weak Group			
Coordination (group)		**Fragmentation (individual dyads)**		**Westerners**	**Africans**
+1	Heritage of common faith/beliefs	−1	Variant faith/beliefs	1, 0	1, 0
+1	Affirmation of unity by ritual/symbol	−1	Brittle, isolating structure; identity relations	.5, −.5	1, 0
+1	Group decisions by majority or consensus	−1	Segmented, personal power decisions	1, 0	1, 0
+1	Obligation of reciprocity among members	−1	Support conditional upon interests	.5, −.5	1, −.5
+1	Social links reinforce authority (kin, class)	−1	Social links are means to ends	.5, −1	1, −.5
Sum of Group Variables:				**+1.5**	**+4.0**

CONCLUSIONS

Although both Africans and westerners play the egalitarian game with regard to community authority, westerners are more egalitarian in their assignments of role and less committed to group than are their African counterparts (fig. 8.2). Perhaps this is due in part to the greater economic freedom of the western missionary. Most westerners have a bloc of supporting churches and individuals whose loyalty is not to UNIWORLD, but to them as individuals. If his ministry with the team is not satisfying, he can take his bloc of financial support and go elsewhere—either to a different mission field or to a different agency. The African has more at risk in challenging group norms. If he does not conform and must leave the agency, his means of support might be cut off entirely. He is faced with finding a new identity, job, and means of support. Because they are at greater risk when they leave, Africans place higher value on identity in the group and on conformity to headquarters' policy and requirements. David, the African leader who left the organization, found his expectations dashed as he sensed that Jonathan, the western field leader, undermined his relationships with headquarters and spoiled his reputation.

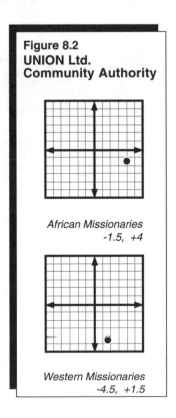

Figure 8.2
UNION Ltd.
Community Authority

African Missionaries
-1.5, +4

Western Missionaries
-4.5, +1.5

Research Questions 8.1
Grid and Community Authortiy

High Grid	Low Grid
+1 *Hierarchy of power units.* To what extent do people distribute authority and power through subunits within the centralized hierarchy? or	−1 *Aggregate interest clusters.* Do people reject authority and hierarchy? Do they form aggregate interest clusters, dispersing when their interests are satisfied or diverge?
+1 *Central unit decisions.* Are people empowered to make decisions for others? To what extent is the locus of decision making reserved for or controlled by the central power units? or	−1 *Decisions negotiated situationally.* Do members retain independent power, forcing a negotiation process? Are people forced to bargain and dialogue to reach collectively significant decisions?
+1 *Leaders delegate power.* How much power is delegated to subordinates, and in what specific ways? Are subordinates free to exercise power within a structure of accountability? or	−1 *Leaders exercise aggregate power.* Is the leader's power composed of individuals who grant support? Is the leader's control limited by individuals who may withdraw granted power at any time?
+1 *Leader exercises power independently.* To what extent do the highest leaders exercise independent power, and how is that power limited, if at all? or	−1 *Members retain independent power.* Do people have control over their labor, finances, and other resources, reserving independent power for personal use?
+1 *Members allocate power centrally.* To what extent do members participate willingly and supportively with the central authority? or	−1 *Power granted reciprocally.* Do individuals manage their resources and labor to support or withhold support from leaders? To what extent is personal reciprocity an expectation when a person gives to another control over resources or labor?

Research Questions 8.2
Group and Community Authority

Strong Group	Weak Group
+1 *Heritage of common faith/beliefs.* To what extent are heritage and tenets of faith given high value and profile among participants? or	−1 *Variant faith/beliefs.* Do people reject heritage and hold beliefs as variant as individual participants? Do they reject any attempt to promote a common faith or belief as an imposition upon others?
+1 *Affirmation of unity by ritual/symbol.* Do people employ ritual and symbol as a means to affirm group unity and identify? or	−1 *Brittle, isolating structure.* Are symbols weak, rituals of marginal value, and group integration like brittle glass? Does conflict of interest lead to fragmentation and the isolation of individuals from one another?
+1 *Group decision by majority or consensus.* Are decisions for the group controlled by a majority at least, and by consensus at best? or	−1 *Segmented, personal power decisions.* Do individuals or interest groups impose decisions or overpower the opposition of others? Can a minority overpower the majority?
+1 *Obligation of membership support.* Does authority for leaders grow out of group consensus? Are members expected to support the group? If they fail to support or reciprocate, are group relations damaged? or	−1 *Support conditional upon satisfaction of interests.* Do individuals support leaders in return for satisfaction of personal interests? Are claims for loyalty rejected on the basis of rights to individual freedom?
+1 *Social links reinforce community authority (kin, class).* Do people submit personal interests to valued relationships of kinship, community, and social class? Do people cultivate relations through several social links from overlapping relationship? or	−1 *Social links are means to an end.* Do people minimize the social obligations of kinship, class, and faith, and use them only to the extent that they enhance personal goals and interest?

Conflict, Political Interests, and Cultural Bias

Case of Moses

When his father-in-law saw all that Moses was doing for the people, he said, ". . . Why do you alone sit as judge, while all these people stand around you from morning till evening?"

Moses answered him, "Because the people come to me to seek God's will. Whenever they have a dispute, it is brought to me, and I decide between the parties and inform them of God's decrees and laws."

Moses' father-in-law replied, "What you are doing is not good. . . . You must be the people's representative before God and bring their disputes to him. . . . But select capable men from all the people—men who fear God, trustworthy men who hate dishonest gain—and appoint them as officials over thousands, hundreds, fifties and tens. Have them serve as judges for the people at all times, but have them bring every difficult case to you; the simple cases they can decide themselves. . . . If you do this and God so commands, you will be able to stand the strain, and all these people will go home satisfied." (Exod. 18:14–23)

Case of Jacob and Laban

Laban said to him, "Just because you are a relative of mine, should you work for me for nothing? Tell me what your wages should be."

Now Laban had two daughters; the name of the older was Leah, and the name of the younger was Rachel. Leah had weak eyes, but Rachel was lovely in form, and beautiful. Jacob was in love with Rachel and said, "I'll work for you seven years in return for your younger daughter Rachel."

Laban said, "It's better that I give her to you than to some other man. Stay here with me." So Jacob served seven years to get Rachel, but they seemed like only a few days to him because of his love for her.

Then Jacob said to Laban, "Give me my wife. My time is completed, and I want to lie with her."

So Laban brought together all the people of the place and gave a feast. But when evening came, he took his daughter Leah and gave her to Jacob, and Jacob lay with her. . . .

When morning came, there was Leah! So Jacob said to Laban, "What is this you have done to me? I served you for Rachel, didn't I? Why have you deceived me?" (Gen. 29:15–25)

Leadership and Settling Disputes

Situations of social conflict provide the test of effective leadership in every society and social environment. In our opening case study Moses was overwhelmed by the number of people coming to him to resolve their disputes. His leadership was ineffective because he had not developed a strategy to reduce his case load to a manageable size and to focus on those conflicts for which he was the appropriate person to judge. His father-in-law observed his dilemma and provided some wise counsel for restructuring the process and delegating power to trustworthy men. Moses demonstrated his wisdom by accepting this sound advice and implementing it immediately.

The process that Jethro suggested to Moses was not the only option available. Jethro suggested a plan that changed the social environment of Israel to a hierarchical (higher grid) system of adjudication for the resolution of disputes. In their comparative study of the disputing process, Laura Nader and Harry Todd (1978, 9) identify seven distinctive procedures for settling disputes that occur around the world: adjudication, arbitration, mediation, negotiation, coercion, avoidance, and "lumping it." Each of these requires somewhat different social structures, procedures, and styles of leadership for settling conflicts.

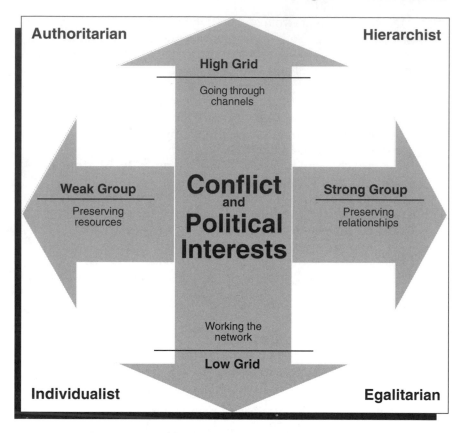

Nader and Todd note that most societies provide several procedures with which members engage one another in conflict and disputes. These procedures differ in terms of the presence or absence of a third party, the nature of the third party's intervention, and the type of settlement. It is the argument of this chapter that a given social environment predisposes the individuals and the groups within it to employ particular kinds of procedures for settling disputes. In the development of the model that follows, the text presents how the factors of grid and group establish value parameters within which people seek to resolve interpersonal and group conflicts.

Going Through Channels

The concept of going through proper channels is part of the everyday life of most American people. When this value provides the rationale for legitimate social behavior, nothing will cause greater conflict than the violation of this rule. People in educational or government bureaucracies become extremely agitated when one of their subordinates fails to go through the proper channels in dealing with a particular issue.

Formal and institutional channels characterize high grid social environments. The procedures used to settle disputes reflect this format and institutional emphasis. An individual in a bureaucratic structure who is in a position of power over subordinates may use that power to achieve a particular outcome in a dispute. Coercion is possible when an individual holds power over others and feels free to use it to achieve the outcome desired.

In most institutional situations, a rule of law governs relationships between the members. When such rules are explicit and known by the members, they often turn to a third party to intervene on their behalf in matters of dispute. The judges of the Old Testament supply an ancient example of adjudication of disputes between members of a society. Moses established the precedent in his role of judge over the people of Israel during their exodus from Egypt. From that time on, the leaders in Israel all were recognized as having authority to hear and settle disputes among the members of the society.

Adjudication and arbitration are "authority rule" processes. In both cases a third party has the authority to settle a dispute and the individuals involved must abide by it. Adjudication has behind it the authority of the law, whereas arbitration has only the consent of the principal parties to abide by the decision of the arbitrator.

Working the Network

Working the network characterizes the dispute processes of low grid social environments. In this context the procedures are informal and personal. There are no formally organized channels; individuals have autonomy to act in their own interest apart from the constraints of institution and law. Networks are personal rather than formal and may be expanded or contracted as individuals build relationships or break them. It is useful to describe the dispute process in a low grid social environment as finessing the outcome. While in the high grid social environment individuals resort to power, law, and authority for the resolution of the conflict, in a low grid social environment the primary focus of dispute is stratagem. Individuals employ diverse procedures and relationships to achieve the resolution of conflict and their personal objectives. This is not to say that power is not part of the process, but rather individuals may not resort to structural power to achieve their objectives.

Jacob's disputes with his father-in-law, Laban, are an illustration of the finessing process. When Laban substituted Leah for Rachel, Jacob had no recourse. He accepted Leah and renegotiated his contract with Laban to obtain Rachel. Laban in this situation finessed Jacob by secretly bringing Leah to him rather than his choice, Rachel. Jacob resorted to the same type of stratagem in his relationships with Laban, using strategy to increase his flocks rather than Laban's and to break away from Laban's household. Both men used informal and personal stratagem to accomplish their objectives with one another.

Negotiation and mediation are processes that are amenable to low grid social values. Laban negotiated with Jacob after he had finessed him by giving him Leah. Both parties agreed to another seven years of labor and to other economic considerations. Mediation involves the intervention of a third party to aid in the negotiation process and may be utilized in either a high or a low grid social environment. The object of mediation is to obtain the consent of those in conflict by crafting a resolution acceptable to all parties.

Other low grid strategies include personal posturing in an attempt to intimidate one's foe or physical duel. The cowboy shoot-out at high noon or the classic European duel are examples of personal processes that deteriorate to a show of personal power.

Individuals in a low grid social environment are constrained both by values for the public good and by their own personal interest. An individual may choose to lump it because he has no choice in a continuing relationship or because the pressure of the public good is an adequate constraint. Similarly, an individual may choose to avoid or to withdraw from a conflict, recognizing the personal power of the other party or one's inability to pursue a dispute to a desired end. The maintenance of the public good is informal and personal. Relationships in the network are broken by withdrawal or sustained by lumping it when the individual finds such action to be to personal advantage.

Priority of Resources or Relationship

Nader and Todd (1978, 18–19) note that disputes about scarce resources produce a recurring dilemma about priority of persons or resources. In some societies, individuals give higher priority to obtaining and holding resources, even at the cost of social relationships, whereas in others, individuals readily sacrifice resources to acquire and maintain social relationships. These value differences are correlated with variables of strong and weak group. In a weak group social environment, people form numerous relationships, based on simple, single-factor links. For example, college students and professors have a relationship based upon a contract by each for a given class. The cashier in the bookstore has a contract to transact exchanges of money for books with the customers. These simplex relationships are characterized by a single functional link that brings people together for a common activity. Disputes in such contexts usually result in individuals valuing the resource more than they value the relationship.

When individuals are connected to one another by two or more social links, social scientists term these relationships multiplex, for they grow out of a strong emphasis on group. For example, Joab, the general of King David's army, was connected to David by at least three other social links: he was David's sister's son, a long-term friend, and an ally. When individuals are bound together in multiplex relationships they tend to choose the priority of relationship over either principle or resource in a dispute. This factor helps us to better understand David's actions toward Joab during his lifetime. Joab violated David's wishes on several significant occasions (2 Sam. 3:27; 14:19; 18:14), but David did not take action against Joab. Some Bible interpreters have called this a weakness on David's part, but they fail to recognize the multiplex social ties that bound David and Joab together. David punished Joab through his son, Solomon, after his death (1 Kings 2:5–6).

In strong group social environments, people engaging in disputes often rely on negotiation or mediation to settle their conflict. These processes generally lead to compromise outcomes. In contrast, people in weak group social environments turn frequently to adjudication or arbitration to resolve their differences. These procedures result in win or lose decisions rather than compromise.

Vulnerability as Weakness or Strength

These different processes for settling conflict have distinctly different implications for personal vulnerability. Marvin K. Mayers (1987, 160) shows how personal vulnerability may be perceived either as weak-

ness or as strength. People are less likely to express their own vulnerability or the vulnerability of others when they perceive personal vulnerability as weakness. Exposing vulnerability is acceptable in weak group
social environments. Adjudication and arbitration drag individuals into
open conflict and expose their failures and conflict to public scrutiny.
The win or lose decisions also clearly highlight the vulnerability of individuals involved.

In contrast, the strong group social environment protects the vulnerability of individual members. The processes of negotiation and mediation serve to equalize power relationships and to protect the dignity of
persons in conflict. The compromise outcomes are often structured
around the protection of the vulnerability of the participants.

When relationships are simplex, people can be rather careless about
exposing the vulnerability of others. However, when relationships are
multiplex the exposure of weaknesses in one's close friends and kin may
lead to broken relationships that have far-reaching social consequences.
Because people know one another over their lifetimes, as did David and
Joab, they exhibit careful concern and protection of self and others. Joab,
for example, was loyal and helpful to David, even when David exhibited weakness as a warrior (2 Sam. 12:27–28), deception and murder in
his personal life (2 Sam. 11:1–17), and ineffectiveness as king (2 Sam.
14:1–3).

Grid: Going Through the Channels or Working the Network?

The characteristics of social structure are once again central to the
fieldworker's understanding. To understand process for settling disputes,
one must determine the presence or absence of judges, arbitrators, and
mediators, and the accepted public procedures for managing disputes.
In high grid structures, the authority of rule and the importance of the
structure become paramount in resolving disputes. The process of dispute settlement is linked inextricably to the institutional structure.

The characteristics of low grid dispute settlement are its informality
and its lack of social structure. Individuals build personal networks of
relationship out of contact and exchanges with other individuals in society. The informality and the lack of institutional support, accompanied
by the autonomy of individuals, produce a very different type of dispute
management. In the variables that follow we will identify some of the

questions that a fieldworker should ask to discern whether the processes at work in the social environment emphasize strong or weak grid values.

Are there formal, institutional channels (+1) or are channels informal (–1)?

In our opening case study, Moses set forth the formal channels through which the people of Israel should appeal for the settling of their disputes. This basic pattern of dispute settlement was carried into the period of the kings. Such formal institutional structures for the settlement of the dispute may be found in many different cultures of the world. In the islands of Yap, chiefs had to proceed on formally recognized channels of communication between villages and leaders, or their requests could legitimately be ignored. The formal channel *(tha)* became an institution of great power in Yap political activity and in the settlement of disputes. The modern bureaucracy of the American legal system has its formal institutional channels through which a dispute must proceed. American attorneys are trained in the specific rules of the institutional process and earn their living by leading individual litigants through the system.

When a person living in a middle-class neighborhood complains to city hall about the unkempt yard of a neighbor, she uses a formal channel. If she decides to talk to a relative or to the wife of that neighbor, she is lodging an informal complaint. Using an informal social connection may accomplish the same goal of having the neighbor address the condition of his front yard. Jacob used personal kin ties to Laban to handle his conflicts. He had nowhere else to turn.

Do people attempt powering (+1) or finessing the outcome (–1)?

Americans who threaten lawsuits do so because they anticipate that this structure will allow them to achieve an outcome they could not accomplish by less coercive means. Yapese who use the *tha* hope to influence a decision they could not achieve or prevent with their own power.

The idea of finessing is that one uses craftiness, negotiation, pressure, and power in strategic ways to accomplish one's objective. To what extent do people deal with each situation in a unique way, and does the actor become a key strategist in working toward an outcome? The urban American who talks to her neighbor's wife or relative about the poor condition of their yard is attempting to finesse an outcome rather than to power it. The Deni wife who shouts angrily at her rival across the village plaza is pressuring an outcome by suggesting that she can play the same seductive game. Laban used deception to accomplish his goal with Jacob.

151

Is there codification of rules (+1) or only a sense of the public good (–1)?

When Jethro, Moses' father-in-law, advised him to set up a hierarchical system for the settling of disputes, he warned Moses to select capable men "who fear God, trustworthy men who hate dishonest gain." Perhaps one of the reasons that Jethro was so cautious in this matter of appointment was his understanding that their role in settling disputes would legitimize a position of authority and dominance in the community. If they were not men of good character, they could not be trusted to occupy such a legitimate, prominent role. People who occupy roles of mediation or arbitration acquire the force of law to legitimize their decisions. As every American who has received a traffic ticket knows, the police are most often legitimized by the legal process in American society. The judge accepts the testimony of an officer against the protest of the driver, making the officer dominant in relationship to the citizenry. Public disputes are settled by the dictums of either authority rule or majority rule through the structure. Laws in American society are passed by majority rule and are implemented by authority rule.

In the case of Jacob and Laban there was a clear power differential between the two. Laban was the senior man who had extensive livestock and two marriageable daughters. Jacob was a young man who had nothing. Throughout this story we see Jacob converting his junior powerless role first into Laban's son-in-law and then into a wealthy, powerful head of a large extended family in competition with Laban. Throughout this process, Jacob used his strategic abilities to gain financial resources and to build his personal power base so that he could separate from Laban. Using relationships with others to equalize power is a common ploy in low grid social environments. Deni Indians use multiple relationships to Brazilian patrons as an excuse to avoid working for each. Deni chiefs have influence to the extent that they are able to motivate people by example and charisma, yet they have no power to arbitrate or even mediate a dispute.

Do people use institutional (+1) or personally directed process (–1)?

Both adjudication and arbitration are third-party processes. Adjudicated disputes are settled by a third party (i.e., the municipal judge) who has the authority to make and impose a decision upon the litigants. Arbitration is power vested in a third party by the principals themselves to make a decision on their behalf (i.e., salary arbitration in professional baseball). In both of these processes, authority is institutionalized and the litigants are subject to the decision of that authority. Moses and his appointees served to adjudicate disputes in Israel and thus institutionalized the judicial process.

The alternatives to institutional dispute settlement are the various forms of personal process. People may resort to public posturing and through such posturing attempt to intimidate a disputant into lumping it or withdrawing. When such posturing is not effective or is deemed inappropriate by the participants, negotiation may provide an alternative means of dispute settlement. In low grid social environments, these are the only alternatives available to individuals. Individuals negotiate in a face-to-face relationship and any settlement is agreed to by both parties. On some occasions when a settlement cannot be resolved by posturing or negotiation, individuals may resort to personal duels. These duels may be social, economic, or physical (as in the case of Alexander Hamilton and Aaron Burr in the early history of American government).

Do people use institutional (+1) or personal time/agenda (–1)?

The novel *Bleak House* by Charles Dickens provides a marvelous example of institutional time in the settlement of disputes. Dickens describes the case of Jarndyce and Jarndyce regarding a disputed will that attorneys carried in the British courts for years. The judges and the attorneys established the times for hearings, the delay of process, the movements for new information, and perpetuated the case over so many years that by the time it was resolved all the resources of the estate had been spent to support the legal process. In several of his novels, Dickens is acerbic in his criticism of the British judicial process, particularly in reference to its use of institutional time; cases are perpetuated indefinitely to the great distress and loss of both the plaintiff and the defendants. All of the western courts, whether they represent Latin legal code or the common law of British and American courts, set the time for hearings and the agenda as determined by law and customary legal processes.

When people choose to settle their disputes within the context of their own relationships or outside of the institutional alternatives available to them, they are free to employ personal time and agendas in the resolution of these matters. In a low grid social environment no external rules intervene, nor do external parties prescribe time and agenda. Usually, individuals are opportunistic, selecting a time that serves their interest to lodge a dispute. The Deni wife chooses a time when enough people are around to insure a public hearing of her grievance. People select time and agenda in accord with opportunity and willingness of the opponent to respond.

Group: Preserving Relationships
v. Preserving Resources

In every dispute in human society, the issues of relationships and resources are always present. Since human motives are extremely complex and the circumstances that surround the disputes are also highly variable, it is impossible to predict how human beings will act in relationship to these issues. In the disputing process one must sacrifice either relationships or resources. It is extremely difficult to find a solution that will allow the litigants to sustain all that they wish in either relationships or resources.

One of the key factors pressing individuals toward one or another kind of solution is the strength or weakness of the value for group. In a social environment in which there is strong value for group, the pressure to reach a decision that will preserve relationships is great. The very nature of group relationships, involving multiple ties between persons, pressure for consensus decisions, and concerns to protect vulnerability and avoid confrontation, increase the cost of breaking relationships and the pressure upon people to preserve them. In contrast, in a weak group social environment the weakness of relationships, the freedom to make independent decisions, and the ease of exposing vulnerability and engaging in confrontation allow participants to press for preserving their resources and fulfilling their economic as opposed to their relational interests. In the variables that follow we will identify some of the questions that a fieldworker should ask to discern whether the processes at work in the social environment emphasizes strong or weak group values.

Are relations characterized by multiplex networks (+1) or aggregate factions (−1)?

Earlier we noted how difficult it was for David to punish Joab for violating David's instructions and murdering two of David's enemies. David had the same problem when his son Absalom attempted to steal his kingdom from him. Even after Absalom raised an army and drove David from his palace, David was reluctant to act against him. Perhaps David was unusual in the strong personal commitments he exhibited to those people who had been close to him. However, he was consistent in that he

154

treated Saul in the same manner. David refused to harm those men with whom he had close relationships and from whom he had received significant support and help at one time during his political career.

In the case of Abimelech and the men of Shechem (chap. 8), aggregate factions were predominant. Gaal led one of the factions to rob anyone who passed by that city. He also organized the people to rebel against Abimelech, and this rebellion precipitated a major war between the forces of Abimelech and the men of Shechem. Different aggregate forces appeared to have specific political and economic objectives. Even relationships within Abimelech's family seemed unimportant in the dispute that emerged.

Is conflict resolved by group consensus (+1) or by independent actors (–1)?

The idea of consensus decision making is that the leaders and the members of the group have been consulted and their decision with regard to the resolution of the conflict is one to which they are in general agreement. When Boaz decided to redeem Naomi's land and marry Ruth he had to do so in consultation with village elders and obtain agreement of the other heir who had priority over his right. The Aukan in Surinam have similar processes for settling disputes in their communities. However, the Aukan use divination to appeal to the ancestors for the authoritative cause and consequences of a particular problem. Gideon's gold ephod was apparently used in a similar manner: to divine information that would be authoritative in settling disputes among the people of Israel.

Independent decision making occurs when people feel little or no obligation to appeal to others in authority to help them resolve the dispute. We have already cited Jacob's disputes with Laban in this regard. The Deni in Brazil operate in similar fashion, usually carrying their disputes into the public in the form of open confrontation and argument. However, the disputes are not resolved by consensus; they are resolved when the people involved tire of the public debate and the ongoing hostilities. Sometimes they achieve no solution at all, but merely have the opportunity to vent their frustrations.

Do leaders protect vulnerability (+1) or expose vulnerability (–1)?

In a strong group environment, full information is rarely disclosed, and culpable individuals often are absent from the proceedings or in the background while a spokesman intervenes on their behalf. Dialogue on the subject involves circumlocution and indirect accusation and

155

response. When David plotted to have Uriah killed on the battlefront and then took Bathsheba, Uriah's wife, as his own wife, no one dared confront him except Nathan the prophet. Nathan did this in an indirect manner, telling David the story of a rich man who took the little ewe lamb from a poor man. After David responded with great anger, Nathan named David directly for his sin with Bathsheba. Such practices are common in strong group social environments, where social relationships are of highest priority.

The Deni represent the opposite pattern in exposing the vulnerability of others. When Deni have a dispute they usually go to the top steps of the ladders leading into their houses and in full voice rail against the offenders across the village plaza. If an offender happens to be a member of one's own household the person will go to the house of another villager opposite and begin public accusation from that position. The Deni do not hesitate to expose the weaknesses and challenge the credibility of their opponents. Every aspect of their dispute is made public so that others in the village can hear and take sides. If one of the two involved feels that public opinion is mounting against him or her, that person may storm in violent protest from the village, proclaiming the desire never to return again. Paul and Barnabas illustrate this type of conflict in their dispute over John Mark in Acts.

Are disputes settled by broker/mediation (+1) or by display of personal power (–1)?

Mediation played an important role in the life and political career of David. The incident of David's dispute with Nabal in 1 Samuel 25 describes how Abigail, Nabal's wife, plea bargained with David for the life of her family and husband. Abner attempted to mediate between David and Ishbosheth, and Joab mediated between David and Absalom. In some societies mediators or brokers are renowned individuals of social prestige or religious prestige.

The process of settling legal cases in American courts is one that encourages the display of personal power and a contest of wits and eloquence. American attorneys gain great public fame for their ability to win cases that the public generally agrees they should have lost. Through their charisma, knowledge of the law, and personal wit they have been able to gain decisions in the court that counter public opinion and wisdom. Such a contest was made famous in 1995 when O. J. Simpson was tried for murder, and the trial was televised. Such trials are win-lose struggles.

Is there confrontation avoidance (+1) or open confrontation (−1)?

Avoiding confrontation saves the face of both the litigant and the defendant. One of the most interesting cases of avoiding confrontation in Scripture is the dispute between David and Absalom prior to Absalom's rebellion. After Absalom had killed his brother Amnon, David refused to see Absalom or to allow him to come peacefully back into Jerusalem. This decision was one that caused David great personal pain, yet he knew this was the appropriate action to take. After several years Joab convinced David to allow Absalom to return to his home and ultimately to receive Absalom in his court. Rather than seeking a reconciliation between father and son, Absalom used the face-to-face meeting to justify his own action and humiliate his father, David. By refusing a confrontation, David saved the life of his son. By pressing for a confrontation, Absalom succeeded in humiliating his father.

In weak group social situations open confrontation is not only acceptable, it is legitimate. People use open confrontation to form factions and to build power careers. Factions gain power and individuals realign their loyalties on the basis of these open confrontations and assessments of interest and loyalty. Violation of public norms leads to public criticism and response. Confrontations are not friendly, but when they are over, friendly relationships are readily restored. Factions are quite common among university and college faculty, even in Christian institutions. In many parts of the Christian community open confrontation is deemed to be spiritually appropriate. Sometimes these confrontations do result in the resolution of disputes. However, at other times factions form, leading to the splitting of churches, the dividing of faculties, or the breaking of Christian organizations. Open confrontation always has potential for precipitating social factions.

UNION Ltd.: Conflicts and Political Interests
by Donna R. Downes

Case Study: David, Jonathan, and UNIWORLD Administration

In the early 1980s, UNIWORLD decided to appoint an African director for the UNION Ltd. team in an effort to internationalize its leadership. This man, David, had a variety of spiritual gifts (mercy, pastoring, giving, and teaching, among others), but lacked ability to cope with the administrative issues of importance to the western members on the team.

One of the westerners, Jonathan, confronted the director to address the problem, an approach that greatly offended David. David defended his response, saying that the younger man had no right to challenge him as UNIWORLD's appointed leader without going through proper channels; that they needed to bring in objective mediators to talk about the issue from both sides; and that they should try as much as possible to restrict their conflict to private meetings. "There was no need to show our dirty laundry to everyone," said David. On the other side, Jonathan wanted to "bring the issue before the entire team to decide" and to leave mission authorities and other parties out of the affair.

As the years went on, the problem escalated and the UNIWORLD mission authorities finally did step in, but not before terrible damage had been done to the relationship between Jonathan and David. By then, David said that Jonathan only wanted power in the mission, and Jonathan countered by saying that David was ineffective as a leader and could not be trusted. Where David had been visibly and verbally angry with Jonathan, David's approach to the formal leadership was one of servanthood, submission to authority, and peaceful talk. "I am willing to do whatever it takes to restore unity to the team and to go forth together in ministry," he said. Jonathan, however, often leaned toward exposing David's vulnerability: "We should simply put this whole issue to a team vote and see if David should step down. We've got to get things out in the open so that David can see his problems more clearly."

The mission authorities eventually removed David from leadership, and the lot fell to Jonathan, who was willing to serve. David later resigned because he felt "betrayed and lied to" by the mission and could not serve under the new leader. The mission concluded that David had not been honest about his desire to do anything to work toward unity, since he was unwilling to work with Jonathan under any circumstances.

Analyzing the case study through observation and interviews, we again find Africans and westerners have significant differences in their understanding of the game being played. Applying the diagnostic questions, the differences show Africans much stronger (+3.7) in commitment to group than the westerners (−.9). However, the Africans' zero grid score (see table 9.1), according to Michael Thompson (1982), suggests that individuals are trying to achieve equilibrium between two conflicting social environments. The Africans appear to be adjusting their hierarchist game for settling disputes to the lower grid corporate values of UNIWORLD International.

THE GRID DIMENSION

Both formal and informal channels for communication and conflict resolution exist within UNIWORLD International and UNION Ltd. Formal channels tend to be used in communication between the team and headquarters, and the informal channels for communication within the team. However, Africans tend to resort more to UNIWORLD policy statements and formal channels (+1), especially in times of conflict. While they use informal channels (−.5) for one-on-one team communication, they feel less secure with western-style informal channels under stress. The westerners, in contrast, frequently address confrontational issues using informal channels only (−1) and even avoid the formal channels (+.5) when possible.

Similar differences occur in the western/African exercise of power in conflict resolution. Both groups occasionally resort to powering the outcome (+.5) through headquarters, regional-level personnel, or the team director. Westerners prefer private face-to-face negotiation, finessing the outcome (−1), and are somewhat embarrassed to resort to higher authority. Because the African team members have not learned the western finesse game, they are less likely (−.5) to turn to it. This ambiguity is evident in the following comment by an African: "I was uncertain about

Table 9.1
Conflict and Cultural Bias in UNION Ltd.:
Western v. African Missionaries

High Grid		Low Grid			
Going Through Channels		**Working the Network**		**Westerners**	**Africans**
+1	Formal, institutional channels	−1	Informal channels	.5, −1	1, −.5
+1	Powering the outcome	−1	Finessing the outcome	.5, −1	.5, −.5
+1	Legitimizing dominance	−1	Equalizing power	.5, −.5	1, 0
+1	Institutional process	−1	Personally directed process	0, −1	.5, −1
+1	Institutional time/agenda	−1	Personal time/agenda	0, −1	0, −1
	Sum of Grid Variables:			**−3.0**	**0**

Strong Group		Weak Group			
Preserving Relationships		**Preserving Resources**		**Westerners**	**Africans**
+1	Multiplex network of relations	−1	Aggregate factions	1, 0	1, −.5
+1	Consensus decision making	−1	Independent decision making	1, −.5	1, 0
+1	Protecting vulnerability	−1	Exposing vulnerability	.3, −.7	1, 0
+1	Broker/mediation	−1	Display of personal power	0, −1	1, −.3
+1	Confrontation avoidance	−1	Open confrontation with equals	0, −1	1, −.5
Sum of Group Variables:				**−0.9**	**+3.7**

Note that .3 has been used twice here to indicate a present but reluctant application of that criteria; .7 has been used to designate a strong leaning toward that criteria, moderated somewhat by its antithesis.

how he would take it. It seems that any time we talk, all we ever do is yell at each other. I cannot and will not do that anymore!"

Westerners also feel ambivalence, as is evidenced by favoring legitimate dominance (+.5) as well as equalization of power (−.5). The discrepancy can be traced to UNIWORLD's policy of appointing certain leaders on field, regional, and international levels, and the tendency of field members to resist and even scorn the appointees. The Africans prefer to legitimize formal leaders (+1) because "we must give him a chance to speak even if he says nothing great. He is a leader in the church and we must recognize him."

Although the Africans are comfortable with using the institutional process (+.5), they understand the UNIWORLD value for resolving disputes on the field through a personally directed process (−1). All conflict resolution in the team follows the personal time/agenda (−1) of the individuals, be they African or western.

THE GROUP DIMENSION

Within UNION Ltd. team relationships and ministry have priority over accomplishment of individuals' goals. Hence, westerners (+1) and Africans (+1) seek to avoid factions in the team. On occasion African team members have felt threatened regarding their authority on African ways, and have used bloc voting and influence tactics to demonstrate

160

their solidarity (–.5). In decision making, team consensus (+1), even on controversial issues, is preferred over independent decision making whether by Africans or westerners. However, westerners (–.5) on occasion circumvent the prescribed system of consensus because of their task orientation. UNIWORLD's philosophy of consensus management tends to hold this independence in check.

Westerners display their personal power (–1) in open, one-on-one confrontation (–1). Jonathan has said that open confrontation is biblical, and mediated confrontation "wastes time" and "beats around the bush." Westerners lean toward using candor and openness in conflict, exposing vulnerability (–.7), although some are sensitive to protecting vulnerability (+.3). The Africans seek to avoid public airing of private conflict (+1), and face-to-face confrontation (+1). They prefer mediation (+1) to resolve conflict, yet, in an effort to adapt to UNIWORLD's organizational culture they make occasional use of personal power (–.3) and open confrontation (–.5). The African style of open confrontation takes the form of responsive questioning rather than the assertive challenging common with the westerners.

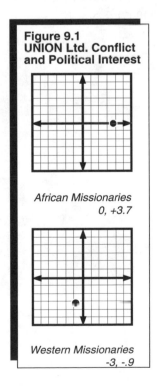

Figure 9.1
UNION Ltd. Conflict
and Political Interest

African Missionaries
0, +3.7

Western Missionaries
-3, -.9

Conclusions

Given the wide distance between Africans and westerners, one can easily see that communications problems will continue within UNION Ltd. (fig. 9.1). The westerners approach conflict from an individualist game cosmology—one-on-one, open, and each for his own. The Africans rely on group loyalty (their UNION Ltd. extended family of sorts) and an uncertain hierarchy to carry them through conflict. While westerners know the theory of valuing team relationships and of resolving conflict for the sake of team, they trust their individualist game instincts (–0.9) rather than the team when they are under pressure.

Although Africans have some fairly structured channels for resolving conflicts and communicating about important issues outside UNION Ltd., in the organization they have adapted to the organization model. They appear to be trying to achieve an equilibrium between the hierarchist and the egalitarian games, manipulating each to his best interest within various social environments (Thompson 1982). Their individualist western colleagues don't play by the rules of either, although they too seem to be struggling to reach an equilibrium, but between the individualist and the egalitarian games.

Research Questions 9.1
Grid and Conflict, Political Interests

High Grid	Low Grid
+1 *Formal, institutional channels.* To what extent can/do people define institutional channels through which communication must effectively proceed? or	−1 *Informal channels.* What alternatives, other than formal channels, are available to individuals for settling disputes? Do people create personalized networks and utilize these to manage interpersonal conflict?
+1 *Powering the outcome.* Do people attempt to power the outcome by the use of the institutional structure? Do people turn to courts, judges, supervisors, or other authorities to seek restoration and to achieve a win-lose decision? or	−1 *Finessing the outcome.* To what extent do people rely on stratagem rather than structure to accomplish their objectives?
+1 *Codification of rules.* Do officials and leaders use channels to legitimize dominant-subordinate relationships in the society? Do people have written or oral codes (custom law) against which legitimacy or relationships and action are measured? or	−1 *Sense of the public good.* Do people use relationships, work the network, to subvert the powerful? Are individuals constrained by a sense of the public good and by the aggregate interests of others with whom they compete?
+1 *Institutional process.* Do people settle disputes predominantly by the processes of adjudication or arbitration? or	−1 *Personally directed process.* To what extent are people limited to only those strategies that individuals can control, such as posturing or negotiation?
+1 *Institutional time/agenda.* To what extent is the time factor in settling disputes defined by the institutional context? Do authority figures in the structure place individual cases on the agenda? or	−1 *Personal time/agenda.* Is the time agenda of dispute settlement usually set by individuals, following their interests, needs, and convenience?

Research Questions 9.2
Group and Conflict, Political Interests

Strong Group	Weak Group
+1 *Multiplex network of relations.* Do decisions settling disputes give higher priority to relationships or resources? What evidence do you find that people value relationships within the group more than the resources in dispute? Which resources precipitate disputes among competitors? or	−1 *Aggregate factions.* Are resources in dispute a higher priority than the relationships of the contestants? Do individuals readily break relationships and realign with a leader or faction in support of their interests? Do factions have specific political or economic goals?
+1 *Consensus decision making.* To what extent does the group demand consensus decision, limiting the authority of individual leaders? or	−1 *Independent decision making.* Do individuals make decisions independently of others? How commonly are disputes settled by private bargaining?
+1 *Protecting vulnerability.* Do the participants carefully safeguard the vulnerability of the litigants? Do people cover their group vulnerability by placing blame on a deviant member of their group? or	−1 *Exposing vulnerability.* Do people challenge and undermine competitors by exposing their weaknesses and challenging their credibility? Is exposing vulnerability accepted as part of the game?
+1 *Broker/mediation.* What role do mediators play in social disputes? Who are the mediators—persons of senior status, of high respect, and articulate? Are plea bargaining and compromise the strategies of mediation? or	−1 *Display of personal power.* Is public display and contest part of dispute? Do parties calculate power and use strategy to win? Do people define these contests as win-lose struggles? and withdraw or delay to gain advantage?
+1 *Confrontation avoidance.* Do people work to avoid confrontation in disputes? Does the public view confrontation as disruptive and to be avoided? Do individuals value public decorum even under the most aggrieved circumstances? or	−1 *Open confrontation with equals.* Do people value open confrontation? Are confrontations the social fuel that facilitate dispute resolution?

Ritual, Social Interests, and Cultural Bias

Balak Summons Balaam

Now Balak son of Zippor saw all that Israel had done to the Amorites, and Moab was terrified because there were so many people. Indeed, Moab was filled with dread because of the Israelites.

The Moabites said to the elders of Midian, "This horde is going to lick up everything around us, as an ox licks up the grass of the field."

So Balak son of Zippor, who was king of Moab at that time, sent messengers to summon Balaam son of Beor, who was at Pethor, near the river, in his native land. Balak said:

"A people has come out of Egypt; they cover the face of the land and have settled next to me. Now come and put a curse on these people, because they are too powerful for me. Perhaps then I will be able to defeat them and drive them out of the country. For I know that those you bless are blessed, and those you curse are cursed."

The elders of Moab and Midian left, taking with them the fee for divination. When they came to Balaam they told him what Balak had said. (Num. 22:2–7)

Hezekiah Purifies the Temple

Hezekiah was twenty-five years old when he became king, and he reigned in Jerusalem twenty-nine years.

In the first month of the first year of his reign he opened the doors of the temple of the LORD and repaired them. He brought in the priests and the Levites, . . . and said, "Listen to me, Levites! Consecrate yourselves now and consecrate the temple of the LORD, the God of your fathers. Remove all defilement from the sanctuary. Our fathers were unfaithful; they did evil in the eyes of the LORD our God and forsook him. . . . Therefore, the anger of the LORD has fallen on Judah and Jerusalem; he has made them an object of dread and horror and scorn, as you can see with your own eyes. This is why our fathers have fallen by the sword and why our sons and daughters and our wives are in captivity."

The goats for the sin offering were brought before the king and the assembly, and they laid their hands on them. The priests then slaughtered the goats and presented their blood on the altar for a sin offering to atone for all Israel, because the king had ordered the burnt offering and the sin offering for all Israel. (2 Chron. 29:1, 3–9, 23–24)

Ritual and Cultural Bias

Ritual is the habitual practice of activities that carry significant meaning to people in a society and that are used for collective or individual responses to issues of social, moral, and spiritual importance. Ritual may also serve as a key teaching activity through which people learn of their heritage, reinforce their relationships to one another and to God (or gods) or ancestors. Ritual takes many diverse forms, yet all rituals have symbolic importance to the participants. However, sometimes the practice of ritual becomes so routine that people no longer know the meaning of the symbols, nor are they able to articulate the meaning to themselves or to outsiders. Nevertheless, the mere performance of ritual often sustains the social purpose for which it was originally created, even when the symbolic importance and meaning has been lost.

Our purpose in this chapter is to study the characteristics of ritual as they are framed by social interests and relationships. Mary Douglas (1970) argues that ritual and cosmology grow out of fundamental relationships in family and society. She points to the distinction between positional and personal family relationships as a basis for understanding the role of ritual in society. Based upon an analysis of the nature of control in the family structure, she poses two distinctive approaches, the positional and the personal.

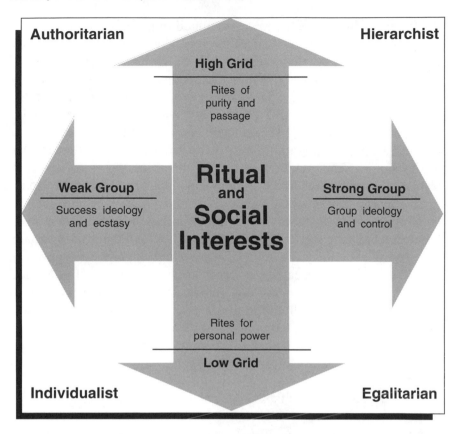

In the positional family structure, control is exercised through the definition of social roles in the family and the structuring of obligations and interaction through those role relationships. The positional family structure emphasizes relationships of power and submission. As individuals grow up within the family and reach critical stages of transition, members hold rites of passage for those individuals to initiate them into the new stages of structured relationship. The rightness of relationships becomes a matter of structural good and evil and individuals who follow the rules contribute to the collective purity of the family group. Individuals who violate the rules are polluting and a disgrace to the positional structure.

When broader social environments follow similar structural patterning, the value system and ethos or cultural bias of the positional family are replicated in larger structural arrangements. For example, in the New Testament Jewish world of Jesus, the tax collectors, the prostitutes, and the thieves represented the lowest polluted dimension of society. The only people who were lower were foreigners or lepers. Above this polluted level of society one found the poor and the landowners, and above these the Pharisees, and above these the doctors of the law and the members of the Jewish elite, the Sanhedrin. The society was ranked in stages of pollution, purity, and power. The value system that characterized this social structure emphasized good and evil, with the Pharisees and the rulers characterized as good, and those in the lower ranks as sinners. One achieved purity and goodness by keeping the rules of the law, and each level of society had its marks of membership and rituals of transition.

One finds a similar situation in the islands of Yap. In Yapese society, men progress through a series of stages of increasing purity and power, based upon relative age and the inherited authority of their family estate. An individual male reached the position of highest purity and power in his old age when he became the oldest surviving male and titular head of his family estate. Women, in contrast, dropped from a position of neutrality to extreme pollution at the onset of menses and gradually progressed to a state of neutrality again at menopause. Women who bore children were relieved from the extremes of pollution and as they matured were gradually allowed to reassociate with the unpolluted sector of society.

The personal system of family control relies upon sensitizing the child to the feelings of others and encouraging the child to consider her or his own feelings. When this is carried over into the wider society, the result is a relative lack of structure and flexibility in social roles. A person is identified by name and by personal characteristics rather than by a collective role category. Unique individuality and giftedness are highly valued. People do not channel interests through social roles, but rather encourage people to develop according to their inclinations. The feelings of others are most important, and social control is achieved by expressions of personal, face-to-face interests and consideration.

In the personal family and community, ritual is not cultivated and is often denied. Roles are not sharply defined, and people may move freely from one role to another. In Genesis Jacob chose a life around the camp and in the kitchen with his mother, while Esau chose a life in the fields with his father. In such a flexible situation, rituals of transition have no meaning or purpose. Rules about relationship are loosely defined, if they exist at all, and without rules, ritual reinforcement is unnecessary. The types of ritual most commonly found are those that emphasize an unstructured existence and support personal development and personal power. In Genesis Jacob used fresh-cut poplar branches in the watering troughs as ritual to insure larger numbers of speckled or spotted animals in the flocks of sheep, thereby increasing his personal wealth. His wife Rachel stole her father's idols in an attempt to take the power of her father's house with her. The cultural bias that emerges values individual craft within a cosmology where humans may negotiate with the supernatural.

Grid: Rites of Purity and Passage or Rites for Personal Power

The objective of grid analysis is to determine how people define the roles of individuals in ritual. The high grid social environment is characterized by structured relationships of power and rites of purity and passage. These structures and rites originate in the positional family and extend to the total framework of society. Within the community, pollution, purity, and power begin with male and female distinctions and are then elaborated in a hierarchy. Men are high and receive honor; women are low and without honor. Men are considered pure and women are considered polluting, particularly upon the onset of menses. Power is granted in greater degree to men than to women. Similar patterns are elaborated in the wider structures of the community, so that high and low in the hierarchy are good/evil or pure/polluted, and rituals mark transitions or contact of high and low.

People in low grid social environments define the roles of individuals in terms of their access to personal power. Growing out of the social environment of the family whose focus is on personal control, members seek avenues to enhance their personal power. Often these people deny the power of ritual altogether, yet they unwittingly embrace ritual practices when they support their personal objectives. The following questions provide diagnostic criteria through which a researcher may analyze the elements of grid in social environments.

Is power hierarchical (pollution/purity) and dangerous (+1) or unstructured and malevolent or benign (−1)?

High grid social environments generally define power in terms of stages of relative power. Sometimes these stages have associated with them the values of purity and pollution. In other situations they may not. Individuals must pass through these power stages as part of their personal careers. The structure is positional, and individuals are valued

169

according to their places in the power structure. Access to higher positions of power usually is associated with increasing expectations for purity as well. Rituals of purification may be associated with transition through these stages.

In the case of Hezekiah, the king is highest, setting the agenda. The priests and Levites are just below him, and the people below them. Defilement is the critical problem, particularly in the temple and in reference to its rituals. Because of this defilement, God has responded to the people with fierce anger. Judah and Jerusalem have become "an object of dread and horror and scorn."

In the low grid social environment people see power as deriving from a number of benign power sources. The social environment is unstructured and the power sources are available to the motivated individual. These power sources are not considered dangerous, but rather quite beneficial. It is a matter of the individual discovering those power sources and tapping them for the personal quest.

In the case of Balak and Balaam, both seem to view God and man as beings open to persuasion. Balak recognizes that Balaam has power to bless and to curse, and offers to purchase that power with great gifts. Balak is persistent in seeking to gain a curse against the people of Israel. Power is there to be accessed and turned to one's purpose.

Is ritual led by a hierarchy of specialists (+1) or by ordinary people (–1) with access to spiritual power?

In positional social structures, relationships between individuals often involve structural and supernatural danger. To help members cope with such dangers the society provides a hierarchy of specialists who mediate as spiritual leaders and magicians to provide protective ritual. In the case of Hezekiah the priests mediated between the exceedingly dangerous holy God of Abraham, Isaac, and Jacob and the ordinary world of Judah and Jerusalem. These priests directed the Levites in the cleansing of the sacred temple and vessels, in the performance of sacrificial rites, and in sin offerings to atone for the people.

The power practitioner in the low grid social environment has no special relationship or structured position in society but is a common member with special spiritual experience or insight. This person has achieved a measure of power and serves as a broker for other individuals who lack it. In the tribal societies these individuals are called shaman. Balaam seems to have been this type of spiritual leader. The purpose of his sacrifices on the mountain has nothing to do with defilement. Rather, the offering is an attempt to gain the attention and favor of God. Balak knows that Balaam is renowned for his power to curse or bless, and he calls for the best man to curse Israel.

In a modern industrialized society, the television evangelist, the backwoods uneducated preacher, and the Jesus movement evangelist are low grid brokers of power. They have no structural position to sustain their role, but rather derive their influence from their access to spiritual power that is manifest to their followers in their public speaking and ministry.

Is the focus of ritual social transition (+1) or spiritual vision and power (–1)?

Passage from one level to another is an important feature of high grid social environments. People in high positions always begin in lower ones and must move to their high status. Rituals mark these transitions and prepare individuals to assume their new authority. These rites of transition include offerings to supernatural spirits, periods of abstinence from sexual relationships and work, isolation from society, instruction from elders, and collective public rituals to mark their change in status. The story of the installation of Aaron and his sons (Lev. 9) to the office of priest is an exemplary case. Such rituals were employed by the Hebrews to mark the transitions into the roles of priesthood or into the supporting roles of levitical service in the temple. Hezekiah instructed the priests and Levites to consecrate themselves in preparation before they could enter the temple to work there.

The search for power, rather than position, is the goal of ritual in a low grid social environment. Individuals seek power through a unique spiritual experience. Tribal shaman or peasant diviners often commit extensive time to a vision or a spirit quest to acquire a familiar spirit. Once they have achieved this spirit visitation, they serve their fellow man through this acquired power. Balaam was clearly a man of such power. He had access to God that was not common among other men. He "went off to a barren height" where God spoke directly to him with a message for Balak. In the urban world, the quest for vision or spiritual experience is often expressed in the "second blessing" of the Christian charismatic movement, a vision or word of prophecy, speaking in tongues, or some other spiritual encounter or power.

Is the outcome ritual purification (+1) or curing/restoration (–1)?

Power and purification are inextricably linked in high grid societies. Individuals who aspire to positions of power are subject to the rites of purification prescribed by the social structure. For example, the American presidency requires a higher level of moral behavior than that demanded of the ordinary citizen. (Witness the fall of Gary Hart in the 1988 presidential campaign.) Rites of purification may be elaborate, such as those prescribed in Jewish tradition, or may be fairly perfunctory. Most high grid societies place some value on purification. Keeping from contact with decaying bodies, containing the flow of menstrual blood, removing human waste, and conducting rituals of personal hygiene and other means of purification are common features of contemporary American society. Rites of spiritual purification may also be required in certain institutions.

The case of Hezekiah shows a great preoccupation with purification. The priests report that they have "purified the entire temple" including the altar, table, and utensils used in service. Following this work they offered sacrifices for consecration of the temple, the altar, and finally the king and the assembly of people. The king and priests seek the purification of the people and atonement for their sins.

In spite of the fact that low grid individuals deny the value of ritual and scorn its practice, the pervasiveness of human problems and illness leads to rituals of curing and restoration. The shaman or medicine woman is predominantly a curer in his or her application of spiritual power. Much of the Christian charismatic movement has focused upon rituals of curing. Faith healing is a major aspect of the Vineyard movement in Southern California, and the leaders practice healing regularly in the Sunday evening services. The leaders seek spiritual restoration as well as physical healing, drawing people into a deeper relationship with God. Rituals of spiritual restoration may be even more important than the rites of curing.

Balak has not asked Balaam to cure, but he has asked him to solve a problem. The elders of Moab describe the people of Israel as a dreaded plague, a horde that "is going to lick up everything around us." They call upon Balaam as the one who can solve the problem through his access to spiritual power.

Does ritual protect by mediation or reversal (+1) or punish by curse, sorcery, or witchcraft (−1)?

Pollution, purity, and power inevitably involve danger. Those who are pure are always subject to loss of purity by contact with polluted persons. Those who have power are always threatened by others with power and by the drain of the populace on their personal powers. Ritual and magic are often used to mediate the danger that individuals experience in these roles. The washing of hands and the washing of eating utensils were rituals to protect the Hebrew people from the polluting aspects of society that could cause sickness and even death. Sometimes Christians in contemporary American society make prayer a magical ritual to protect them from some perceived or physical danger. The ritualizing of prayer mediates for individuals experiencing great anxiety. Rites of reversal are sometimes employed in society to mediate between high and low, or to alleviate the tensions that grow between the leaders and their people. The layman preaches, and the pastor sits in the pew; the men cook, and the women sit around and talk.

Hezekiah attributed failure in war and the captivity of the sons, daughters, and wives of Judah to the abandonment of the temple by their fathers. The purpose of the opening, cleansing, and ritual purification of the temple was to reestablish their covenant with God and to turn away "his fierce anger." The ritual served to mediate between God and the king and his people.

The beneficial power that is characterized by the low grid social environment also has its dark side. The shaman who learns the use of power for curing may turn that same power against those with whom he is at enmity and become a practitioner of sorcery. The familiar spirit to which the shaman has attached his personal star may become a vengeful spirit leading him into acts of witchcraft and social conflict. What once was benign power has now become malevolent and of great danger to other individuals in society.

Balaam knew and exercised the power of sorcery. On the third attempt of Balak to curse Israel we read, "Now when Balaam saw that it pleased the LORD to bless Israel, he did not resort to sorcery as at other times, but turned his face toward the desert" (Num. 24:1). He had apparently tried on the two earlier occasions to exercise his power to harm the people of Israel. On each of those occasions he had failed, since this was not in the purpose of God. Of course, Balak was angry and refused to pay Balaam his wages. Balaam said, "I told you so." In their minds, God was capricious, refusing to respond to Balak's generous sacrifices and Balaam's sorcery.

Group Ideology and Control
or Success Ideology and Ecstasy

The objective of group analysis is to determine whether ritual serves to mark insider/outsider distinctions or the distinctiveness of persons. When a social environment is strong group, the story of the group becomes a very important part of tradition. This story is told and retold, and in the retelling elaborated to emphasize the nature and importance of group relationships. A brief illustration of this is the group ideology surrounding the founding of an Anabaptist denomination. The denomination has split numerous times, but in spite of these splits, traces its ancestry back to the founder in Germany, nearly three hundred years ago. Individual members of local congregations boast of their genealogical connections to the founder, and each current group operates under the illusion that its particular theological position and present ministry practice would be that most approved by the founding father. The group story is told to support the legitimacy of present members and their connection to the historical past. The importance of the past is critical to the membership and provides the continuity that sustains group identity.

Success stories and ritual that recognize unusual persons and their achievements characterize weak group environments. The Book of Judges in the Old Testament is an excellent illustration in which the hero judges provided the single integrating force. Each judge leads the people successfully against external oppression, and for a time they enjoy peace and prosperity. In contemporary society the hero/success ideology is played out in the television evangelist or the New Age movie star. In either case, people who are individualists, seeking meaning and symbol, turn to public heroes for their models. The stories are about impoverished, hard-working individuals who achieve a special blessing of God or gain access to new self-actualizing power to accomplish career, economic, and public success.

Does the ideology and power of ritual focus on group (+1) or on heroes and success (−1)?

The case of Hezekiah centers upon the people of Israel and their current plight caused by their ancestors and the judgment of God. Hezekiah referred to the fathers, their actions in the past, and the consequences for those living in the present. The priests were descendants of Aaron, and the work they did was a continuation of that initiated by Aaron. Hezekiah stated that the power of God will not return to Israel until the people have repented and consecrated themselves. The notion of covenant came from the Abrahamic covenant between the people of Israel and God. They sacrificed the sin offering for the whole people.

Balaam is an example of ritual focused on a success story. Balak chose Balaam because of his record of success. Balaam's protests did not matter, as his reputation had preceded him. When he came, the people of Moab expected him to destroy the people of Israel.

Do people focus upon rituals of collective consecration to God or ancestors (+1) or upon personal power and ecstatic experience (–1)?

Another facet of sustaining group identity is the practice of collective consecration, prayer, and fasting with the object of gaining favor from the group deity. The Pharisees in Judea practiced regular fasting to gain and sustain communion with God. Yapese practiced prayer and fasting to gain the goodwill of their deceased ancestors and to obtain the favor of a cult spirit in their region. Collective fellowship during prayer and fasting increased the solidarity of these groups and the control of the leadership over the members.

In the case of Hezekiah the observance of the Passover meal and celebration signified group membership, history, and identity (2 Chron. 30). The Passover marked the identity of the tribes of Israel, having common ancestry to Abraham, Isaac, and Jacob, and the experience of deliverance from Egypt. This special meal, called the Feast of Unleavened Bread, symbolized the group and its history with God.

In contrast, Balaam was a man with spiritual power for sale. Two groups were in conflict, to be sure, but the power that both Balak and Balaam sought was to be gained by Balaam's special personal relationship to God. In the success paradigm individuals seek a unique union with the supernatural through collective or personal experiences. Individuals may go on extended spirit quests in nature, or work through mediums, or become involved in collective religious events. The individual experience often results in some particular moving spiritual encounter. The charismatic Protestant or Roman Catholic may have a unique experience such as speaking in tongues or the second blessing of the spirit. The New Age quest may have a unique experience of self. In these cases the emphasis is on unique individual revelation and expression.

Do revelation and divination yield authoritative knowledge for a group (+1) or personal knowledge and competitive ambivalence (–1)?

People in every culture seek superior knowledge and power from God or other supernatural beings. Dreams, visions, and direct voices are one source of revelation. More commonly, people have used divining instruments through the centuries to ascertain "God's will." Old Testament leaders, priests, and prophets used the ephod, casting lots, and other instruments to divine the will of God. In Yap, priests and magicians used the coconut palm leaf and other hand-manipulated devices to ascertain supernatural information. On special occasions an elaborate divining ritual was employed to glance into the future of human political and social relationships. The key distinction in strong or weak group lies in whether the knowledge sought enhances the authority of the group or of the persons who achieve it.

Where group is strong, the knowledge gained from God or from the ancestors reinforces group boundaries and enhances the survival of its members. Hezekiah sought an answer from God regarding Sennacherib's siege against Jerusalem. He took the letter sent to him by the emissaries of the invader and spread it out before the Lord in the now purified and functioning temple. The Scripture reports that he prayed to the Lord (Isa. 37:14–38) and the Lord answered him through the prophet Isaiah. The answer was definitive: the Assyrian king will not enter the city! The text reports that a plague struck the Assyrian camp that night; Sennacherib withdrew and was slain shortly after returning to his capital, Nineveh. The people of Jerusalem were delivered and the kingdom of Judah saved.

Where group is weak, the knowledge gained from God or other supernatural sources is controlled by an individual and may be used for whatever ends that person desires. In the case of Balaam, Balak believed that Balaam had such personal power. The story tells how Balaam and Balak went to three different mountains, taking three different views of the people to be cursed, and offered three major sacrifices to God in hope of winning his favor. Balak believed that God could hear his request and that Balaam could curse Israel; and toward that end he killed many animals in anticipation of God's pending favor. The decision went against him, and he departed in frustration and despair.

Since not all individuals are successful and not all spiritual experiences provide optimum health and well-being, the weak group social environment fluctuates from spurts of optimism and fatalism. In times of well-being, optimism leads individuals in their quest for success. In times of disappointment and personal failure, one explains one's plight as the lack of luck. To be lucky or unlucky is part of the ambivalence of the success ideology. People often commit themselves to such activities as buying lottery tickets in light of this optimistic-fatalistic perspective.

Do symbol, ritual, and sacrifice serve as covenant for a group (+1) or are they efficacious primarily for the individuals who perform them (−1)?

People in strong group environments employ ritual to teach and perpetuate the symbols and doctrines of covenant relationship between them and their spiritual ancestry. Circumcision and ritual sacrifice in the Old Testament focused upon the covenant between God and the people of Israel; if they obeyed his commands he would make them a great nation. The Book of Leviticus describes burnt offerings given as a fragrance to God, meal offerings that served both as a pleasing aroma and as an offering of first fruits to the Lord, fellowship offerings in which people enjoyed feasting with one another and with the Lord, and the sin offering, which served to appease the wrath of God for violations of the ritual and moral law. While the people in my local congregation no longer provide offerings and sacrifices to God, the regular practice of communion service four times a year, which includes a fellowship feast, footwashing service, and the taking of the bread and cup in commemoration of the sacrificial death of Christ, provides precisely the same symbolic equivalent.

The case of Hezekiah illustrates well how these offerings served both to mediate between God and man and to reaffirm the special history and position of the Hebrew people in relationship to one another and to their God. Once the temple had been purified, the people gathered before the Lord to offer a sin offering "for the kingdom, for the sanctuary and for Judah" (v. 21). Following this event, Hezekiah invited them to bring sacrifices and thank offerings, "and all whose hearts were willing brought burnt offerings" (v. 31). The significance of the burnt offering was that the people could not eat the meat; rather it was offered totally to God as an act of worship.

The symbolic world of the low grid social environment is highly individualistic. Each person creates for himself or herself the doctrines of his or her religious experience. The outcome of this is that there is no strong collective theology in a weak group social environment. Balak and Balaam each had his expectations of God. Balak did not understand why Balaam refused to curse Israel, and he was persistent in pressing his cause. Balaam in turn had no success in convincing Balak that the matter was out of his control. Their theologies were in conflict, and neither was able to convince the other.

Theological conflict is characteristic of individualistic social environments. A criticism often leveled at the Pentecostal movement is weak theology. Where such criticism is warranted, "weak theology" often arises out of the very nature of the strong personal relationship with God. The charismatic believer sees the word of God and the word of prophecy from the indwelling spirit to be the key expressions of his or her spiritual experience. The word of prophecy is the ecstatic individual experience with God, and from these words the Scriptures are interpreted and understood. Doctrine tends to be individualistic rather than collective and coordinated.

Are the characteristic spiritual responses of people framed in terms of confession, sanction, and restoration (+1) or of celebration (–1)?

The strong group context places high value on conformity, sanctioning of deviance, and restoration of individuals or the group to right relationships. People define "sin" in reference to group standards and interests. Rituals of confession and sanction respond to the collective sins of the group and the sins of individuals. The Book of Leviticus details the burnt and sin offerings required of the people of Israel. The sin offering required public confession, affirming the accountability of person and group and restoring individuals to good faith and standing. Individuals who fail to confess may be subjected to rites of ordeal to determine their innocence or guilt of the violation of group rules, as happened among the Puritans of New England. Some contemporary Americans subject one another to the ordeal of open confrontation, which serves somewhat the same purpose. The rituals of exorcism also appear in strong group social context in which a contrary spirit may be seen as a cause of aberrant social behavior. The Aukan of Surinam practice extensive rituals of exorcism to bring deviant persons into control of the group.

Hezekiah understood the need for group accountability, confession, and repentance for sin: "Our fathers were unfaithful; they did evil in the eyes of the LORD our God and forsook him." All of the people were therefore accountable, and the punishment was also collective. The sin offerings addressed the guilt of the whole people, atoning for them as a corporate group and restoring them to favor with God.

In contrast, the weak group context employs ritual primarily for celebration. People emphasize celebration rather than confession; worship rather than penitence; fellowship above moral duty and responsibility as members. Sin and sanctions are personal matters between an individual and his God. When people come together, they do so to express their personal experiences, which may include confession, but without group accountability and sanction. Their success stories encourage others, and their trials and failures serve as warnings, but each is responsible alone to God.

One of the most significant contributions of the charismatic movement to Christianity has been its contribution to collective worship. The celebration of worship, the joy of individualistic expression of worship to God, the optimism of hope and the reassurance of success through faith, provide an exuberance and collective joy. The charismatic movement has contributed the gift of celebration to contemporary Christianity. These celebrations are both individualistic and collective. They allow the individual symbolization of the event and the ecstatic individual experience. At the same time, they provide collective support for the reaffirmation of belief and a confirmation of individual theology.

Ritual in Churches and Christian Organizations

Reviewing these features, it is my conclusion that the universal church of Jesus Christ is as diverse and multiplex as the social environments in which it occurs. I have defined ritual here as the habitual practice of activities that carry significant meaning, are used for response or teaching, and have symbolic importance to the participants. The order of service in a Baptist church, or the "worship time" of a Vineyard service have clear and meaningful structure or nonstructure for the participants. "Unstructured" symbols and practices are as much social products as structured symbols. The nonliturgical churches would deny that they have any ritual at all; yet in the terms spelled out here it is evident that the nonliturgical groups respond in socially predictable ways.

Many charismatic churches typically embrace an individualist game prototype of low grid and weak group. Independent fundamentalist churches more typically follow the egalitarian prototype, whereas the national mainline denominations of Protestant and Roman Catholic churches are variations upon the hierarchist game. The megachurches of the 1990s in Southern California tend to be organized around the authoritarian game prototype, resulting in congregations administered by strong leadership, but with weak group connections. In all of these, God may be glorified and his work may be carried out. The varying forms of worship and the affirmation of individual and group are useful tools for the continuing work of the church. God is not limited by human social environments and the characteristics of society to accomplish his divine purpose.

The case study by Donna R. Downes that follows shows how forms of ritual in an international mission team also reflect the structure of social relationships. The diagnostic questions developed above are used by Downes to analyze ritual behavior in UNION Ltd.

UNION Ltd.: Ritual and Social Interests
by Donna R. Downes

The study of ritual interests continues our analysis of the struggle between two value systems. The Africans' grid score (+.5) near midpoint reflects their continuing ambivalence between the hierarchist game and the egalitarian ethos of the team. Westerners also show a tendency toward the center on this variable (−1). For the first time both Africans and westerners scored identically in their group (+3.0) commitment, which is consistent with their philosophical commitment to an egalitarian team and their unity built upon faith, doctrinal, and ministry commitments (see table 10.1).

The Grid Dimension

In UNION Ltd., the director is neither a mediator between headquarters and teammates nor the holder of power. All members have rights to open communication with headquarters and equal power and rights within the UNIWORLD community. Therefore power and transitions are generally unstructured and unclear, which is fine with the westerners (+.5, −.5), but discomfiting to the Africans (+1). No one really knows how leaders are chosen, and leadership (in the sense of team director or headquarters staff) is considered by many to be a burden rather than a goal to be sought. Furthermore, removing an inept member is a long and difficult process.

Personal vision and growth (−.5), a sacrifice of oneself to God, and a personal calling to leadership are common emphases within UNI-WORLD. When members commit offenses, westerners (−1) and Africans (−.5) believe in the principle of restoration. The process of restoration involves weeks and/or months of counseling and a period of time to resolve personal issues before reentering mission work.

Both Africans and westerners have similar views (+.5) regarding emphasis on corporate prayer. Members see regular morning prayer, pre-conference prayer, and other times of prayer as crucial to their ministries. While team members believe in prayer mediating danger, as a team they also believe that God can choose to completely reverse satanic activity, restore individuals to full fellowship in the team, and heal broken lives. Hence they are constantly seeking an equilibrium between the two polarities of the grid scale.

Table 10.1
Ritual Variables in UNION Ltd.: Perspectives
of Western v. African Missionaries

High Grid		Low Grid			
Rites of Purity, Passage		**Rites for Personal Power**		**Westerners**	**Africans**
+1	Power hierarchical, dangerous	−1	Power unstructured, malevolent/benign	.5, −.5	1, 0
+1	Hierarchy of ritual specialists	−1	Commoner leaders of ritual	0, 0	0, 0
+1	Focus is social transition	−1	Focus is vision and power	0, −.5	0, −.5
+1	Outcome of ritual is purification	−1	Outcome of ritual is curing, restoration	0, −1	0, −.5
+1	Ritual protects by mediation/reversal	−1	Punish by curse, sorcery, witchcraft	.5, 0	.5, 0
Sum of Grid Variables:				**−1.0**	**0.5**

Strong Group		Weak Group			
Group Ideology and Control		**Success Ideology and Ecstasy**		**Westerners**	**Africans**
+1	Ideology, power focus on group	−1	Ideology, power focus on heroes, success	1, 0	1, 0
+1	Group consecration re: gods or ancestors	−1	Ecstatic individual experience	1, −.5	1, −.5
+1	Authoritative knowledge for group	−1	Personal knowledge and ambivalence	1, 0	1, 0
+1	Symbol, ritual, and sacrifice as covenant	−1	Symbol and ritual serve individuals	.5, −.5	.5, −.5
+1	Responses framed as confession, sanction	−1	Responses framed as collective celebration	1, −.5	1, −.5
Sum of Group Variables:				**+3.0**	**+3.0**

The Group Dimension

UNIWORLD and UNION Ltd. together have a rather extensive and well-developed group ideology (+1). Hardly a team meeting goes by that the members don't recall where the ministry has come from, what their distinctives are, and where they are going. The stories of beginnings, the miracles that brought them all together—all are part of this established tradition for both Africans and westerners. The team stresses group prayer (and sometimes fasting) (+1) over individual efforts because of the unity and camaraderie that group activities of this type will bring. However, believing that the individual's life and growth in God will strengthen the ministry of the team, the team also encourages individual experiences (–.5) with God. Authoritative knowledge comes from Scripture and from "sensing God's peace," "seeing God open doors," or receiving "particular illuminations of God's Word" (+1). The team stresses both collective symbols and offerings (+.5) (or money, material possessions, and time) as well as individual symbols and experiences (–.5). Neither is a requirement, however. Last, the group is highly valued as a place for public confession (+1) of sins, prayer and forgiveness—especially with relation to sins the members commit in attitudes or actions toward one another. While they also celebrate collectively (–.5) their individual expressions of their relationships with God, the emphasis is definitely

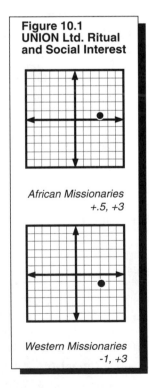

**Figure 10.1
UNION Ltd. Ritual
and Social Interest**

African Missionaries
+.5, +3

Western Missionaries
-1, +3

on group worship and purification and how such activities strengthen the group.

Conclusions

The team unity of Africans and westerners emerges clearly in the analysis of ritual, which gives focused attention to the practices surrounding their common core of beliefs and ministry (fig. 10.1). The fact that westerners are a bit lower grid and more committed to personal vision for ministry is not surprising. Western missionaries often commit to a vision and then find an organization to fit. On this variable westerners show strong identification with the egalitarian game endorsed in UNIWORLD international policy. Africans retain their ambivalence, on the line between the hierarchist and egalitarian games. This ambivalence stems perhaps from their service in a mission in their home nation where the hierarchist game is a dominant prototype in family and community life.

Research Questions 10.1
Grid Interests and Ritual

High Grid: Rites of Purity, Passage	Low Grid: Rites for Personal Power
+1 *Power is hierarchical and dangerous.* To what extent is power structured as high and low? dangerous, requiring mediation? Are people distant from power deemed "dirty, impure," and people close "clean, pure"? or	−1 *Power is unstructured, malevolent/benign.* To what extent is power loosely defined, broadly available, and both malevolent or benign? Is spiritual power something sought to improve personal or collective life?
+1 *Hierarchy of ritual specialists.* Do leaders constitute a hierarchy of specialists with access to spiritual power? Do these leaders serve as brokers of knowledge and ritual for individuals or the group? or	−1 *Commoner leaders of ritual.* To what extent are ritual specialists ordinary members of the community? Are common people free to carry out rituals according to the felt needs of individuals or the group?
+1 *Focus is social transition.* Does the ritual process mark social transitions (e.g., birth, marriage), and prepare people for reentry into society in new social roles? Does ritual have public outcomes? or	−1 *Focus is vision and power.* Is the ritual process one of personal quest for vision or power to benefit individuals or a group? Is spiritual experience focused upon individuals, either separately or in groups?
+1 *Outcome of ritual purification.* Do ritual events have as their explicit purpose the purification or restoration of an individual to a socially and spiritually pure role in the social environment? or	−1 *Outcome of curing, restoration.* Do ritual events have as their explicit purpose the curing of physical, psychological, or spiritual maladies and the restoration of persons to a healthy life or to normal relationships in a group?
+1 *Protect by mediation and reversal.* Does ritual have the explicit purpose of mediation of dangerous situations for individuals or the group, such as ordination, anointing, sacrifice, exorcism? Do rituals of role reversal diffuse tension in society? or	−1 *Punish by curse, sorcery, or witchcraft.* Can you identify events in which individuals act on their own behalf or on the behalf of others to resolve or mediate danger through or by the use of ritual such as cursing, witchcraft, or sorcery?

Research Questions 10.2
Group Interests and Ritual

Strong Group: Controlling Ritual	Weak Group: Success Ritual
+1 *Ideology and power focus on group.* Is power located in group-focused ritual and symbols? Do the stories reflect group identity, interests, conflicts with outsiders, and control over errant individual behavior? Are the stories familiar to members? or	−1 *Ideology and power focus on heroes, success.* Is power located in persons and private ritual and symbol? Do stories tell the exploits, success, and failure of heroes from the past? Do people point to the heroics of past players as a model for their hope for success?
+1 *Collective consecration re: gods or ancestors.* Do members engage in group rituals of denial, consecration, or taboo? Is fasting and prayer a group activity to seek direction from God, gods, or ancestors? or	−1 *Ecstatic individual experience.* Are fasting and rituals of denial part of a personal spiritual quest? Do individuals engage in private or public worship/prayer in quest for power or ecstatic experience?
+1 *Ritual provides authoritative knowledge for a group (+1).* Do rituals of divination or some other approved methodology provide authoritative knowledge for a group, serving its goals and protecting its members? or	−1 *Personal knowledge and competitive ambivalence (−1).* Do individuals control ritual and its knowledge, using it for personal ends? Does the ambivalence about knowledge lead to both optimism and fatalism?
+1 *Symbol, ritual, and sacrifice serve as covenant for a group.* Does the group have covenant identity with god or ancestors? Do leaders give offerings or sacrifices in support of group interests and duty to their god? Do sacrifices stay the wrath of gods or ancestors for sins committed by the members? or	−1 *Symbol and ritual serve the individual performers only.* Do people define, each in an individual way, their relationship with the supernatural world, and the ways and means (fetish, rite) by which they can enhance and draw upon those relationships for their personal life?
+1 *Responses framed as confession, sanction, restoration.* Do people expect confession for sin or deviance from group norm? Are deviants subjected to public sanction, ordeals, or exorcisms to determine their guilt? Is restoration a group action? or	−1 *Responses framed as personal or collective celebration.* Do people emphasize celebration, rather than confession; worship rather than penitence; fellowship above moral duty and responsibility as members?

Cosmology and Cultural Bias

Eliphaz

Then Eliphaz the Temanite replied:
"Are you the first man ever born?
   Were you brought before the hills?
Do you listen in on God's council?
   Do you limit wisdom to yourself?
What do you know that we do not know?
   What insights do you have that we do not have?
The gray-haired and the aged are on our side,
   men even older than your father.
Are God's consolations not enough for you,
   words spoken gently to you?
Why has your heart carried you away,
   and why do your eyes flash,
So that you vent your rage against God
   and pour out such words from your mouth?

"What is man, that he could be pure,
   or one born of woman that he could be righteous?
If God places no trust in his holy ones,
   if even the heavens are not pure in his eyes,
How much less man, who is vile and corrupt,
   who drinks up evil like water!

"Listen to me and I will explain to you;
   let me tell you what I have seen,

what wise men have declared,
hiding nothing from their fathers
(to whom alone the land was given
when no alien passed among them);
All his days the wicked man suffers torment,
the ruthless through all the years stored up for him." (Job 15:1, 7–20)

Micah's Idols

Now a man named Micah from the hill country of Ephraim said to his mother, "The eleven hundred shekels of silver that were taken from you and about which I heard you utter a curse—I have that silver with me; I took it."

Then his mother said, "The LORD bless you, my son!"

When he returned the eleven hundred shekels of silver to his mother, she said, "I solemnly consecrate my silver to the LORD for my son to make a carved image and a cast idol. I will give it back to you." . . .

Now this man Micah had a shrine, and he made an ephod and some idols and installed one of his sons as his priest. In those days Israel had no king; everyone did as he saw fit.

A young Levite from Bethlehem in Judah, who had been living within the clan of Judah, left that town in search of some other place to stay. On his way he came to Micah's house in the hill country of Ephraim.

Micah asked him, "Where are you from?"

"I am a Levite from Bethlehem in Judah," he said, "and I am looking for a place to stay."

Then Micah said to him, "Live with me and be my father and priest, and I will give you ten shekels of silver a year, your clothes and your food." So the Levite agreed to live with him, and . . . the young man became his priest and lived in his house. And Micah said, "Now I know that the Lord will be good to me, since this Levite has become my priest." (Judg. 17:1–3, 5–13)

Mary Douglas (1970, 1982) in her works on cosmology investigates the relationships between the nature of social interaction and the symbolic ordering of the world of culture. Her original thesis proposed that the variables of grid and group produce four distinctively different cosmologies with related beliefs and values. Following Douglas, Aaron Wildavsky (1984, 195–97), in a seminal study of the leadership career of Moses, proposes that conceptions of god and religious belief are inextricably tied to the social regimes of leadership. The approach taken here builds upon the works of Douglas and Wildavsky.

Opposition, Boundary, Danger

Anthropologists and linguists have long observed the tendency of humans to organize their world in opposite linguistic categories. Binary coding—hot/cold, wet/dry, day/night, east/west, good/evil—seems to be a universal feature of human conceptual systems. Edmund Leach (1976) notes how opposites such as clean and dirty, noise and silence, may have analogous associations with psychological and ritually important concepts such as impotence and potency or sacred and profane.

The structuring of the world in series of binary oppositions is illustrated most graphically in Genesis 1. In this text we see a whole series

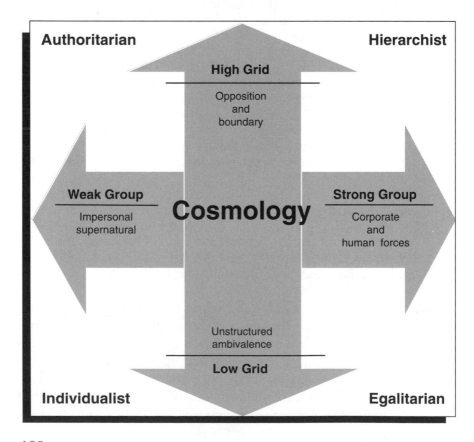

of opposite categories unfold in a description of the order of God's creation. Light is separated from darkness, water above from water below, morning from evening, land from sea, and so on. These opposites define an order and framework of the created world.

Leach and Douglas note the importance of boundary and threshold in such a conceptually divided world. These boundaries may be of both space and time. A graphic illustration of this found in Genesis is "inside and outside" of the garden of Eden. When Adam and Eve are driven out of the garden, cherubim and a flaming sword guard the way to keep Adam from returning to eat of the tree of life.

With the notion of boundary one then finds the notion of danger. To move across boundaries implies significant danger; when humans approach such a situation, they must guard their behavior with great care or perhaps with ritual protection. For example, in Leviticus (9, 10) Aaron and his sons prepared for ministry in the tent of meeting before the Lord. They observed elaborate rules of dress, preparation, and sacrificial offering to enter into the presence of the Lord. However, Aaron's sons, Nadab and Abihu, violated the rules, offering unauthorized fire before the Lord, and were immediately consumed by fire from God. The lesson that Moses teaches from this incident is that ordinary humans may not cross the boundary into the holy place of God, and Aaron and his sons, the chosen priests, must observe carefully every rule and prescription required. Unauthorized behavior leads to immediate destruction.

Many societies have elaborate cosmologies composed of binary distinctions, symbolic categories, boundaries of inside and outside, and significant rituals of purity and danger. Douglas (1966) has described this at length in *Purity and Danger.* The reader is encouraged to pursue that volume for further detail.

Ambivalence and Benign Cosmos

Not all societies characterize the world in a highly structured binary system. While all languages are built on binary features in their sound systems, and most languages construct linguistic binary categories, some societies clearly depart from the high structured cosmology described. When Gordon Koop (1986) and I inquired of the Deni about the origins of the universe and the origins of the Deni, they had no answer. When we asked for stories about their ancestors, they remembered nothing beyond their own life experiences. They related many stories of individual Deni they had known, describing encounters with malevolent creatures and spirits in the jungles. They told in detail the story of each individual and his or her tragedy or triumph. However, an elaborated cosmology was not a part of their thought. They expected that the world around them would support their needs and activities. When sudden disaster befell them, they attributed it to malevolent local spirits, yet they anticipated that the spirits in another location would allow them to lead successful and normal lives.

The Deni knew nothing of the bounded categories of good and evil, pure and impure, or sacred and profane. To the contrary, the world around them was one of ambivalence. It could be good or bad, and only experience would prove the point. A shaman in the village might have a vision from a familiar spirit indicating that a given location would be hospitable for them. However, this provided no promise, and events in that place might prove suddenly disastrous. These people did not see the world as either predictable or essentially good or evil. People did what they needed to do to survive, seeing their lives as similar to those of the creatures in the jungle.

Grid: Opposition and Boundary or Unstructured Ambivalence

The high grid social environment is one in which the cosmology is highly structured with features of symbolic opposition and boundaries of space and time. The diagnostic criteria that follow reflect some of the specific characteristics of opposition and boundary. The criteria focus on qualities of being, relationship, and space and time.

The low grid social environment is one in which structural distinctions in the cosmos are unimportant. People have concepts of spirits, gods, and other powers, but they are not carefully organized in structured ways. The relationships of these beings and powers to people are ambivalent, potentially good or evil, and may be useful or harmful to them. Human activity, then, is couched in terms of this ambivalence and the necessity of flexibility and individual effort in responding to them.

Do sharp boundaries separate God, spirits, and humans (+1) or is the supernatural accessible and benign (−1)?

In a high grid social environment, the differentiation between God, spirits, and humans is a key structural feature. The specific way in which a society or culture will define each of these varies. For example, in Yap, the creator gods are distant beings that have little to do with the contemporary Yapese world. They appear in the origin myths and are part of the Yapese thinking about a distant afterlife. However, spirits are very much a part of the world of the living. Spirits and humans oppose one another, and Yapese believe that every activity must be framed within the ever-present danger of hostile spirits.

A different but parallel cosmology is developed in the argument of Eliphaz presented at the beginning of the chapter. He makes very clear the separation between God and humans as he questions Job, "Do you listen in on God's council?" God doesn't even trust his holy ones, so "how much less man. . . !" He says nothing of the spirit world apart from God, but authority in the human world resides with "the gray-haired and aged . . . men even older than your father." Boundary and danger are emphasized in Eliphaz's explanation of the torment of the wicked who defy God.

The spiritual world in a low grid social environment is one of potentially benign power. The shaman in the Deni society seeks to gain access to the spirit world and to acquire the beneficial power of spirit beings. Deni know that spirits can sometimes harm and are sometimes malevolent, yet they generally look to the spirit world for assistance. The cosmos is a place of support and aid for human subsistence.

Micah, in the second biblical case, sought to win the favor of God through his economic and social action. His mother acted first, setting aside silver "to the LORD for my son to make a carved image and a cast idol." She assumed that God would favor her. After Micah completed this work, he induced a Levite to live with him and serve as priest. He concluded, "Now I know the LORD will be good to me," believing that his actions were all that was necessary to acquire the benevolence of God.

Are male/female roles characterized by strict boundaries (+1) or ambivalence (–1)?

The male/female distinction is one that is given strong emphasis in a high grid social environment. Eliphaz ignores female/God relationships in the dialogue. The focus of his discussion is the relationship between a male and God. The Yapese case provides further illustration; they define male and female space, male and female economic activities, and male and female spirits. Yapese men work on the sea and must deal with jealous female sea spirits. Yapese women work on the land and must deal with active, virulent male land spirits. In each case, Yapese men and women struggle with nature and with spirit beings who may thwart their efforts at will.

Male and female in the low grid social world is a loosely structured distinction. Men and women are not confined to a highly structured division of labor or to a specific set of sex roles. For example, Micah steals from his mother, and his mother in turn makes the decision to use her silver to make idols. Deni men and women exchange roles for the fun of it or for convenience when a spouse is incapacitated. Relationships of men and women are not dangerous, but rather of mutual support and benefit. Cooperation is loosely structured and role reversal is common and beneficial.

Are transactions across boundaries dangerous (+1) or potentially benign but unpredictable (−1)?

The high grid social environment involves relationships between people across structured positions. When people engage in relationships with people of the same category, they feel secure and expect to benefit. However, when people relate across structure, they anticipate danger or even disaster. Eliphaz derided Job's defense of his piety and innocence before God. He argued that Job was suffering because he had sinned against God (a boundary violation), and then declared his innocence. In the Yapese social setting, people structure boundary crossing male/female relations with rules that protect them from inherent cosmological danger. The relationships between spirits and humans entail greater risk and require public ritual and careful personal preparation before an individual may try such an encounter.

In a high grid social world of a complex society such as America, transactions within a social category are relatively neutral. For example, in a university, faculty relations to faculty are considered normal and nonthreatening. However, the dean walking into a faculty member's office brings to the faculty member a slight tinge of anxiety. When the president walks into a faculty member's office, he anticipates that this is an occasion of unusual importance. The faculty member will react in either fear or awe at being honored with such a visit. Interaction across boundaries is unusual and significant.

Low grid is characterized by unstructured space, categories of relationship, and social transactions, leading in the extreme, according to Wildavsky (1984), to states of either anarchy or equity. Leaders and followers mingle freely and no significant social distinctions are made in their public appearance or behavior. Differential behavior to leaders is nonexistent and exchanges between leaders and followers are unstructured. Leaders may not rely upon followers, but must continually seek to renew their support. Duration of relationships is unpredictable and people look at social transactions for their potential benefits. The more one can expand one's sphere of transactions the more likely one is to gain social power. No one is excluded as a potential partner in exchange relationships.

Micah illustrates social and religious anarchy. He freely stole eleven hundred shekels of silver from his mother. They together made idols to represent God, notwithstanding the law of Moses against such. Then he installed one of his sons as a priest, followed by a transient Levite. He made up his own rules as circumstances changed, and negotiated with his mother, his son, and the Levite to accomplish his purposes.

Are space and society structured (+1) or unstructured (−1) in terms of pure, sacred/polluted, profane?

Space and other features of the social environment are frequently marked as sacred and profane. Sacred space is also pure, and individuals and activities that pollute are excluded. Profane space in contrast is open to all members of a society and is frequented by both the pure and the polluted. People may be classified as pure or polluted and activities may also be classified in this manner. Purity is the more vulnerable of these two qualities and great precautions must be taken to protect that which is pure from destructive contact with the polluting and the profane.

Eliphaz denied that a man can be pure, saying, "What is a man that he could be born pure, or one born of a woman that he could be righteous?" His whole argument against Job was based upon marked separation between the purity and righteousness of God and the sinfulness of humanity. Micah in contrast demonstrated no sense of the sacred in his social relationships or his relationship with God. He constructed his own shrine, and perhaps that became sacred for him; the text is not clear. The notion of purity is not reported in any of his actions, but rather he "did as he saw fit."

Space relationships in the low grid social environment are loosely structured. People do not share common distinctions between inside and outside or between pure and polluted. In fact, ideas of purity and pollution are usually nonexistent. Space is unbounded and people move freely in space and time.

Are violations viewed as pollution, sin (+1) or are standards ambivalent and negotiable (−1)?

Sin in high grid society is most frequently associated with a violation of rule and boundary. In the Book of Leviticus God consumed Nadab and Abihu by holy fire because they violated a rule of worship. In the same book Moses differentiated between intentional and unintentional sins, requiring different offerings for different sins. The Israelites had to offer sacrifices for being polluted and for intentional sin. They became polluted by touching a dead body or by violating some dietary law. Sin, in contrast, was the violation of moral law.

Eliphaz and his friends ardently sought to convince Job that his trouble stemmed from sin. Job's denial was inconceivable to them, since their cosmology had no other explanation for these disasters. Eliphaz appealed to the wisdom of the fathers to support his conclusion. Micah in contrast was amoral. Stealing from his mother was of little regard. She attempted to curse the thief, but when she discovered it was her son, she blessed him. Their cosmology reflects much ambivalence.

Ambivalence with regard to sin and deviation is characteristic of low grid social behavior. Such social settings have few if any social rules and the idea of sin is understood only with great difficulty. Because of the highly individualistic characteristic of social relationships, it is very difficult to define deviant behavior. While broad categories of acceptable behavior exist, and people complain about deviations from these broad-ranging expectations, they find it difficult to understand a narrowly defined standard of sin and deviance.

Strong Group: Inside/Outside; Ancestral and Wisdom Focus

The inside/outside distinction is a significant feature of those social environments in which group is strong. Membership in a group is crucial to social identification, and insiders have obligations and constraints to one another that grow out of that membership. Outsiders, in contrast, are often considered nonhuman, and a different set of social values and rules applies. Douglas notes that the inside/outside distinction often results in a cosmological dualism of good and evil. Those who are inside are inherently good, and those who are outside are inherently evil.

Ancestors may be insiders and outsiders. Because of their kinship with the living, they constitute a special set of relationships in the supernatural world. At the same time, because they are dead rather than living, they have crossed a significant boundary. Relationships with ancestors are inherently dangerous. Ancestors may relate to humans in a punitive or a benevolent way, varying with a high or low grid social context.

In high group social environments, ancestors are the authoritative source for wisdom and social norm. The people turn to the structure and rules of their ancestors for the code of conduct for today. Among the people of Yap in Micronesia (Lingenfelter 1975) the word for customary law is *yalen,* which may literally be interpreted as "from the womb." The authority of parents is positional and powerful in Yap society, and while they may die, their authority continues as ancestral spirits. Such an authoritarian position of ancestors is reflected across a wide variety of societies, including the Anabaptist case study referred to earlier.

Weak Group: Millennialism and Impersonal Forces

Douglas (1982) argues that millennialism and emphasis on renewal are important parts of low group social environments. Citing the frequent eruption of cargo cults in New Guinea and Melanesia, she argues that these particular movements grow out of highly individualistic competitive environments. In these settings, Big Man leaders compete for followers by engaging in extensive agriculture and pig production and then outgiving competitors with luxurious feasts and challenges to rivals. Douglas notes that successful leaders must continually assert themselves against rival clubhouses, districts, and regions. The Big Man gains his power not only by his sheer physical and economic force, but also by his ability to engage demons or other supernatural forces to work for him. It is his access to supernatural forces that furnishes the hidden key to the Big Man's success.

The cargo cult phenomena in New Guinea and Melanesia is one in which individual Big Men lead people into variant forms of Christianity or other cults obtained through a vision or prophetic encounter. The Big Man then promises to his followers extraordinary supernatural access to material goods and power if they are willing to follow him. Each cargo cult has its own variation of cosmology and cargo promises. However, all cargo cults hold in common the view that the leader has discovered the secret route to a millennial era of prosperity and he and his followers will have exclusive rights to that cargo when it comes.

Such social environments are characterized by the highly individualist pursuit of wealth, intense competition with other individuals within that environment, and a reliance upon external forces for assistance to supplement the individual charisma and effort. The concept of *mana* among Pacific Islanders labels that impersonal force that makes the difference between one leader and another. The Muslim worlds of southeast Asia and south Asia have the concepts of Adat and Haqq that connote a similar impersonal power. While the specific features of these cultures and social environments differ markedly from that which we see in New Guinea, the emphasis on individualism, the intense competition among leaders, the impersonal quality of power, and the success orientation are similar.

To what extent does the cosmology focus on the power and authority of ancestors (+1) or upon impersonal forces (–1)?

In a high group social setting, the importance of ancestors cannot be minimized. Ancestor focus is a key feature of the social environment, whether framed in terms of clan or lineage, or the founding fathers of a religious group such as the Seventh-day Adventists or the Plymouth Brethren. Ancestors are authoritative, prescribing the doctrine and ritual for society and the rules of morality that govern social relationships. Eliphaz nails his argument with Job upon just such authority: "Wise men have declared, hiding nothing from their fathers (to whom alone the land was given . . .)."

Individuals in a low group social environment turn to personal relationships with supernatural beings or powers for support in their daily activities. The collective identity of ancestors or the collective power of group has no significance for them. The sheer force of the individual personality, pursuing allies that may be gained in the cosmos, is paramount. This was precisely the object and the work of Micah. His mother's money, an idol, and a priest were instruments in his quest for favor from God.

Individuals actively seek means to access these external forces such as luck, *mana,* or astrology. A characteristic of the New Age movement in contemporary America is that individuals may turn to any supernatural medium or force to gain self-power and, thereby, economic and social success. In the New Age movement any kind of force, any supernatural being, is viable and permissible. No doctrines are excluded except perhaps those of exclusive Christianity or exclusive Islam.

Are the categories of the cosmos framed in terms of inside/outside, good/evil dualism (+1) or categories of self, persons, and power (–1)?

A key feature of high group social environment is the inside/outside distinction. Group membership is critical and widely known. Outsiders are considered deviant and threatening to the group. The insider/outsider distinction becomes one of dualism with regard to good and evil. Insiders are by definition good, while outsiders are suspect and potentially evil. Eliphaz speaks of the fathers "to whom alone the land was given when no alien passed among them." In his cosmology, aliens were part of the company of the godless. Job was in danger of becoming part of that company because of his refusal to confess his sin. Eliphaz and his friends are relentless in pressing this viewpoint upon Job.

Micah, in contrast, constructs his own god and liturgy. His priest is the most convenient person available. He does recognize the priority of the Levites for leading worship, but any Levite will do. Micah illustrates how the categories of cosmology and of society may be redefined in terms of the individuals view of the world.

The low grid environment allows each individual to create his or her own cosmology and doctrine. Again, the American New Age movement is one in which each individual produces an individualist theology and world view. These self-made theologies are constructed out of the collective syncretic beliefs of individuals in dialogue with one another.

Does the cosmology emphasize control and conformity (+1) or renewal and millennialism (–1)?

The high group social world is one regulated by members. The group is careful to discipline its membership and to exclude those who violate its rules. The strong emphasis on conformity is essential to the daily well-being of the social group. Individuals who deviate are punished by exclusion or by other means to sustain group cohesion and unity.

Eliphaz is caustic in his rebuke of Job because Job will not accept the collective judgment of his peers. He argues with Job, "Would a wise man answer with empty notions . . . ? But you even undermine piety and hinder devotion to God. Your sin prompts your mouth; . . . your own lips testify against you." Eliphaz appeals to corporate knowledge, "what wise men have declared," to correct Job in his folly. Job's friends cannot comprehend his obstinacy, and they appeal for his repentance so that God will heal and restore him to his wife and community.

Micah has no one to correct him. The text states that "in those days Israel had no king; everyone did as he saw fit." While the details are sparse, Micah apparently sought prosperity through his own private cult. Further, no one challenged him. In the sequel in Judges, five Danites stopped for the night and inquired of God through the Levite if their journey would be successful. The Levite assured them of the Lord's approval; prosperity was theirs. With this encouragement they rounded up six hun-

197

dred men, stormed the small city of Laish, burned it to the ground, and killed its peaceful inhabitants. They occupied the territory and rebuilt the city for their own.

The preoccupation with success and the quest for a better life characterizes a weak group cosmology. The New Age movement in America epitomizes this philosophy. Tending to be millennial in their orientation, people define themselves as potential gods. Through the process of self-realization they are able to achieve their fullest potential. This belief is millennial in that it focuses on potential and on the renewal of persons and prosperity for individuals.

Are cultural symbols powerful, efficacious (+1) or weak, individualistic (–1)?

The symbols of a high group social environment play a crucial role in group definition and continuing existence. For the Anabaptists the specific form of baptism and communion provide powerful and efficacious symbols of membership. These same people will split their groups over deviation from the rules and practice of these symbols. For example, among a group of American Brethren, a split emerged in the 1980s between churches who admitted members without rebaptism and those who did not. They split over the symbolic power of the form of baptism, which marks for some their commitment as a group to doctrinal integrity.

Eliphaz was concerned with Job's language, saying, "Why do . . . you vent your rage against God and pour out such words from your mouth?" He then described in detail the fate of men who behave in such manner. "All his days the wicked man suffers torment, . . . terrifying sounds fill his ears; . . . distress and anguish fill him with terror; . . . because he shakes his fist at God and vaunts himself against the Almighty" (Job 15:20–25). Apparently Job had violated the manner in which men may talk to and about God. His words were so out of character that his friends fear for his life.

The story of Micah and the Danites reveals men without fear of God or of violating cultural norms. On the way to their conquest at Laish, the five Danites decided to steal Micah's idols for their new city. They handily accomplished the theft, and they persuaded the Levite to come with them. "Isn't it better that you serve a tribe and clan in Israel as priest rather than just one man's household?" they said (Judg. 18:19). When Micah pursued them, they threatened him, so that he gave up and returned home. Because of their success that the idols foretold, the Danites set up Micah's idols and his priest in the rebuilt city to become the center of a new cult.

The symbols of low group are individualistic. Each individual or collective may define symbols of personal value to them, yet these symbols have relatively little wider social impact. The Danites had no interest in Micah's idols until they consulted them, with positive effect, regarding the success of their venture. People may form collective groups sharing symbols of mutual interest and benefit, but the weak ownership of these symbols by members of these collectives inevitably leads to varying interpretation and diverse expression and divisions. For example, the focus of the New Age on eclecticism means that any symbol will do and any means of gaining personal power is acceptable.

To what extent are beliefs and rituals collective (+1) or personal (–1)?

The performance of collective rituals that reinforce key doctrines and beliefs is central to the maintenance of group identity. For Anabaptists the regular performance of their communion ritual affirms their distinctive doctrines. Further, communion and baptism provide the unifying public events around which the group unites and mobilizes for continued support and growth. Similar activities may be identified in other social groups. The annual rituals of the reading of the Torah and of sacrificial offerings in Israel were crucial to the identity of the tribes of Israel. The regular observance of the Sabbath marked the ritual event that distinguished Israelites from outsiders around them in Canaan.

In the case of Eliphaz and Job, we have no data on the ritual lives of these men. In the case of Micah, the one ritual noted was the request of the five Danites regarding the success of their journey. Micah's idols and cult were certainly limited to one household, until they were stolen.

In weak group environments, as illustrated by Micah, ritual and religion become a very personal matter. Individuals may choose to meditate, pray, or do nothing. The religious system may involve regular meetings or no meetings and elaborated ritual or no ritual. The religious system works for the individual and provides the connection to supernatural forces necessary for individual goals. When the idols worked for the Danites, they stole them, enshrining them as their own gods.

UNION Ltd. Cosmology, Meaning, and Cultural Bias
by Donna R. Downes

As one might expect, the cosmology of evangelical missionaries is similar, be they western or African. Although UNIWORLD accepts people from a variety of denominational backgrounds, the majority are evangelical and noncharismatic and stress a personal relationship with Christ as paramount in life and ministry. They see God as a personal God, not exactly benign, but "working all things for good for those who love him and are called according to his purpose." Further, they seek to mobilize laity, train leadership for the church, and release the church from "oppressive traditional" structures that inhibit the priesthood of the believers or the ministry of the laity.

The Grid Dimension

A few differences did appear in the sums of grid for westerners (–3) and Africans (–1) (see table 11.1). However, for all UNION Ltd. staff members, God is personal, dwelling within each of the team members, and accessible (–1). God is not benign, but he is sensitive to and willing and able to answer the individual prayers and needs of those who love him and seek his help.

Africans and westerners do show differences in the way they perceive male/female boundaries. The westerners on the team believe in limiting church and spiritual leadership roles for women (.5, –.5), but they are less strict than the Africans. Africans (+1) show a consistent high grid view of male/female roles and say that westerners exhibit uncertainty about women in leadership, the workplace, and spiritual roles.

Transactions between people inside UNION Ltd. or UNIWORLD International or even outside the organization are seen as healthy and beneficial (–1). Personal boundary and space are signs of insulation from others and neither are valued by Africans or westerners in UNION Ltd. Westerners are generally more open in their willingness to be "transparent" and to expose themselves to the possible ridicule or criticism of the team. They do so in the name of self-expression.

Westerners and Africans do not agree on the sacred and profane dimensions of the cosmos. Westerners (–1) see things more ambivalent than Africans (–.5), although neither have a well-defined structure. Both Africans and westerners have some ambivalence regarding what sin is or is not, but the reasons behind this ambivalence are different. Westerners (+.5, –.5) view lying (e.g., making promises one can't keep) as moral sin and an extreme violation of group and scriptural standards, yet countering authority or face-to-face conflict is an

Table 11.1
Cosmology in UNION Ltd.: Perspectives of Western
v. African Missionaries

High Grid	Low Grid		
Boundary and Opposition	**Unstructured Ambivalence**	**Westerners**	**Africans**
+1 Boundaries separate God, spirits, humans	−1 Supernatural accessible, benign	0, −1	0, −1
+1 Male/female boundaries	−1 Male/female ambivalence	.5, −.5	1, 0
+1 Transactions dangerous	−1 Transactions benign or unpredictable	0, −1	0, −1
+1 Cosmos structured by sacred/profane	−1 Cosmos unstructured	0, −1	0, −.5
+1 Violation viewed as pollution, sin	−1 Standards negotiable, ambivalent	.5, −.5	1, −.5
Sum of Grid Variables:		**−3.0**	**−1.0**

Strong Group	Weak Group		
Group Cosmology and Group Power	**Success Cosmology and Personal Power**	**Westerners**	**Africans**
+1 Power and authority of ancestors	−1 Impersonal forces at work	.5, −1	.5, −1
+1 Inside/outside, good/evil dualism	−1 Categories focus on self	0, −.5	0, −.5
+1 Emphasis on control, conformity	−1 Emphasis on renewal, millennialism	.5, −1	.5, −1
+1 Powerful, efficacious symbols	−1 Weak symbols	.5, −.5	.5, −.5
+1 Collective ritual, religion	−1 Personal ritual, religion	.5, −.5	.5, −.5
Sum of Group Variables:		**−1.5**	**−1.5**

individual expression, not arrogance or lack of submission. Africans (+1, −.5) are tolerant of unkept promises as "all in the will of God," yet view open conflict and lack of submission to authority as violations of scriptural standard.

The Group Dimension

On the sum of group scores Africans and westerners show identical responses (–1.5). In UNION Ltd., as in many organizations, there is a commitment to the past, to their forebears (.5, –1) and to their values. But such commitment is not so high as to squelch individual illumination, wisdom, and independence in direction. Both the African and American teammates encourage an independent spirit that moves away from tradition and ancestral ties.

UNION Ltd. emphasizes cooperation, ecumenicism, and unity with diverse church groups; inside/outside (0, –.5) is relevant to "team" but does not in any way restrict working relationships with others. Individual personal commitments are highly valued, but are constrained as well by the evangelical leanings and doctrines of UNIWORLD.

The team believes that human beings make a difference in the world; we are guided by scriptural standards (.5, –1), but stress personal response to God's will and his guidance in the Holy Spirit. The emphasis on the potential for renewal is high. After all, why would anyone become a missionary if he didn't believe he could make a difference in the world?

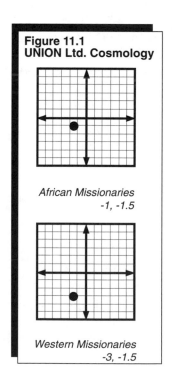

**Figure 11.1
UNION Ltd. Cosmology**

*African Missionaries
-1, -1.5*

*Western Missionaries
-3, -1.5*

As for symbols (.5, −.5), UNION Ltd. and UNIWORLD have a few, such as service awards, "UNIWORLD" pins, attendance awards, and a few other things that symbolize one's commitment to the group. The symbols are not strong. UNION Ltd. doesn't throw a person out because he has not symbolized the ideal team behavior.

On the variable of personal v. collective religion (.5, −.5), the team is ambivalent. Personal religion is a given, and all appear to believe in the individual's celebration of his own relationship with God. But the team also values group-centered, collective worship and prayer, believing that those times strengthen the team and its ministries.

Conclusions

The analysis of cosmology suggests that the team belief system is influenced most by commitments to an individualist evangelical theology, which is inconsistent with other social and economic commitments team members have made (fig. 11.1). Africans (−1, −1.5) and westerners (−3, −1.5) profess an individualist game cosmology, which is in conflict with their philosophy of egalitarian team ministry. The tendency toward the center point for group (−1.5) is perhaps a reflection of these inconsistencies, balancing individualist beliefs with their goals for corporate ministry.

Research Questions 11.1
Grid in Cosmology

High Grid: Boundary and Opposition	Low Grid: Unstructured Ambivalence
+1 *Boundaries separate God, spirits, humans.* Do people make sharp distinctions between God, spirits, and the human world? Is crossing boundaries dangerous or impossible? How do people mediate between God, spirits, and humans? or	−1 *Supernatural accessible and benign.* Is the spirit world open to manipulation and potentially beneficial to humans? To what extent is the universe considered a beneficial and giving resource for human life?
+1 *Male/female boundaries.* Are the life roles and identities of men and women sharply defined and symbolically and socially separate? or	−1 *Male/female ambivalence.* Are the roles assigned to men and women flexible, so that they may sometimes do the same task or exchange tasks? Are the life roles and identities of men and women negotiable?
+1 *Transactions across boundaries are dangerous.* Do participants perceive danger and feel threatened by social exchanges with others who have higher or lower positions? Are such relationships met with anxiety or apprehension? or	−1 *Transactions benign, or unpredictable.* Are social exchanges calculated in economic terms without an overlay of symbolic meaning or social distance and conducted on the basis of personal relationship rather than social status?
+1 *Cosmos structured by sacred/profane.* Do people single out places and people that are holy and to which everyone should give deference and respect? Are people required to bow to symbols or idols? or	−1 *Cosmos unstructured.* Do people speak to others of title or position without formality or perceived difference? Are children free to approach parents or other adults? Is respect based upon reputation and relationship, without emphasis on symbolic identity?
+1 *Violation viewed as pollution, sin.* Do people have a sense of loss and pollution when certain rules are violated? What is needed to restore purity? To what extent do they expect discipline and punishment for violation? or	−1 *Standards ambivalent, negotiable.* To what extent are social standards open to negotiation? Do people defend their character and integrity even when caught in a wrong? Are standards for social behavior a matter of personal conscience rather than rule or group expectation?

Research Questions 11.2
Group in Cosmology

Strong Group: Group Cosmology and Power	Weak Group: Success Cosmology and Personal Power
+1 *Power and authority of ancestors.* Do people revere and honor ancestors or historical figures? In what ways are these people remembered, honored, consulted? To what extent is group identity tied to heroes of the faith, founding fathers, ancestors? or	−1 *Impersonal forces at work.* Is God defined as distant, transcendent? Is supernatural power largely impersonal, and subject to human manipulation? To what extent is the supernatural beyond human understanding?
+1 *Inside/outside, good/evil dualism.* Do people have a collective identity, based upon traditions of the fathers? Are outsiders suspect and even evil? Do people define themselves by symbols, rituals, or statements of faith? or	−1 *Categories focus on self.* Is the individual quest for spirituality, access to higher power, highly valued? more so than a corporate faith? Is personal spiritual fulfillment more significant than the definition of a collective statement of faith?
+1 *Emphasis on control, conformity.* Do people control their personal and collective lives? Does the group discipline its membership and exclude those who violate its rules? Is conformity essential to the daily well-being of the social group? or	−1 *Incipient millennialism, revival.* Do people focus on renewal in relation to god(s) for each individual in society? Is achieving one's fullest potential part of the goal of life? Is progress essential? Do people seek prosperity now and/or in a new millennial era?
+1 *Powerful, efficacious symbols.* Are symbols crucial to the daily life of people and reinforced in a ceremonial calendar? Do people refer to symbols and mark appropriate or deviant behavior in relationship to them? or	−1 *Weak symbols.* Is symbolic behavior relatively absent in daily and ceremonial life? To what extent do individuals have the freedom to define symbols in their own terms and according to their own interests?
+1 *Collective ritual, religion.* What specific rituals do the participants emphasize as critical to group membership and identity? How does participation distinguish members from nonmembers? or	−1 *Personal ritual, religion.* Do individuals set their own worship, prayer, or other practical agendas? Is variability tolerated in religious commitment and expression?

Cultural Bias in a Mission Organization

Donna R. Downes

UNION Ltd.: Conflicting Biases and Interests

Western and African missionaries have embraced somewhat different values in reference to each of the social, economic, and religious variables considered in previous chapters. The challenge before us is to understand the meaning of the variation discovered through this analysis. Figures 12.1 and 12.2 present a graphic representation of the value variations and differences of Africans and westerners in UNION Ltd. In this chapter I will attempt to give some explanation for the distributions as a whole and to project what might be happening within the UNION Ltd. social environment as Africans and westerners minister together.

First, it is obvious that two very different configurations are present for westerners and Africans. While the westerners seem to oscillate horizontally between the individualist and egalitarian games, the Africans oscillate vertically between the egalitarian and the hierarchist games, with variant weak group responses to family authority and cosmology.

For the westerners, the oscillation between individualist and egalitarian games is not a surprise. Following a western cultural pull toward individual autonomy, we expect a weak group orientation in the most personal variables in the missionaries' life—family, religious beliefs (cosmology), and disputes and conflicts. In these areas they value privacy and personal control. But, as UNIWORLD missionaries, they have chosen to identify with an organization that stresses ministering in team.

To blend as a team, they surrender authority, labor, and resources to team ministry. Their exchange relationships are important for building group unity as is the group observance of ritual. The westerners have learned to identify with and rely on group because it is their supportive structure for ministry in a foreign land.

The pull toward a higher group orientation on the team does not affect how westerners view their family authority or how they handle disputes and conflicts. Family structure is their own business; they are unwilling or unable to allow the organizational culture or the host culture to influence it.

Although one might expect a western missionary to show some tendency toward an authoritarian game, common to international mission corporate cultures, UNIWORLD relies on other values to motivate and lead its members. UNIWORLD considers itself an organization always in transition, and considers such transition healthy. It instills a strong sense of group identity and loyalty in the recruits. Apparently this loyalty takes a bit better with the Africans than it does with the westerners, but they also evidence a fairly high degree of loyalty.

Figure 12.1
UNION Ltd. African Missionaries

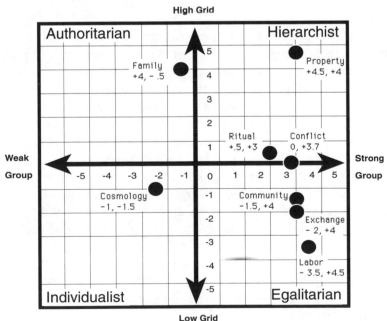

207

Figure 12.2
UNION Ltd. Western Missionaries

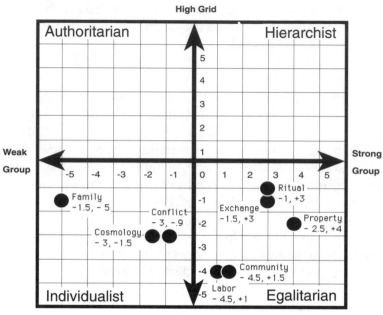

The prominent role of family authority throughout the study is of significance. The Africans' higher grid orientation to family was replicated throughout most of the variables, and they appear to carry their family values into the team social environment. For example, Africans have high regard for the symbolic value of property, which confers authority and prestige in their extended families and communities. No such value was evident among the westerners, who viewed property as utilitarian. The Africans' idea of preserving the image of team unity (like the cohesive bond of extended family) was far more important than the westerners' desire to express individual opinions or gain individual justice. The Africans project family or group bond into UNIWORLD and UNION Ltd., while westerners do not. The Africans placed high value upon relationships in their labor expectations and exchange agreements, which are never merely instrumental, but also symbolic. The mission recognizes the power of African family relations, setting policies that take nonwestern missionaries out of their local environment to avoid family authority conflicts.

Since strong reliance on identity with group is so important to African team members, whether it be the UNION team group or their own extended family, the weaker group score for family authority is a surprise. Perhaps because all African team members live in urban households, apart from their extended families, and have also spent lengthy periods in America, they prefer a weaker group family structure. However, they face the tension of meeting the expectations of their extended families. Perhaps this tension forces them to view the team as an extended family on whom they can rely in times of need.

Two major issues divide westerners and Africans that arise from their different cultural biases regarding family authority. First, the issue of income causes conflict, in spite of the fact that both receive the same salary. Because of the westerners' lack of family obligations, they can save more money, give more money, and spend more money on possessions than can their African teammates. So, westerners take vacations at tourist hotels, dine out, and hold memberships at health or sports clubs. The African team members rarely opt for a few days of vacation at a tourist spot. They pour their disposable income into family needs and spend their vacation time in the countryside working on the family farm.

This discrepancy in western v. African lifestyle choices occasionally becomes a problem, especially when the western team leader requires an African teammate to take a vacation "alone" with his wife. Also, the African teammates to sometimes wonder how the westerners can spend so much money on leisure. "Can the salaries really be equal?" some may question. The westerners on the team might do well to attempt to explain how they are independent from their families back home, so that their African teammates may better understand some of the economic discrepancies that occur.

The second major issue is time management and ministry. Because African grandparents often live with their children and make family demands, African team members struggle with team work time and family time. In the traditional western organization, rules limit time away from work to tend to family needs (purchases of land, legal matters, hospital visits, marriage negotiations, birth and deaths). For example, team rules allow an employee to take one day per month for personal family leave in the case of death or sickness. Because Africans value families above work, they may take five or six days per month away from scheduled work. Western teammates question their dedication and productivity.

The UNION Ltd. western team leader recently estimated that one African team member spent at least a third of his available work days last year settling family legal disputes. "Should their supporters be paying for that?" he questioned. "Is it right that he collects his monthly salary like the rest of us and does only two-thirds of the work he should do?" Obviously, the difference in orientation between western and African views of family authority affects their working relationships and mutual respect.

Other areas of conflict are evident (figs. 12.1 and 12.2). The Africans' high grid values about property (+4.5) conflict with the westerners' low grid values (−2.5). UNIWORLD has encouraged African team members to limit their property ideals to their private lives and let UNIWORLD's corporate culture dictate values regarding team property. In spite of this, team members have disputed about office location, loaning of books and personal properties, and property maintenance.

The African team members also struggle in their attempt to resolve conflict. In their own traditions they expect a much higher grid orientation to the resolution of disputes and conflicts. In an attempt to cope with UNIWORLD's lower grid values process, they give greater emphasis to group unity, relying on the loyalty of the group for protection in conflicts. The westerners, living in their individualistic families, have little idea of the tension Africans are feeling in this area. Their "biblical" view of the confrontational, one-on-one approach is the norm for them and the acceptable approach within UNIWORLD as a whole.

There appear to be three major factors that must be addressed for the UNION Ltd. team (and perhaps other UNIWORLD teams) to become more effective in their group ministry:

1. The Africans have a much higher need for and value attached to their corporate group identity than do the westerners.
2. The Africans live in a state of uncertainty and tension between UNIWORLD's corporate values, their own traditional values, and the varying values of their western teammates.
3. Westerners in UNIWORLD place a high value on UNIWORLD's low grid orientation, but that orientation causes friction and tension for the Africans.

Addressing the Issue of Group Identity

UNIWORLD is somewhat unusual among mission organizations because of its strong emphasis on team ministry—not just a team of individuals doing their own thing, but a team that actually sets goals together, plans together, prays together, and operates together in ministry. This group orientation is attractive to the Africans on UNION Ltd.'s team, but less so to the individualistic westerners.

Perhaps UNIWORLD should prepare its African team members more carefully to understand the nature of western individualism and high commitment to a task, rather than to an organization. At the least some discussion must take place on how teams, having members with distinctly different values, can operate effectively within a nonwestern context. Should UNIWORLD, for example, adopt the values of the local African culture and their African teammates in the management of the field ministry? Should UNIWORLD expect a strong group orientation from its western staff when they are accepted as missionaries?

Westerners need to recognize more clearly the kind of commitment UNIWORLD makes when it recruits African staff. As UNIWORLD becomes their corporate identity, Africans expect more confirmation of that identity—recognizing their status in the organization as well as reinforcing their membership in and value to the group. To suggest that UNIWORLD's western recruits be required to make greater commitment to a team identity is appropriate, but such a requirement might not work. UNIWORLD already spends several months trying to train its recruits to operate as a team. The organization cautions individualists to change their ways, but the mission has little power to enforce such a value.

Recognizing the Africans' high need for group identity and the team philosophy of UNIWORLD, westerners had best follow the command of Paul to the Philippians (2:3) to esteem others better, and stretch more to adopt high group values and goals. Westerners also need to inform African recruits about and discuss with them the virtues of the individualistic orientation of their colleagues. For Africans the security of knowing that UNION Ltd. will become a part of their extended family offers them hope that their job and ministry will not be jeopardized if they occasionally violate the corporate cultural rules. Westerners, in contrast, are accustomed to separating work from private relationships, and viewing work relationships as extended family creates potential conflicts of interest. Some open discussion of this issue during missionary training may help to facilitate mutual understanding and to make individual expectations a bit more realistic.

Addressing the Conflict Between Corporate and Individual Values

One strategy for reducing team conflict is to make the western missionaries fully aware of the tricultural tensions Africans face as they attempt to operate according to the values of UNIWORLD's corporate social environment, their own traditional social environment (especially their family environment), and the traditional social environments of their western teammates. All three will occasionally be at odds, and in an egalitarian game like UNIWORLD's, it is difficult for the Africans to see which standards or norms they must follow. The westerners also face tricultural tensions, so the team would benefit from open dialogue about such issues.

The area of disputes and conflicts is especially problematic, for the Africans find open confrontation particularly offensive. This is the style valued by the westerners on the UNION Ltd. team. While UNIWORLD may value a higher group commitment, the westerners are unable or unwilling to draw on team resources to help them negotiate in conflict. In their view, mediators get in the way, rather than help resolve conflict. So the Africans are faced with a dilemma:

1. to address conflict within someone else's cultural framework, which is a difficult thing to do when emotions are high and personal feelings are on the line;
2. to rely on group loyalty to carry them through the conflict; or
3. to resort to their own cultural norm for resolving conflict.

None of these answers are very effective for the African. The westerner is faced with similar dilemmas. In such a personal area like conflict resolution, it is difficult to ask someone to step out of his "comfort" value orientation and to operate in another. So what is the answer?

A practical beginning might be more time in training of recruits regarding intercultural conflict resolution, perhaps using game theory. Also, the team needs to discuss these issues together so that Africans and westerners can gain a better understanding of their differences. While understanding will not remove the problems, it may at least help people to deal with their conflicts effectively.

The team and mission could also assist Africans to resolve conflicts arising from their dual commitments to family and work. Although UNI-WORLD attempted to skirt this issue by assigning Africans to field teams outside of their home countries, that solution is not attractive to Africans who desire to minister in their own countries. Further, the fact that an African is located in another country does not diminish obligations to his family. The African's family ties cut across distance and time. How should a western mission organization like UNIWORLD accommodate such value differences, or should it even attempt to do so? Such a question must be addressed by international organizations that desire to have multinational teams.

Addressing the Issue of a Low Grid Team Orientation

Overall, in the measurement of the eight grid/group variables, the Africans have shown some leaning toward a hierarchist social game. Since UNIWORLD has encouraged a low grid approach to ministry, team, and organizational identity, some additional training for Africans in understanding and working within UNIWORLD's corporate culture is essential. Perhaps teaching acceptance of differences in the nonessentials and unity on essential team processes such as conflict resolution is a viable strategy for team development.

It is one thing to ask UNIWORLD members to operate within the corporate cultural bias, but it is quite another to ask team members to operate in ways that conflict with values they hold deeply. The central question for any mission organization is, By whose values will missionary teams conduct themselves—the values of the host culture, the "sending" culture, or some hybrid? The attempt to form a hybrid is certainly attractive, but it is doubtful that people can operate for long in such tension. The question is indeed a puzzling one.

It is fitting to end this case study on such a question, for while the study of cultural bias gives much insight into the social roots of value conflicts, it cannot provide the answers to those difficulties. The resolutions to the problems must come first from recognizing that the conflicts exist and then a collective commitment to find ways of resolving the difficulties within the particular social context under study.

Postscript

About a year and a half after this case study was completed, the author had a remarkable opportunity to use what she had learned from the grid-group analysis to assist the UNION Ltd. team to build forgiveness and reconciliation with its former African leader, David. Applying the diagnostic tools used in this case study helped the entire team work through the conflict in a way that brought inner peace and joy to all the participants.

A year and a half passed after David resigned in frustration from the mission. During that time the western teammates and the one African family remaining on the team sensed some frustrations in their ministries. Bound to their past mistakes, and unforgiven, they felt tentative in much of the ministry they attempted. Jonathan, the western leader who replaced David, eventually transferred to other responsibilities in the mission, and a new westerner was appointed director of UNION Ltd. The new director saw the need for beginning with a clean slate, learning from past mistakes, and trying to go forward from what they had learned.

He called an all-day meeting of the UNION Ltd. team to pray and to discuss the future together. During the course of the morning, as the team prayed, one teammate declared that their inability to forgive and forget the past was blocking the effectiveness of their ministries. The whole team readily agreed, and in a prayerful spirit asked the Lord to reveal to them what sin in each team member needed to be forgiven. They also asked for wisdom regarding what needed to be done to put the past to rest. Over a three-hour period of prayer and tears, each teammate felt conviction regarding wrongs, each confessed, and each felt forgiveness.

But the question remained: How could the whole team put an end to this historic conflict with David, their former leader? They knew they must go to David in a way appropriate to him and ask forgiveness and seek reconciliation. By this time David had begun a new mission organization, having just received his official government charter.

After quiet discussion, the team decided to give David honor as the new leader of his organization and as the founding director of UNION Ltd. They agreed to go as a team to ask forgiveness openly, even if that meant doing so before his family and ministry team in order to acknowledge his authority and leadership role. They also knew that a significant symbolic gesture and ritual were important if they were to achieve reconciliation.

214

They set up an appointment to visit David in celebration of the government registration and charter of his new organization. On the appointed day they gathered as a group, and went to his office/home, bringing a live sheep as a gift—a sign of biblical reconciliation, and a symbol of the sins forgiven between David and UNION Ltd.

The visit achieved everything they had hoped. David had invited his family and organizational members as expected. He saw and understood the symbolic value of the sheep and arranged for a traditional handing over of the sacrificial sheep. They had a time of prayer, forgiveness, reconciliation, food, fellowship, and dedication of his new organization and office. David's symbolic authority, leadership, and importance had been restored. The laughter, the joy, and the inner peace were evident in all as they left David's home that day. Since that time David and his teammates have attended two UNION Ltd. celebrations where he has been honored as the founder of that team.

Today in the UNION Ltd. office a rock stands to mark this event, an Ebenezer to reconciliation. The words on the rock are "It Is Finished!"—a constant reminder to all on the team that God brought reconciliation and forgiveness that day between UNION Ltd. and David.

Interestingly enough, from that time to this day, the ministry of UNION Ltd. has flourished and grown in a way unexpected. In fact, UNION Ltd. is in the process of turning the ministry over to leading Africans who have come alongside the team and made their increased ministry possible. God honors the pilgrim, imperfect though we be. May we learn more about what it means to be God's pilgrim people.

Ideas
and Interests

The Dynamics of Culture

> Then God said, "Let us make man in our image, in our likeness, and let them rule over the fish of the sea and the birds of the air, over the livestock, over all the earth, and over all the creatures that move along the ground." (Gen. 1:26)
>
> Now the serpent was more crafty than any of the wild animals the LORD God had made. He said to the woman, "Did God really say, 'You must not eat from any tree in the garden'?"
>
> The woman said to the serpent, "We may eat fruit from the trees in the garden, but God did say, 'You must not eat fruit from the tree that is in the middle of the garden, and you must not touch it, or you will die.'"
>
> "You will not surely die," the serpent said to the woman. "For God knows that when you eat of it your eyes will be opened, and you will be like God, knowing good and evil." (Gen. 3:1–4)

Anthropologists have approached culture from at least three distinctive perspectives: culture as mental or symbol systems, culture as material systems, and culture as the ideological expression of social systems. Proponents of each of these approaches have argued that their perspective most accurately represents the real world of sociocultural systems. Some "mentalists," such as Clifford Geertz (1984) and D. M. Schneider (1984) have argued that each cultural group has shaped its world through cognitive and social processes, employing unique cultural categories and

216

propositions that are unlike any other in the world. Materialists, such as Marvin Harris (1964) or Eric Wolf (1984), explain culture and human history through economic processes, which, they argue, are the causal forces from which all social and ideological systems follow. Social systems theorists, such as Meyer Fortes, Mary Douglas, Anthony Giddens, and Peter Berger derive forms of economic and cultural life from social structure. Others, like Richard Adams (1975) and Margaret Archer (1988), have sought to blend these perspectives into comprehensive theories of society, economy, and culture.

This chapter seeks to develop a biblically informed theory of culture drawn from Scripture and the observations of those who are students of cultural life. We will begin with a discussion of *ideas* that frame the concepts and logic of cultural life. We will review briefly some of the idea systems that make up the great religious traditions of the world, while recognizing that the creativity of the human mind allows for countless variation and elaboration upon them.

We will then follow with a discussion of *interests*, focusing upon the material and social dimensions of cultural life. Human interests derive from the biological, economic, and social necessities of human life, and are framed within the five distinctive yet universal social game prototypes. Across the diverse environments of the world and through human

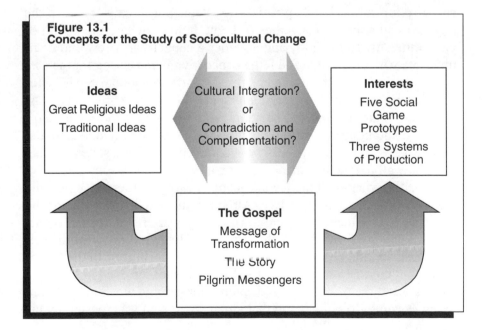

Figure 13.1
Concepts for the Study of Sociocultural Change

Ideas
Great Religious Ideas
Traditional Ideas

Cultural Integration?
or
Contradiction and
Complementation?

Interests
Five Social
Game
Prototypes
Three Systems
of Production

The Gospel
Message of
Transformation
The Story
Pilgrim Messengers

history, these ways of life have been expressed through at least three broadly defined systems of production, each of which results in unique configurations of ideas and interests.

Finally, we will examine the relationships between ideas and interests as they are expressed in the dynamic contexts of sociocultural life. Rejecting the theme of the integration of culture around one of the three perspectives advanced by anthropologists, I will argue that people employ their ideas and interests in social activities in a dialectical fashion, and that contradiction and complementation are the norm for cultural logic and social interaction. The chapter will conclude with a discussion of the gospel as a message of transformation, which in its presentation will both contradict and complement the ideas and interests of those who hear it.

Creation and Culture

Created in the image of God—what can this mean? The text in Genesis makes a number of observations: dust and breath; male and female; to rule over the fish, birds, and creatures; to occupy and care for the garden; to name the living creatures; to obey God's single command. Each of these items identifies certain characteristics that are part of the human capacity for cultural and spiritual life. "Dust and breath" refer to the physical and spiritual capacities of being human, where the breath of God brings life to the body and signifies a capacity to know and communicate with God. Male and female, occupying and caring for the garden, and ruling over the living creatures signify the human capacity for society and economy—material and social life in the garden. The last two features are naming and obeying: naming signifies the capacity for language and communication, obeying the capacity to understand and choose between good and evil. The account ends with the statement that "God saw all that he had made, and it was very good" (Gen. 1:31).

Yet in the opening of the second act of the story, the serpent enters the scene to engage Adam and Eve. Although the serpent was one of the creatures over which they were to rule, they were ruled instead by his guile. When confronted with the choice to obey God or to fulfill their own curiosity and desire, both Adam and Eve succumbed to the lust of the flesh ("the tree was good for food"), the lust of the eye ("pleasing to the eye") and the pride of life ("desirable for gaining wisdom"). Before the story can unfold, the good that God had created was twisted by his

218

creatures to serve the desires of their flesh. In the exercise of their capacity to think and choose, they accepted the ideas of the serpent as truth, and acted accordingly to disobey the one command given by God. The immediate outcome was spiritual death—separation from their creator—and eviction from the garden into a cursed world of toil, suffering, and physical death. Their created capacities for language, ideas, economy, and biological and social reproduction remained, but under the curse of sin and separation from God.

The temptation of Jesus in the Gospels (Matt. 4:1–11, Luke 4:1–13) provides a parallel yet contrasting picture to the preceding analysis. Satan tempts Jesus in a similar manner, urging him to turn a stone into bread (lust of the flesh), to seize the kingdoms of the world (lust of the eyes), and to demonstrate his power to defy death (pride of life). Satan's comment on the kingdoms is provocative: "I will give you all their authority and splendor, for it has been given to me, and I can give it to anyone I want to. So if you worship me it will all be yours." The kingdoms—Rome, the Han dynasty in China, the Mayan and Peruvian kingdoms—were splendid; yet they belonged to the master of rebellion, Satan the tempter. Jesus could have them merely by submission in worship to their master. Knowing of the suffering and death before him, this must surely have been an appealing prospect; yet, unlike Adam and Eve, Jesus rejected these temptations, defying Satan by appealing to ideas, commands in the written Word of God. Jesus thus affirmed the power of the Word of God in Scripture and established the ground for human reconciliation to God through his righteous life and subsequent death and resurrection.

Ideas: A World of Differences

All human beings have ideas. We learn ideas from others, we create propositions of our own as we learn, and through our ideas we frame the context—definitions, meanings, and motivations—for our daily lives. Each of us reflects at various times and places about the world around us, and in our reflections we form propositions and draw conclusions about God, nature, people, society, and the course of our lives. As we participate in the events of social life, we evaluate situations, we seek to determine which course of action is appropriate, and we articulate ideas and explanations that rationalize our decisions in each.

Ideas are part of the collective experience of human beings, and as they are shared by people across time and space, they form the basis for human communication in society. Ideas flow from the creativity of the human mind, with its powers of classification, abstraction, analogy, and elaboration. The ordinary and the gifted persons in each culture create and recreate stories of creation, paradise, disaster, murder, and conflicts of the gods and humans in their attempts to frame a meaningful and satisfying existence. The unique history, whether written or oral, of each society frames the foundation categories, propositions, cosmology, and explanatory events of its world view.

World view is fundamentally a system of ideas, of logical relationships, through which actors in a sociocultural arena explain and rationalize their thoughts and actions. What do we mean by "logical" relationships? Archer (1988) asserts that people connect their ideas into meaningful, noncontradictory propositions, inasmuch as they are capable of doing so. For example, we evangelical Christians believe that God is truth. From that proposition, we frame other propositions; for example, as Christians we are sons and daughters of God, and therefore we should be truthful because we belong to the One who is Truth. That we should be truthful is a logical extension of our ideas about God and our relationship to him. We also believe that God created the world and everything in it. From this basic proposition we generate a series of propositions about the creation in logical relationship to God as creator. For example, God saw his creation, and it was good; we are God's creation, therefore we are of positive value in God's sight.

Propositions about the world and the logical relationships between them provide the substance of cultural systems. While we do not have space here to develop an analysis of idea systems in depth, Ward Goodenough's (1981) essay on culture develops a useful, descriptive model of linguistic categories, propositions and beliefs, and the logic that produces a cultural system. Readers who wish to explore this further will also benefit from Paul Heibert's extensive writings in this area (1978, 1986) and from the works of Charles H. Kraft (1981), Marvin K. Mayers (1987) and Donald K. Smith (1992) on cross-cultural communication.

Of critical importance in our understanding of ideas is that while humans are wonderfully creative, they have from the beginning of time been deceived by the ideas of the master of deception, the serpent in Genesis 3, the father of lies (the devil) in John 8:42–47. The human quest for truth is therefore always corrupted by our yielding to the same temptations of the flesh described for Adam and Eve. The idea systems spun out in every culture reflect the tension between the human desires to know and to satisfy their interests. Knowing is never interest free, but is always structured within the biases that arise from our living and walking "in the flesh" (Rom. 8:5–7).

The Great Traditions: Ideas That Have Shaped History

Over the long history of human society and culture certain intellectual traditions have gained widespread human acclaim and adherence. These traditions illustrate how systems of ideas have been created by human beings and have emerged with powerful force to achieve the loyalty and commitment of literally millions of followers. These idea systems reflect a creativity and diversity of expressions of the human mind.

Most familiar to us is the Judeo-Christian heritage of which we are part. The Bible provides the historical record of the significant ideas and themes that constitute this great tradition. The Jewish Torah or the Old Testament articulates the dominant theme of monotheism, and God's justice and law governing human relationships. The Jewish people claim a covenant relationship with their God, and Christians have understood this covenant relationship to be fulfilled in the person and work of Jesus Christ. The predominant thesis of the Christian faith is the sinfulness of all human beings, the gift of redemption through the sacrificial death of Jesus Christ on the cross, and the hope of eternal life through the resurrection, ascension into heaven, and the expected return of Jesus. Salvation is not only for the Jews, but for all people, and the Scriptures that carry the revealed message are to be translated into every language for their salvation.

Muhammed took the major works of Christianity, the Old and New Testament Scriptures, and expanded his own revelations in the Koran, the book of Islam. Islam is a religion of law, founded upon the five pillars or commandments that Muslims must follow for a right relationship with God. Islam, like the Judeo-Christian tradition, is absolutely monotheistic, and God is an all-powerful, distant being who wills the destiny of humans. The authority of Allah is expressed in society through the authority of the father and the exclusive solidarity of the family. The Koran is the holy book, authoritative in its original language. To become Muslim is to learn Arabic, to study the Koran, and to adopt the religious, cultural, and social laws of Islam.

On the continent of Asia, Hinduism, Confucianism, and Buddhism have been the great traditions, originating as early as 600 B.C. and dominating cultural life in India, China, and southeast Asia into the present century. All three of these great traditions emphasize wisdom literature and proclaim the perfection of life through spiritual means. The dominant theme of Hinduism is the denial of self and material interests in favor of a spiritual quest. The life of Mahatma Gandhi illustrates powerfully the Hindu mystic and religious pilgrim who sacrifices material life in favor of a higher spiritual essence. Confucianism in contrast sets forth the agenda for human fulfillment in terms of social and moral perfection. Harmony in social life and the submission of individuals to the authority of the group provide its dominant themes. Buddhism, the quest for human identification with ultimate spiritual reality, grew out of Hindu traditions and spread from India into China and southeast Asia over a strong Confucian cultural foundation. Family, ancestors, and offerings to ancestors and gods dominate all three of these religious traditions.

Discussion of dominant world views would be incomplete without reference to recent ideological paradigms growing out of the European Enlightenment. Western scholars sought secular alternatives to religious thought, and Marx and Engels provided an appealing substitute in their *Communist Manifesto.* Marx, Engels, and their followers assumed that human beings are innately altruistic and that the objective and goal of human society is to release this inherent good toward the fulfillment of a utopian, religion-free world. The postmodern scholars have rejected the idealism of both Communist and western socialism, and many have turned to an eclectic pluralistic spiritism. The New Age movements in America and Europe represent a revival of spiritism and the blending of segments of many of these great traditions.

The tribal peoples of the world, living beyond the influence of the great traditions, have generally been characterized as animists. Animism refers to the belief in a pervasive world of spirits inhabiting trees, rocks, and all of the natural world. Animists attribute their good and bad fortune to the idiosyncratic and unpredictable power of the spirits. People seek the mediating services of ritual and of spirit-possessed men or women who can provide protection and obtain power from these pervasive spirits. Illness is the most common manifestation of discontinuity between the human and spirit world. Shaman or other religious practitioners acquire the knowledge necessary to help people cope with the inevitable problem of illness.

The label *animist* is too simple to address the complexity of tribal religious systems. Human beings are highly creative in their elaboration and development of idea systems. For example, scholars have observed across the continent of Africa the presence of three central ideas: a "high god," the ancestors or living dead, and humans who have spiritual power for the evil acts of witchcraft. One of these three ideas may be highly elaborated in a specific society and form a thematic core around which people organize their social and religious life. While some people elaborate their world view more than others, most believe that their idea systems are logically and socially coherent.

Missiologists typically use the concept *world view* to refer to the idea system of a culture. However, they have not limited its application to ideas. Rather, they propose a series of connected, concentric circles that ultimately include all of human life. They argue that ritual, social, political, and economic behavior is integrated around these core ideas (see Smith 1992, 251–67).

While I accept the causal importance of ideas, I prefer to keep them analytically distinct from the domain of social and economic interests. Ideas may trigger social and economic responses, but there is no necessary connection between them.

Interests: A World of Similarities

Interests are the wants of individuals that must be achieved through their relationships to others. Before Adam and Eve sinned, it was in their joint interest to name the animals, to care for the garden, and to enjoy food and fellowship together. Once Eve had eaten the fruit of the forbidden tree, it was in her interest to have Adam taste the same. Once both had tasted, and discovered their nakedness, it was in their interest to hide themselves from God, since they had broken his command to them. Most of culture is framed within the context of relational interests.

For example, everyone has a physical need to eat. To fulfill that need one must get food, and acquiring food usually entails relationships with other people. Every society defines a division of labor around food-getting activities. Among peasants in Europe, men had responsibility for plowing and working in the fields, while women processed food in their kitchens, courtyards, and village ovens. In some parts of Polynesia these roles were reversed; women worked the taro plots and yam gardens, while men fished for protein and cooked the main meal of the day. Such social arrangements served the domestic interests of families in these cultures and the interests of men and women regarding shared labor.

Interests always involve relationships within what Archer (1988) calls a sociocultural system. The integration of interests in the social system is not a function of logic, but rather of *power relationships* between people who have differing access to power. For example, in a rural Philippine community Christians and pagans disagree about power surrounding rice planting. The pastors of village churches claim access to the power of Jesus Christ through the Word of God, preaching, and prayer. The animist shaman and ritualists claim access to the power of the spirits of the rice fields and the mountains. Pastor and shaman each denies the power of the other to achieve success in their activities of planting, cultivating, and harvesting rice, the very staple of their livelihood. Where shaman have wide influence and support, animist and Christian villagers follow traditional ritual when planting rice. However, when pastors and Christian leaders have a large enough community of believers to support change, they have successfully contested these shaman and their ideas, leading to new methods of rice cultivation. However, the change did not occur until people sensed a shift in social as well as spiritual power.

Power relationships are always structured within community and are patterned in accord with at least one of the five game prototypes described in chapter 2. People seek to achieve their interests through the power relationships in their community. This is illustrated well in Paul's controversy with the Jewish believers of the party of James who came into Asia Minor to assert their power relationships over new Gentile converts. Paul notes how they demanded the marks of membership (circumcision, Gal. 2:3), observance of a calendar of rituals (Gal. 4:9–10), and adherence to certain eating practices (Gal. 2:12) and standards of conduct (Gal. 2:14).

Paul vehemently objected to these practices. He charged the Galatians with "deserting the one who called you by the grace of Christ" (Gal. 1:6), and accused his fellow Jews from Jerusalem of being "false brothers" (Gal. 2:4). Paul observed these new believers conforming to the interests of an existing social structure, rather than living and walking in the Spirit. He lamented, "Who has bewitched you? . . . Did you receive the Spirit by observing the law, or by believing what you heard?" (Gal. 3:1–2).

Human interests are rooted in the physical/biological needs of persons and the social demands of communities. The Scriptures speak of these biological demands as desires of the flesh and the social demands as the "empty way of life handed down to you from your forefathers" (1 Pet. 1:18). This is not to say that society and cultural bias have no value, any more than we would say that body and flesh have no value. Without body we are dead, and without ideas, society, and cultural bias we cannot live together. Each is essential to the daily existence of persons.

Language, society, and culture are gifts of God's creation and common grace. We cannot live apart from them, nor should we desire to do so. The issue is one of quality of life, "walking in the flesh" apart from God, or "walking in the Spirit" in communion with God. These tensions will be explored in depth as we examine in later chapters how we are all in the grip of our cultural biases, and how these biases define our interests and values for personal and social life. The bad news is that our communities of bias are by nature prisons of disobedience (Rom. 11:32; Gal. 3:21–22); the good news is that in Christ we are under "no obligation to the flesh, to live according to the flesh;" rather, we are "children of God, . . . joint heirs with Christ."

The Myth of Cultural Integration

According to Archer (1988), the predominant theoretical orientation in anthropological thought over the last century is what she terms the "myth of cultural integration." Anthropologists have asserted that cultures are cohesive integrated systems. Americans point to themes around which the religious, political, social, economic, and material life of a people constitute an expanding series of interconnected rings. The British reject the American notion of themes, but assert that social structures constitute the central organizing feature of society, and all other aspects (symbolic, religious, political, and economic) are functionally integrated parts of a cohesive and smoothly working system. The functionalism of Douglas and Michael Thompson, Richard Ellis, and Aaron Wildavsky is a variant of this British approach. They argue that the ideas and values rooted in the dynamics of social environment predispose people to particular myths about nature, blame, or risk, and are reflected in the five ways of life. Archer contends, and I concur, that this is a false picture of the nature of social and cultural systems, a picture that originated in the experiences of ethnographers in isolated, relatively prim-

225

itive cultures and the romantic biases that they brought to their research and interpretation.

If cultures are not integrated systems, then what? Archer is not saying that ideas and interests have no connection; indeed they have very real connections, but not of a cohesive, integrated nature. Archer argues first that ideas influence, but do not determine, interest and power-causal relationships. For example, if I am asked to contribute to support a particular missionary, my ideas about missions, about Scripture's mandate, and about my personal responsibility are important. However, I have limited resources. If I agree to support this person, I may not have money to give to the poor or to another ministry. Ideas influence how I manage these competing interests, but they do not determine what I will do. Relationship with the missionary will probably tip the balance; I give to those with whom I have a trust relationship.

While ideas influence how we respond to interests, interests also create *feedback* into our system of ideas. The relationships we value and the priorities we accept and value ultimately affect how we think about the world and how our ideas are shaped. For example, I invest for a period of ten years in a missionary who is translating the Bible. Over that time the missionary reports regularly to me about the challenges, difficulties, and progress of the translation. I receive letters and occasional phone calls, perhaps even a visit, in which my fellow worker tells me of her ongoing battles with the powers of the spirit world where she works. Years ago I believed that spiritual opposition in the form of demonic presence happened in New Testament times, but isn't a problem today. As I listen to these reports of people in spiritual bondage, and of miraculous deliverance through the Word of God, my ideas about demons and about their relevance for today gradually change. Because this person whom I trust, with whom I have an investing relationship, reports experiences that my ideas didn't allow, I begin to question aspects of my world view. This feedback leads me to change my ideas about the spirit world and how it affects daily life and ministry.

Feedback from experience connected to my interests results in *logic modification*. In other words, I reorganize the way I think because I have obtained new information that I believe, because of my relationships (see fig. 13.2).

Another outcome of this process is adjustment in my interests and relationships. I chose to support individual missionaries because I believe that reaching the world for Christ should be my highest priority. By supporting these people I can become a part of a task that I can't accomplish myself. And so, I restructure how I use my resources, spending a substantive portion for missions. This restructuring in turn brings changes in my sociocultural system by establishing new relationships and a wider sphere of power and influence. The connections within my sociocultural system have been expanded, altered because of ideas that I have about world mission.

The dynamic interplay of ideas and interests inevitably results in contradictions and complementarities in our logic (cultural system) and relationships (social system). For those who have embraced the myth of cultural integration, contradiction is an anomaly and is not allowed as a normal part of life. These scholars see contradiction as disruptive, creating disequilibrium and problems. Archer contends that contradiction and complementarity are an integral part of the way people live and work.

By their very nature, belief systems have inherent contradictions. Sometimes the contradiction occurs in the constructed logic of our beliefs; at other times the discrepancy is between belief and practice. We believe things that we don't practice, and we practice that which we do not believe. Such inconsistencies are part of human life.

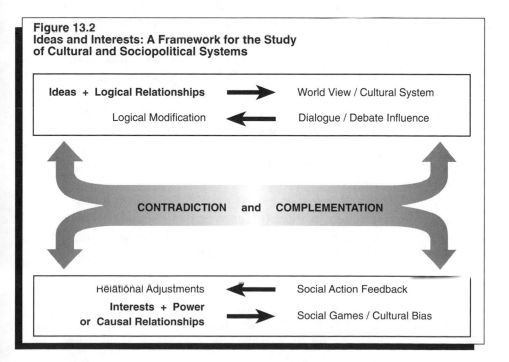

Figure 13.2
Ideas and Interests: A Framework for the Study of Cultural and Sociopolitical Systems

Ideas + Logical Relationships ➡️	World View / Cultural System
Logical Modification ⬅️	Dialogue / Debate Influence

CONTRADICTION and COMPLEMENTATION

Relational Adjustments ⬅️	Social Action Feedback
Interests + Power or Causal Relationships ➡️	Social Games / Cultural Bias

Outsiders who study a cultural system of ideas often find contradiction and flawed logic. Archer states that all people are capable of a certain level of pure logic, in the sense of knowing that A is not B. However, sometimes we choose not to exercise this capability. I remember querying a Yapese man, "In your story of the great flood only one Yapese couple, their children, and one single man survived. Since clan membership is through women, how did the two founding clans of Ngolog and Ngabinaw survive, given that only one woman and her children lived through the flood?" The man said with some irritation that the story of creation and the story of the flood had no connection. Each story had its own didactic purpose, and the Yapese had no intention of constructing a "systematic" mythology as I was proposing. We face similar problems in the application of our texts to constructing a logical world view—for example, a "six-day" creation in Genesis and the "ancient universe" of science; attempts to resolve this contradiction have produced heated arguments over the "six literal days" and the evidence of "ancient" in the earth and universe (Ross 1994).

Complementarities are also part of human life. Some ideas are different, but parallel one another; and because they complement one another, the difference is allowable. For example, giving my life to making money is a secular agenda, having no central place in the command to follow Christ. But if I use that money for God's glory, giving generously to the Lord's work, and so serve the Lord even though I am completely involved in the secular work of obtaining wealth, it is a complementarity. Some would argue that it is a contradiction; but, in my system of logic, and perhaps yours, it is a complementarity. The life of the Christian businessman is not a logical contradiction to the life of the missionary or evangelist. They hold ideas and interests that complement rather than contradict, provided that they are united in a system of beliefs and of supportive relationships.

Cultural and socio-transformations emerge from the complex interplay of ideas and interests. If culture is to be transformed or changed in any way, the change involves contradiction, complementarity, influence, and feedback between the idea system and the social environment. The view of change proposed here follows Archer, suggesting that contradictions may be resolved or sustained and complementarities may persist or be integrated.

While the analogies of world view as concentric circles with a core of cultural themes, or the "cultural onion" with its multiple layers into the heart, have been useful to many, when pushed to their logical ends they fail to encompass the complexity and the dynamism of social and cultural life. Following Archer, our analysis assumes the following:

1. Ideas have logical relationships; people formulate world views.
2. Interests have power/causal relationships; people create socio-economic systems.
3. Ideas influence interests, social feedback influences ideas.
4. Contradictions and complementarities characterize idea/interest interaction.

This framework allows us to focus on how the gospel story challenges the existing ideas and the logic of a people's preconversion world view, yet without necessary connection to their socioeconomic systems. The process of discipling new believers must address the power/causal relationships of the sociocultural system, as well as the theological frames of belief. Biblical transformation involves not only reconciliation with God, but also response to the call of Jesus to "follow me."

The Gospel as a Message of Transformation

The Bible is fundamentally a story. It begins with the account of creation in the Book of Genesis and unfolds with successive stories of God's provision for mankind, their rebellion, and God's judgment and restoration. The opening story of Genesis—the Creator God who made heaven and earth and human beings to have fellowship with him—binds together the text from Genesis to Revelation. From Adam to the final judgment, the story is one of people rebelling against God, and God in his great patience offering mankind his special grace, mercy, and salvation. This message is repeated through the stories of people who have been touched by the Spirit of God. Adam and Eve, Cain and Abel, Noah, Abraham and Sarah, Jacob, Leah and Rachel, Moses, Miriam and Aaron, Naomi and Ruth, Hannah and Samuel, David, and the prophets, all have special encounters with God. In spite of their failings, their doubt, and the rebellion of the people who follow them, God continues to reveal to them his grace and his salvation. The stories of these people and their relationship with God constitute the holy Scriptures and frame the great tradition of Judeo-Christian thought.

The ideas developed in the Scriptures, about the relationship between God and mankind and the salvation that comes through Jesus Christ to all people, have profound implications for history, economy, and the five ways of life. The Scriptures provide the history of God's revelation to humanity. The church provides the history of the outworking of those great ideas as they first transformed the diverse peoples and societies within the Roman Empire and then spread into Asia, Africa, Europe, and the rest of the world.

The gospel challenges each of the five ways that we have described. The message of transformation is neither individualist nor hierarchist, neither authoritarian nor egalitarian. The Great Commandment is to love the Lord our God with all our heart, all our soul, all our mind, all our strength, and to love our neighbors as ourselves. The message of salvation is a message of faith in the person and work of the Lord Jesus Christ. It is not a call to a particular set of social relations or to a particular cultural bias. Even the autonomy game of the hermit cannot escape from the claims of the transforming power of the gospel. Living in isolation from all social relationships is as much in violation of Jesus' call to servanthood as are the extremes of the other four social games. No cultural bias or set of social relationships is untouched by the unconventional ideas of the gospel.

The gospel also questions values of every level of economic life. Whether they live in a tribal subsistence economy, a tributary peasant economy, or an industrial market economy, the gospel calls Christians to a different agenda. Christ commands his disciples to seek first the kingdom of God; his righteousness supersedes the pursuit of wealth, health, and power at any economic level. He instructs his disciples to focus their attention on the coming of the kingdom of God and to commit their lives in wise economic stewardship dedicated to the service of the orphan, the poor, the alien, and the prisoners of society.

All who are touched by this message are called to become messengers, witnesses of the power of the transforming gospel of Jesus Christ. The model set forth for the believer in the Gospels is that of the pilgrim lifestyle of the Lord Jesus himself. The religious pilgrim is called out of society, yet unlike the hermit, remains engaged with it. In his prayer before the crucifixion Jesus stated, "My prayer is not that you take them out of the world but that you protect them from the evil one. They are not of the world, even as I am not of it. Sanctify them by the truth; your word is truth. As you sent me into the world, I have sent them into the world. For them I sanctify myself, that they too may be truly sanctified" (John 17:15–19).

The "Pilgrim" Alternative

In proposing five ways of life, Thompson, Ellis, and Wildavsky speak of the hermit as the primary expression of the autonomy game. Another important variant of the autonomy game is the religious pilgrim. The pilgrim differs from the hermit in that he withdraws from the social structures and politico-economic pursuits of society, yet remains morally and socially engaged. The hermit typically withdraws from society, is disengaged, takes no part in the struggles, and accepts no blame for social events or problems.

The pilgrim understands that the struggles of people in society are compounded by a greater spiritual struggle between the kingdom of darkness and the kingdom of the Son, Jesus Christ. The pilgrim lightens his or her social and economic commitments, responding to Jesus' call to divest one's self of the cares of this world for the purpose of service (see table 13.1).

Like the hermit, the pilgrim is satisfied with a life of suffering. The religious pilgrim sees this suffering as part of the grace of God and is content in whatever social and political circumstances that engagement requires. The contentment of the pilgrim is encapsulated in the apostle Paul's comment in Philippians 4:12–13: "I know what it is to be in need, and I know what it is to have plenty. I have learned the secret of being content in any and every situation, whether well fed or hungry, whether living in plenty or in want. I can do everything through him who gives me strength."

The Christian pilgrim, like the hermit, is impervious to common dangers, yet intimately acquainted with them. The pilgrim is particularly not afraid of those dangers that arise out of social engagements. He or she understands the warning of the Lord Jesus in the gospels: "Do not be afraid of those who kill the body but cannot kill the soul. Rather, be afraid of the one who can destroy both soul and body in hell" (Matt. 10:28).

The hermit is disengaged and socially relevant only to the extent that he or she serves as a critic of the wider society, or contributes reflections from the life of solitude and meditation. In the Middle Ages in Europe hermits were often characterized as madmen or holy fools. The madman was probably a mentally disturbed recluse, and the holy fool, one who was known for flashes of inspired wisdom mixed with obscure folly. Occasionally intellectuals from wealthy families choose the life of solitude for religious reasons, living a life of fasting, prayer, and meditation. These men and women often produced significant works of religious and devotional literature (Ford 1982, 34–35). Sometimes the life of religious solitude was carefully regulated by religious orders or the church hierarchy.

The Christian pilgrim is most significantly distinguished from the hermit in his or her activism in the spiritual struggles of human life and engagement in respective social environments. The pilgrim is one who lives in sustained nonconformity to the cultural biases and values of society, yet remains committed to social reform in the light of higher spiritual principles. The Christian pilgrim understands the profound importance of a loving God, of salvation through grace, and of forgiveness and service as essential to the quality of human life. These values are not fostered by any of the five social games.

The essence of the life of the pilgrim is his or her commitment to the autonomy of discipleship as a follower of Jesus Christ, modeling his or her life after the pattern set by Jesus, and obeying Jesus' commandments

Table 13.1
The Autonomy Game and Cultural Bias

	The Pilgrim	The Hermit
Preferences	Called out/remains engaged	Withdraws/disengaged
Blame	Spiritual struggle—kingdom of darkness v. kingdom of son	No blame/no part in struggles
Envy	Satisfied with grace, circumstances of engagement, Philippians 4	Satisfied with suffering
Economic growth	Engaged servants	Convivial beneficiaries
Risk	Impervious to common risks and those of social engagement, Matthew 10:28	Impervious to common dangers, yet intimately acquainted with them
Apathy	Activist in spiritual human struggles, engaged in respective social environments, yet sustained nonconformity	Disengaged, socially irrelevant

for service and humility in a life of righteous obedience to God. Following Jesus is to identify with him as a pilgrim, in the world, but not of it. Such a lifestyle requires the transformation of interests and power relationships, taking the nature of a servant. The words of Scripture provide the trigger mechanism for changes in our interests, relationships, and lifestyle. This transformation is a lifelong process of accepting God's grace to free us from our cultural bias and learning to walk in his steps.

The one who is truly a disciple of Jesus Christ accepts the command to go into the world and make disciples, "teaching them to obey everything I have commanded you" (Matt. 28:20). The disciples of Jesus uphold a lifestyle constrained by obedience to his word, rather than by cultural bias and the inevitable personal and social interests of economic and social relationships. Disciples surrender their interests to God and lead lives in which the interests of others are as important as their own, or more so. For the pilgrim, social interest no longer has preeminent priority. Rather, one organizes one's life around the word of God and obedience to the commands of the Lord and Master, Jesus Christ.

A Pilgrim Lifestyle in Economic Relations

"Why do you look at the speck of sawdust in your brother's eye and pay no attention to the plank in your own eye? How can you say to your brother, 'Let me take the speck out of your eye,' when all the time there is a plank in your own eye? You hypocrite, first take the plank out of your own eye, and then you will see clearly to remove the speck from your brother's eye." (Matt. 7:3–5)

"Watch and pray so that you will not fall into temptation. The spirit is willing, but the body is weak." (Matt. 26:41)

Conflicts about Labor

American missionaries are typically like their secular American counterparts who work in business and government facilities overseas. In their work with Asians or Africans, they usually introduce new labor requirements and a social organization of labor that is characteristic of their experience at home. Further, since missionaries are often paying the bill for this labor they insist that nationals do it the American way. This means that the national must adapt to the missionary's work schedule, standard of productivity, organization of the work, and system of rewards. Donna R. Downes (chap. 12) has documented how the individualist values about labor of the westerners in UNION Ltd. has undermined the group focus of their mission organization and their personally professed commitment to team relationships.

Although one might rationalize that people in developing nations are entering into economic relationships that have worldwide dimensions and the skills that nationals will learn from missionaries will better facilitate their participation in the world economy, it is usually not the objective of a mission to introduce and implement such extensive social change. These changes are brought about inadvertently rather than intentionally. Further, such changes often lead to tension and frustration between missionaries and nationals, as documented by Downes, and create barriers to the significant growth and development of mission and church ministries.

Christian workers who have a primary concern for the effective expansion of their ministry, as opposed to the economy of their home culture, should do everything possible to adapt to the existing structure of labor among local people. For example, a missionary working with the Deni in Brazil should attempt to contextualize labor relationships into the Deni individualist system of labor. The missionary to Yap should follow the lead of the Roman Catholic priest, who left the construction of the church to the Yapese even though it took nineteen years to complete it. The field-worker who adapts to the existing social game of labor will be most effective in building relationships with local people. Through effective relationships one is able to communicate the gospel, to disciple new believers, and to build a viable dynamic church within the context of the social environment of that particular society.

Missionaries often struggle with the tendency to view their own pattern of labor as more godly than others. The study of Scripture, however, does not support such conclusions. The history of the Jewish people and the Christian church has demonstrated their participation in several social environments of labor. To be effective in serving others, Christian workers then must view their own labor system with a certain degree of critical skepticism.

In the role of a servant to a local community a missionary may be called upon to help people adjust to the changing economic conditions of their nation as it participates more widely in the world economy. Changes in labor relations may be beneficial to people as they seek to compete in the modern world. Expatriates can assist by being cultural brokers, explaining the nature of the new system and its cost and benefits to their fellow workers. This role is legitimate, and it is the obligation of the Christian worker to provide such knowledge and insight if one is able to do so.

Conflicts about Resources

Without question the issue of asking, giving, and control of resources is the most volatile and pervasive source of missionary and national conflict in ministries around the world. In workshops that I have held on five continents the question inevitably arises as to what one should do in situations in which people ask for money or material resources. Because most missionaries come from western countries that have a reputation of being wealthy, and nationals see them as representatives of those wealthy nations, nationals frequently ask for material assistance. While the people asking do not understand the missionaries' financial circumstances, they nevertheless expect the missionary to give. This matter has become so threatening and frustrating to some missionaries that it has destroyed their effectiveness and caused them to give up on ministry to a particular people group.

In the case study of UNION Ltd., Downes makes it clear that while African and western members of the team had differences with regard to property, labor, and exchange relationships, they did not comprehend the cultural pressures and biases underlying these problems. Westerners did not understand or appreciate the fact that African teammates were accountable not only to the team but also to their families, national pastors, and other national interest groups in the wider community. They interpreted disputes or disagreements about property, labor, and exchange relationships as motivated by personal interest, or perhaps even worse, as spiritual deficiency and disloyalty to the team.

When missionaries or national leaders have disagreements with one another over the exchange of money or material goods, the most typical response is to judge the brother or sister in Christ as being unspiritual. Each person involved in the relationship sees his or her own agenda and values as appropriate and biblically justifiable to the situation. As a consequence team members judge one another and develop a critical attitude that undermines their personal and collective ministries.

One missionary team in Asia, George and Ellen, report that the local people came to their door daily to ask for money or material assistance. George and Ellen felt used, abused, and threatened by their neighbors. While feeling obligated to give, they also feared for their personal resources and their ability to meet their financial obligations with the mission. In the community they were seen as rich people, as evidenced by unusual material benefits such as solar electricity and access to the village by missionary airplanes. Moreover, local custom approved seeking patronage from prominent and influential members of the community. George and Ellen felt utterly inadequate to fill this role and despaired of their ability to continue to meet the demands of people around them.

The tension that this couple felt with their neighbors soon spilled over into their marriage. George and Ellen disagreed with one another as to when they should give and how much they should give. Each time a man or woman came to make a request, the result was further conflict and a deeper division between George and Ellen and the local people. Since these financial requests came daily, the source of friction imperiled the future of their ministry.

The problem for George and Ellen and the westerners and the Africans in UNION Ltd. is that they are oblivious to their cultural bias, which then becomes a prison of disobedience. They have grown accustomed to a way of life that they learned growing up in their families and in the communities that nurtured them. This way of life has become for them the best and proper way of life through which they view themselves and others in the world. As a consequence they do not grasp the values of the others with whom they are interacting. Further, their own values are so overlearned that they lack self-awareness and are blind to the teachings of Scripture that might make them more effective in this situation of conflict.

Under these circumstances missionaries are unable to live pilgrim lifestyles. So constrained are they by their particular social game that they are capable of working out their faith only within a social environment that affirms them. Blind and bruised, they cannot even hear the question of our Lord Jesus Christ, "Why do you look at the speck of sawdust in your brother's eye and pay no attention to the plank in your own eye?"

In the context of cross-cultural ministry these words warn us to become aware of our interests and cultural bias. Our biases are those values, priorities, and understandings of nature and the world that grow out of self and social interests. We organize our social game to fulfill our interests through one of the five prototype games available to us. Self-awareness is possible only when we begin to understand the interests and bias through which we perceive the world and organize and evaluate our relationships with others. Only after we have achieved this self-awareness is it possible for us to obey Christ.

Interests lie at the root of cultural bias. The interests of westerners and Africans in UNION Ltd. led to their disagreements about exchange. The interests of the Asian villagers and George and Ellen set the scene for conflict and tension in relationship to material things. In spite of the high commitment of these men and women to their faith and to investing their lives for the kingdom of God, their interests intervene and their customary ways of satisfying those interests dominate their respective behaviors. They seem utterly incapable of following Paul's exhortation in Philippians 2:3–4: "Do nothing out of selfish ambition or vain conceit, but in humility consider others better than yourselves. Each of you should look not only to your own interests, but also to the interests of others."

As I have discussed these matters over several years with students in my classes, they inevitably cry out, "Why is it that we are so bound by our cultural bias? How can we get out of this prison of disobedience? We want to live pilgrim lifestyles; what is keeping us from it? Why is it that we cannot live out the commands that Christ has given us in the Scriptures?"

My response to this question is usually as follows. The very first and most important step is your daily communion with God, and the presentation of your bodies, your life, your culture, your values as a living sacrifice. Without daily communion and fellowship with God, freedom from the prison of disobedience is impossible. All of the cultural research and the application of the tools in this volume will not help. Knowledge does not empower people to action. It only makes them aware of the circumstances around them and the expectations that they have of themselves and that others have of them. The power to be different comes from the Spirit of God.

Usually this answer is not satisfactory. The students desire to have more practical guidelines, a specific set of how-to-do-it instructions.

Disciplines toward a Pilgrim Way of Life

While cultural bias and habits of life produce blindness in all believers, what Paul terms "walking in the flesh," the life of ministry cross-culturally exacerbates the consequences of our blindness as our habits of life create conflict with the habits of others. We may gain sight and insight, first by studying the habits and biases of the people to whom we are called to minister, and then by juxtaposing those habits against our own. Understanding is the first step in the removal of our blindness, addressing the plank in our eyes, before we begin to address the speck in our brother's eye.

Awareness is helpful, but wholly inadequate to bring about change in our habits of life. Habits are so powerful that they persist, almost unconsciously, in the way we approach and live out the routines of our daily existence. Spiritual disciplines are necessary to break the habits of life that hold us in their grip. Dallas Willard (1988, 68–71) writes, "A 'discipline' is an activity that enables us to accomplish what we cannot do by direct effort." The spiritual disciplines provide for serious Christians the how-to of a deeper walk with God and the steps for a life of pilgrimage, a following of the Master.

To achieve a pilgrim lifestyle we must commit ourselves to "having the mind of Christ," which results from a life of intimate and continuing communion with God. As Willard (1993, 50) notes, our communion with God "consists chiefly in a conversational relationship between God and the individual soul who is consistently and deeply engaged as his friend and co-laborer in the affairs of the Kingdom of the Heavens." It is only through this intimate fellowship and working partnership that we are able to "actively understand and cooperate with God's purposes" (Willard 1993, 51) and to identify ourselves with Jesus Christ, walking in his Spirit.

Once we are aware of habits and cultural bias and are willing to do his will, we may then engage in the spiritual disciplines—the plans and practice—through which we break free from our habits and embark on a life of pilgrimage as effective servants of Jesus Christ. The pilgrim lifestyle is characterized in 1 Peter by holiness (1:13); living as strangers in reverent fear (1:17); loving one another deeply (1:22); free of malice, deceit, envy (2:1); submitting to every authority instituted among men (2:13); bearing up under pain of unjust suffering (2:19); and living in harmony with one another (3:8).

Practicing these principles on a daily basis is beyond most dedicated Christian workers. All too frequently malice and envy creep into our relationships, undermining unity and cooperation, as Downes described for UNION Ltd. Love of Christian work so often supplants love of one another. Submitting to those in authority, or to our neighboring villagers when we believe them wrong, is impossible, and the way of suffering is always the choice of last resort. This is why the disciplines of the spiritual life are so essential to a pilgrim lifestyle. Without the planning and practice of spiritual disciplines, we live according to the habits and cultural biases learned in childhood and reinforced in the social games of our education and community life. We desire to live and walk in the Spirit, but all too often find ourselves mired in perpetual defeat, guilt, and despair.

Having, however, the will to follow Christ and an awareness of self-habits and the habits of others, we are able to embark on a plan and practice to break our habitual manner of life in specific acts and goals focused upon obedience to Christ. By forming new habits that are spiritually focused and centered upon investment in the kingdom of God, we enter into the way of pilgrimage modeled by our Lord Jesus Christ.

Removing the Plank

To remove the "exchange" plank from your eye you must ask, "What is the context of asking and giving in this culture and in the culture from which I come?" George and Ellen did not ask this question. Rather they assumed from their own individualist social game that the villagers were greedy, that they presumed the missionaries were rich, and that they could tap this ready source of funds to meet their personal interests. As a consequence George and Ellen became resentful, frustrated, and then emotionally and relationally detached from their neighbors. Out of fear, they rejected these villagers as people from "the spiritual darkness of paganism," while completely misunderstanding asking and giving in the local culture.

To attempt to rectify this, they finally gained courage to ask a neighbor, "How does one make friends in this community?" The neighbor explained, "If people come to my house I always give them coffee and something to eat. Then we sit down and talk together. I have been here for more than an hour and you have offered me nothing. This is not the way you make friends. You make friends by sharing what you have." Within a few moments he had provided a totally new framework within which George and Ellen might interpret the requests of their neighbors.

Why do neighbors ask? In George's and Ellen's situation asking was clearly a reflection of a sense of belonging within the community. To be asked was to be invited to be a member of the community. To respond by giving was to accept that membership and to engage in relationships with others. To refuse was to say that you did not want to belong and did not want to be friends. This kind of asking and receiving is quite different from what you may experience at Fifth and Broadway in Los Angeles. When a homeless man or woman comes up to you and asks for a quarter, he or she is not inviting you to become a member of the community, nor is he or she expecting to give you anything in return. Instead, people are negotiating to see if they can get something that will help them meet their daily substance needs. Their interaction with the stranger on the street is an isolated contact that will probably never happen again. Asking, for these homeless people, is negotiating to see what they can get for subsistence.

For the Christian worker it is essential to understand the social game of asking and giving. Without the knowledge of each social context it is impossible to interpret the situation and to act appropriately within it.

Out of Cultural Bias:
Disciplines for a Pilgrim Lifestyle

Once you can see the plank, the bigger question is how to escape from the prison of disobedience and live a pilgrim lifestyle. As followers of Christ you want to do more than act appropriately in a particular social game; you want to live as Spirit-filled believers, as servants, as ministers of the good news of the gospel to people who are searching. You must ask the bigger question, "How can I help people from any culture, who may lie, cheat, and steal from me, find the Lord Jesus Christ?" It will be difficult for you to determine which person knocking on your door may be seeking friendship or deceiving you. The Scriptures challenge you to give and to receive at risk for the sake of the gospel (Lingenfelter 1992, 105–6).

To embark on the life of pilgrimage you must release, one after another, the possessions, the relationships, the rules, and the values that hold you in their grip. The missionary couple, George and Ellen, were living in the grip of fear that their finances would not be adequate and that they would be used and abused by their neighbors. The westerners in UNION Ltd. lived in fear of being taken advantage of and being embarrassed by public agreements. The Africans in UNION Ltd. lived in the grip of fear that the UNION Ltd. team could lose power in their relationships to national pastors. All carried on their ministries in the grip of particular cultural biases and out of fears rooted in their faith upon the material resources they held. To become free from these biases and fears, these men and women must first clearly identify them and then begin the practice of surrendering them to the Lord Jesus Christ.

The disciplines of *abstinence* (solitude, fasting, frugality, sacrifice) and *engagement* (study, service, confession, submission [Willard 1988]) are useful to practice surrender on the small issues that bind you in reference to property and exchange. Your values about property and exchange are closely related to one another. The attachment that you have to property will determine the degree of freedom that you have to give or not to give it. To be free of your attachment to property you may prayerfully seek God's direction and take simple steps of surrender in reference to the amount, the way you give, and the things you wish to withhold.

To illustrate how the spiritual disciplines may be practiced, let's consider again the case of George and Ellen. Even after they became aware of the context of giving in their community, it was extremely difficult for them to change a style of life learned and practiced over thirty or forty years. George had a strong commitment to service, and Ellen a strong commitment to frugality, commitments that created an ever-present source of disagreement. How could they change years of living with these commitments to be more effective servants of the Master in this community?

For Ellen perhaps the spiritual disciplines most needed are those of sacrifice and service. Having already mastered the skill of frugality, she had developed this practice to the point where it possessed her. What she found most difficult to do was to sacrifice what she had struggled so hard to save. To overcome this Ellen and George may set aside a particular amount of money, dedicated to the Lord, to be used in service to their neighbors. They might redirect their tithe, which they had given to support some other Christian ministry. Perhaps they could go a step further and set aside a sacrifice greater than their tithe to be used specifically for their neighbors. By dedicating this money to God, they are prepared to give when their neighbors make requests. It is very important that when they give, they acknowledge to their neighbors that they are giving because God commanded them to do so and has provided the means.

George, in contrast, has already manifested a desire to serve, but in so doing he has not exercised the discipline of frugality in a way that would honor his wife. Further, in his prior exchanges with his neighbors he has loaned, rather than given in friendship, and never mentioned his debt to God for the funds. With regard to the discipline of frugality George should participate with his wife in setting apart funds to be used specifically for service. Particularly important is the discipline of confession, by which he may give credit to God rather than take credit to himself for his generosity.

The practical outworking of these disciplines for George and Ellen is to make every giving opportunity in the village a moment of sacrifice, confession, and service in the name of the Lord Jesus Christ. This is not nearly so difficult as it might seem at first glance. When people come to a house in a village they expect to sit down, to be served coffee, and to talk. To ask for money without engaging in appropriate social dialogue is offensive. George and Ellen have the opportunity to make their neighbors comfortable, to show that they are welcome, and to hear their request, humbly given, for assistance. Once the request for help has been given, George has the opportunity, and indeed the responsibility, to explain to these people how he and Ellen get their money. The fact that they have any money at all is due to the generosity of scores of Christians in the United States who desire that the people in this community hear the Good News. George needs to explain that all of this money was given first as a gift to God, and then dedicated to the service of sharing the love of Christ with these villagers. George also needs to confess that in the past he and his wife have tended to hold selfishly to the money that they had. But God had rebuked them for their selfishness and told them clearly that what he had given to them was to be used in service to the people of the village. Once this confession has been completed, George and Ellen are free to give, not loan, the money that they have set aside as a sacrifice for service to the people in their community.

The disciplines of frugality, sacrifice, confession, and service are particularly appropriate in helping one practice the surrender of property, money, and the values surrounding them which hold you in their grip. In practicing these disciplines you are engaging in a committed effort to "put off your old self . . . to be made new in the attitude of your minds; and to put on the new self, created to be like God in true righteousness and holiness" (Eph. 4:22–24). In so doing you begin the steps of living a pilgrim lifestyle, becoming free of the cultural biases that are a reflection of the social games by which others have nurtured you. You also will be empowered spiritually to become effective servants and ministers of the gospel.

What about Stewardship?

In the context of this discussion, many students and fieldworkers ask, "What about stewardship? Doesn't Jesus call us to be good stewards of our resources?" My question in return is to ask, "What did Jesus do? Did he engage in holding, protecting, and preserving property?" I find no evidence in the Scriptures that this is so. Further, what did Jesus model regarding stewardship? The evidence is that he had no house, no furniture, no regular source of income, and no material investments for his future. When you read the parables he told regarding stewardship, you see the good stewards investing and achieving double returns for their investment, but perhaps you have failed to see that their *investment was returned to the master for the purpose of advancing his kingdom*. Stewardship is not the holding, protection, and preservation of property or the investment of it for the profit and well-being of the investor. Stewardship is the utilization of the resources that God has given to us to advance his kingdom, which is spiritual. This understanding of stewardship has provided the guidelines and framework for the preceding discussion.

There is no evidence in the New Testament that money and property are to be protected and preserved for the well-being of the holder. In every case where money and property are mentioned, the lesson is that those who hold on to it lose it, and lose their spiritual lives as well, whereas those who give it freely in investment for the kingdom of God gain great rewards. The concept of stewardship then refers to investing for the kingdom of God, not protecting and preserving for your well-being in the present world.

Agents of Transformation?

How then can the missionary become an agent of transformation, rather than an agent of social cultural change? The answer to this question should now be rather obvious. If missionaries are committed to and sustain the values that arise out of the cultural biases of their home society and culture, they will certainly be agents of social cultural change in the communities in which they live. George and Ellen were modeling North American values of frugality, possession, and materialism. While living in a very simple house, they utilized gas for cooking, a solar panel for electric lighting, furnishings for their sleeping and eating comfort, and missionary aircraft for transportation in and out of the community. They obviously had money to purchase all of their food and clothing, with some to spare that could be loaned to people in the community. As such their way of life modeled to the local villagers a standard of living far above that possible for anyone else in the village. However, their lifestyle was not so different from that of more prosperous shopkeepers and employees of the government in the town nearby. A shopkeeper, in fact, was quite impressed with their solar electricity and planned to purchase the same for his own house. If this is all that they modeled to the members of the community, they were without doubt agents of socio-cultural change.

George and Ellen will be agents of transformation only when they effectively put into practice the spiritual disciplines and the pilgrim lifestyle already described. When people in the community begin to see them living in a way different from that of the shopkeepers and the employees of the government, it is possible that some will choose to follow them. This way of life is a life transformed by an intimate walk with God and by the practice of spiritual disciplines in daily life that confound the cultural biases and the values of the world.

This is illustrated graphically in the history of new converts in the Book of Acts. Acts 4:32–33 describes how these new believers did not squabble about their possessions, but "shared everything they had." Luke reports that "from time to time those who owned land or houses sold them, brought the money from the sales and put it at the apostles' feet, and it was distributed to anyone as he had need." Barnabas is then acknowledged as one of those who sold a field he owned and used the income to serve the needs of others.

Justo L. Gonzalez (1990, 83) discusses the character of Christian community developed in these texts in Acts. Focusing on the concept of *koinonia*, he argues that the English translations "fellowship" or "brotherhood" fall short of the fuller meaning of this concept. Luke used *koinonia* to describe Peter's relationship with James and John (business partners, Luke 5:10), and Paul used it in reference to suffering (*koinonia* of his sufferings, Phil. 3:10), to the blood and body of Christ (*koinonia* in the blood of Christ, 1 Cor. 10:16), and to the partnership in giving and receiving that he enjoyed with the believers at Philippi (Phil. 4:15). Gonzalez concludes that "*koinonia* is not simply a spiritual sharing. It is a total sharing that includes the material as well as the spiritual."

From these texts Gonzalez suggests "that Christian community was a partnership that included material as well as spiritual sharing, that this sharing was to be governed by the need of the less fortunate, and that, though voluntary, this sharing and the vision behind it challenged the traditional—particularly the Roman—understanding of private property" (84). He sees such communities occurring broadly in the Roman Empire; "what Luke was describing here was the understanding of Christian *koinonia* that had been at the very heart of Paul's ministry . . . and was still part of the self-understanding of the church—at least of the Pauline churches—everywhere" (86).

The motivation for church planting and Christian service ministries must be located firmly in *koinonia* community and kingdom values, as we see in these texts. If we plan and promote projects whose primary objective is better health, more material goods, and a higher standard of living, our message of mercy is no different from that of any other secular relief and development organization. Christian ministry should promote kingdom values for the transformation of human life.

A Pilgrim Lifestyle in Family and Community

Brethren, our system will not work without the Spirit of God, and I am glad it will not, for its stoppages and breakages call our attention to the fact of His absence.

Charles H. Spurgeon quoted in Willard (1993, 82)

When we lead in the style of the shepherd, our confidence is in one and only one thing: the word of the Great Shepherd coming through us or otherwise to his sheep. We know that they know his voice and will not follow another (John 10:1–14). We do not *want* them to follow another, even if *we* are that other. This supreme confidence, and this alone, frees us to be the ministers of Christ.

Dallas Willard (1993, 80)

Finally, all of you, live in harmony with one another; be sympathetic, love as brothers, be compassionate and humble. Do not repay evil with evil or insult with insult, but with blessing, because to this you were called so that you may inherit a blessing. . . .
> For the eyes of the Lord are on the righteous
> and his ears are attentive to their prayer,
> but the face of the Lord is against those who do evil.

(1 Pet. 3:8–9, 12)

Communities of the Flesh

In his exegesis of the concept of flesh in Paul's epistles Walt Russell (1993) suggests that Paul is referring literally to physical body and social community, that is, a community of the flesh. The Jews defined their community by marks in the flesh, including circumcision as the mark of male membership, observance of days, and rules and regulations having to do with every aspect of economic, social, and religious life. This Jewish community was clearly hierarchist in its orientation, but it certainly had its pockets of dissenters, such as the "sinners" who were tax collectors, prostitutes, and irreligious merchants. However, Paul does not limit his concept of the community of the flesh to Jews, but applies it to all people. "For God has bound all men over to disobedience so that he may have mercy on them all" (Rom. 11:32). Gentiles also belong to such communities, with their marks of membership, observance of days, rules and regulations.

Inasmuch then as believers continue to order their lives in accord with the same social frames employed in communities of the flesh to control and regulate the behavior of their fellow men, they remain prisoners of the flesh. We see this in the case of UNION Ltd. The African leader was frustrated and discouraged by the failure of his colleagues to meet his hierarchist game expectations. The westerners deemed him unspiritual because he did not and perhaps could not conform to their individualist game expectations, matters for which they were willing to fight. Westerners supported their position by citing the institutional culture of UNI-WORLD and their expectation that all members support the egalitarian team culture, not seeing that they failed to live to that model also. Communities of the flesh regulate individual behavior through one of the five social games that people play; and they pressure individuals to abide by their particular game's rules.

Both the African and western missionaries would probably protest my analysis, arguing that they are believers and living lives in accord with the Word of God. However, I rest my case on the qualities Paul cites as the marks of living in the community of the spirit. "But the fruit of the spirit is love, joy, peace, longsuffering, gentleness, goodness, faith, meekness, temperance: against such there is no law. And they that are Christ's have crucified the flesh with the affections and lusts. If we live in the Spirit, let us also walk in the Spirit" (Gal. 5:22–25 KJV). The evidence presented in the case suggests that African and westerner alike are concerned about issues of authority and power, and they are assertive regarding organizational structure that they believe protects their rights and power.

The sad and frustrating fact is that believers can no more escape grid and group than can unbelievers. Living in society is as immutable as living in our bodies; the only escape is to die. This is the first and most important fact for us to grasp. We cannot escape the biases of the five social games or ways of life; whichever one of these arrangements you find most appealing will inevitably "squeeze you into its mold." As you cannot abandon your body with its appetites and needs essential to survival, you cannot abandon the bodies of social life.

Tension in Family Relations

Why are UNION Ltd. missionary families so prone to misunderstanding and tension about differences in family authority structures? Are they different from missionaries in other organizations, or is their experience more common than we would like to acknowledge? What can mission leaders and pastors do to help their people address these misunderstandings and work toward unity in the Spirit?

The fact that all human beings seek to perpetuate their way of life first in the family unit is central to understanding the scope of this problem. Christians are no different in this regard, and perhaps are more preoccupied than non-Christians with this issue because they seek and find in Scripture instructions as to the importance of family for modeling Christian character and teaching children the way of righteousness.

What Christians fail to understand is how much their way of life in the family is shaped by their past experience and socialization into the community of the flesh. Further, they look for solutions to family problems in one of the five social games, rather than seeing all five as prisons of disobedience. Thus the younger African missionary sees the older family as too authoritarian, and the older family sees the younger as too permissive. The westerners see both African families as too directive and all point to the Scriptures to highlight the deficiencies of the others. They fail to see that the teaching of Scripture is not about family structure, but rather about being in the world, but not of It; living in any social environment, but not conformed to it. The challenge of Scripture is to "live by the Spirit" in each and every social environment, and to not be conformed to any.

A Biblical Model of Family?

Very frequently students and missionaries ask me which of these particular types of family is God's choice or a truly biblical model of family. The way they phrase the question demonstrates an inadequate understanding of our prisons of disobedience and the nature of biblical transformation. In this question, students most often focus on the issue of matrilineal family structure and question its validity on the basis of an obvious patriarchal bias in biblical texts. They point to Scriptures emphasizing the authority of the male in the church, and presume that in matrilineal societies it is the women who are in authority.

In fact, there are no known societies in which women exercise general communitywide authority. Male dominance, which is a sin problem in every society, is typical of matrilineal societies as well as patrilineal and bilateral societies. In matrilineal societies, it is a woman's maternal uncle or elder brother who exercises authority for the corporate and domestic group. Men hold positions of authority in the wider community and dominate public as well as domestic affairs. Matrilineality functions primarily in terms of inheritance of property and the organization of corporate groups. While the rule of relationship through women provides the principle of organization, the men in these societies apply those principles and hold authority and control over resources and people.

The question still remains, Can we conceptualize God as a maternal uncle? Only the Gospels of Matthew and John make frequent reference to God as father, and the context of these references may be served well by the caring, familial concept of father known in matrilineal societies. In the Hebrew Scriptures the analogies and metaphors used to describe God are complex and diverse, including several references to the maternal attributes of God—the eagle with her chicks (Deut. 32:11–12) or a mother with a suckling child (Isa. 49:15). The point is, the Scriptures are not limited by singular conceptions of God: the many analogies of language communicate effectively the person and character of God so that matrilineal societies do not suffer disadvantage. The concept of father may, in fact, be a very poor concept to an individual who has had a father abandon him or her in early childhood. Further, the role of father varies significantly in each of the five social games, so that each is both helpful and deficient when used to communicate the character of God. The Scriptures are not limited by our languages or social meanings, but rather through a rich diversity of analogies, metaphors, and parables communicate effectively in any social environment and into any language and culture.

It is my conclusion that the Scriptures are silent on the issue of the organizational structure of family. In no place do we find criticism or judgment of the polygamous families of Jacob and David. These men were chosen by God, and David was characterized as a man after God's heart. Their family structures were patrilineal and multigenerational in orientation, with corporate-focused residence and economic life. Such a family structure is alien to contemporary western Christians, and I expect few would embrace it as an ideal. There is little evidence in the New Testament that would allow us to assess the particular structure of Jewish or Greek families. In a passing reference in the Gospel of Mark (1:19–20) we find James and John leaving their father, Zebedee, in the boat with the hired men. This text suggests a patrilineal, multigenerational, corporate-focused domestic group. However, in the same Gospel (Mark 1:30) Peter's mother-in-law resides in "the house of Simon and Andrew," and in Luke 10, Jesus visits the house of Martha and her sister, Mary. Without external data, we can say little about the structure of family relations in either Jewish or Greek society at the time of Christ.

Out of Cultural Bias:
Freedom in Christian Family

What then can the missionaries in UNION Ltd. do to bridge their differences and misunderstandings and model in their team, and to national pastors and congregations, families that reflect a pilgrim way of life? The answer is not to be found in either the positional authoritarian or the personal egalitarian types of family structure. Nor is the answer found in bigenerational, husband/wife-focused families, or in the multigenerational parent-focused families. Rather, one must look to the Scriptures to find how each of these organizational frames is to be transformed by life in the Spirit.

The teachings of the New Testament with reference to the quality and character of family relationships are very clear: the Christian is called to domestic relationships that are qualitatively different from those evident in the world around them. The Greek practice of arranged marriages, which served to establish a family's public esteem and a man's personal prestige, often resulted in women married to men without their consent, men married to women they did not love, and children manipulated by their parents for perceived economic or social gain. Such behavior led to domestic relations of tension and conflict. In Ephesians 5–6 and in Colossians 3, Paul challenged Greek men, women, and children to be different, calling upon wives to submit to their husbands as the church submits to Christ, husbands to love their wives as Christ loved the church, and children to obey their parents in the Lord. The Bible teaches that the quality of relationships in a Christian family, regardless of its structure, are to be different from the relationships common in the world. It does not promote multigenerational or bigenerational, or positional authoritarian or personal egalitarian forms of family life, but rather commands Christians to esteem others better than themselves in their domestic life as well as in the life of the church and the larger society (Phil. 2:1–5).

This is not to say that family structures are all of equal value in terms of their structure and social arrangements. Emmanuel Todd argues fairly eloquently that particular types of family structure contribute to higher literacy rates and economic development. Todd (1987, 18–21) suggests that patrilineality produces family and social systems that exclude women, and in some cases become antifeminist, circumstances that he finds obstructive for economic development. Matrilineal systems exalt the kin of the wife and see the mother alone as responsible for the existence of her children, a circumstance that again is a disadvantage for development. The bilateral family system, however, gives equal value to the women in the transfer of inherited property and recognizes the contribution of the mother in the genetic and psychological makeup of the child. Todd argues that societies that give high status to women with strong parental authority have maximum potential for educational and economic development. Todd's argument is complex and rather peripheral to our purpose here. Yet, it is useful to note that the low esteem held for women in some cultures may in fact be a product of their domestic organization and ideology.

Todd's point is that some family types are better suited to the development of literacy and the development of the material life of their members and the larger society. However, these goals are not the objectives set forth by Christ for his church. Jesus said, "My kingdom is not of this world" (John 18:36). As much as we would like to promote literacy and the economic prosperity of the people with whom we work, this is a socioeconomic agenda that has little to do with the plan and command of Jesus to "make disciples of all nations" (Matt. 28:19).

Paul challenges Christians, "Don't let the world squeeze you into its mold" (Rom. 12:2 *Phillips*). To be transformed means that our family relations reflect his presence. To walk in the flesh is to defend and perpetuate one of the five social games; to walk in the Spirit is to lose our way of life for the sake of the gospel. Family structures are the human instruments of biological and social reproduction, perpetuating the way of life of its members.

"If anyone comes to me and does not hate his father and mother, his wife and children, his brothers and sisters—yes, even his own life—he cannot be my disciple. And anyone who does not carry his cross and follow me cannot be my disciple" (Luke 14:26–27). Jesus is not speaking here of hating the *persons* who are our father, mother, brother, sister, or child. This would be inconsistent with his command that we honor our father and mother. Rather he is addressing the obligations of family life that are embodied socially in the role expectations of father, mother, brother, sister, and child, that is, grid and group. When we vigorously defend our family game—our plan and practice of raising our children, our ideas of authority and discipline, and our practices of labor and money sharing—we are dismissing this very direct command of the Lord. This is precisely the error trapping members of UNION Ltd. and so many other dedicated believers in conflict. Whatever path we choose in organizing our family relations, only Christ can transform our relationships and empower us by his Spirit to join with him in the work of his kingdom. The outcome we desire can never come through our choice of structure, authority, and discipline; it is a work of God, accomplished by the power of his Spirit. *To place trust in our family game is idolatry.*

The disciplines of the Spirit may help us break the habits of life that hold us in their grip. Begin with the question, To what extent have we made our family way of life an idol and refused to surrender family issues to Christ and to the people we serve? Africans in UNION Ltd. demanded control of unruly western children. Westerners in UNION Ltd. deplored the excessive control and quenching of the spirits of docile African children. Both prefer their habits of life, and they have come to believe that their family game is God's way. Neither is able to rejoice in the differences of their fellow workers, since to do so questions their own strategies for raising children who are pleasing to parents, successful in life, and pleasing to God. If indeed the outcome is the work of God's Spirit, then Africans and westerners alike must hate the processes they have designed to produce good children, learn from one another about blind spots in their chosen family game, and work together to establish the "unity of the Spirit through the bond of peace." The first discipline needed to achieve this is that of study—learning from one another; the second is confession—acknowledging the judgmental attitude and criticism; the third is sacrifice—surrendering each of the fetishes we have established to insure the proper outcome for our children.

Tension in Community

Mission organizations have a culture, a social game, that more often than not becomes a prison for its members. The concerns and preoccupation of the flesh (human interests expressed through structured social relations) drive the daily lives of the mission and national church community. Leaders speak of those who do not follow or who act to undermine their leadership; team members find fault with one another and with the mission and its leadership. All can cite Scripture to justify their point of view, but only a few find a way to work in peace with whomever the Lord provides as leader and team member.

This becomes especially critical in an understanding of community authority and leadership. In the case of UNION Ltd. we see substantive disagreements about the way authority should be structured and the way leaders should lead. The issues that divided focused upon financial support, obligations of reciprocity, institutional culture, and individual freedom and conformity. Willard (1993, 79–80) suggests that Christian leaders are trained to be sheep dogs rather than shepherds. "The sheep dog nips and harasses the sheep, while the shepherd simply calls as he calmly walks ahead of the sheep." Too often the goal of leaders is to exercise the power given to them in Scripture, and by the organizational structure of their team or congregation to achieve conformity in the sheep. Leadership becomes manipulation, management, and, when necessary, powering the outcome desired by using the Scriptures as a scourge on the sheep.

What then is the answer to our dilemma? The solution comes in our intimate, personal walk with God, surrendering our physical and social appetites and needs to the Lord Jesus Christ. Paul writes, "There is therefore now no condemnation to them which are in Christ Jesus, who walk not after the flesh, but after the Spirit. For the law of the Spirit of life in

Christ Jesus hath made me free from the law of sin and death. For what the law [grid and group] could not do, in that it was weak through the flesh [body], God sending his own Son in the likeness of sinful flesh, and for sin, condemned sin in the flesh: That the righteousness of the law might be fulfilled in us, who walk not after the flesh, but after the Spirit" (Rom. 8:1–4 KJV). The function or purpose of society is to regulate the behavior of individuals and groups so that people may live, reproduce, and work together toward a sense of common or public good. The options of grid and group define the total range of choices open to human beings to achieve public good or righteousness in the flesh. The cultural history of human experience confirms the words of Scripture; there is no law that achieves righteousness, but only law that condemns the members and the society that has framed it.

Disciplines for Communities of the Spirit

The *ideas* of the Scripture and the disciplines of the Spirit lead us in the way to "walk in the Spirit" and be transformed in our *interest* relationships. We must begin by asking God to show us those areas of our lives where we are in bondage to the flesh. Through the study of Scripture, the prayerful examination of our own lives and interests, or the loving counsel of a friend, God will reveal to us the areas we have failed to surrender to him. Perhaps we are unable to give up a plan or course of action that we have chosen. Or perhaps we see no value in the perspective held by a dissenting brother or sister in the Lord. Or perhaps we are pained by our fellow team members who seem incapable of flexibility and unable to adapt to new circumstances.

Whatever the bondage, the act of spiritual discipline is to plan and practice, through the power and direction of the Word of God, releasing that habitual behavior to Christ and allowing him to lead us in his way. For example, if the bondage is a plan of action we have chosen, the disciplines of submission (Eph. 5:21) to the plans of others and service (Gal. 5:13) in support of their plans may be the only way to gain spiritual freedom. Or, if we see no value in the perspective of a brother, the discipline of confession of our arrogance, and watching (Isa. 26:8) for the ways in which God brings forth fruit in that brother's life, will bring us around to Christ's perspective on that person. If we have put too much confidence in the structures of our organization and the power that accrues to leadership, the disciplines of solitude and silence may be necessary to break our preoccupation with this way of life, and the disciplines of study and worship may help us refocus upon following the Great Shepherd.

One thing is certain. We cannot transform others or their culture. But we can be transformed by having the mind of Christ and by being continually renewed in our intimacy and fellowship with God and with his church. As believers we also have the privilege of participating in *koinonia,* the fellowship of believers characterized by submission to one another in Christ. In that fellowship marks of membership, celebration of days, and roles and rules of practice have no central place. We live as aliens and strangers—our finances, social status, family security, place of ministry, culture of organization, and power of leadership are peripheral to following Christ.

The more we are able to live in intimate and personal relationship with God, and imitate Christ in our life and ministry, the more frequently God will employ us as his co-workers, agents of transformation in a fallen world. Our battle is a spiritual one, and our objective is to invest our lives and resources as servants in the kingdom of God.

Disputes in Communities of the Flesh

I am reluctant to discuss these issues one more time in print, since I have addressed this subject in both *Ministering Cross-Culturally* (1986) and *Transforming Culture* (1992). Yet the issues are so volatile and pervasive in Christian ministries that perhaps something more can and should be said. When two fellow workers for the kingdom of God are incapable of being reconciled with one another, and when their communication consistently breaks down into a shouting match, something is deeply wrong. If it happened only in the one case cited by Downes, then perhaps we could explain it on the basis of two unfortunate brothers in circumstances similar to those of Paul and Barnabas, who had best go separate ways. However, that scene can be replicated everywhere in the world that westerners come into contact with high group social environments. My wife and I have observed veteran missionaries and national pastors in our graduate classes on missions engaged in the same heated debate, and at times they lapse into shouting at one another.

I return to the theme of prisons of disobedience and plead with my western and nonwestern colleagues to comprehend your prisons! As long as we insist that our way of handling conflict is biblically sanctioned, we are doomed to remain in the prison of disobedience and to continue to strangle our ministries with unresolved conflicts leading to personal bitterness and rejection of one another.

The westerner who embraces individualism and open confrontation is blind and callous to the techniques for communication required in high group contexts to demonstrate sensitivity and caring. Not only are we blind, but also we are arrogant and judgmental; to quote Jonathan, these techniques "waste time and beat around the bush." I recall my own experience of trying to confront with love and care on Yap, and failing utterly, in spite of my very best attempts, because I did not understand the how of high group communication and confrontation. I was just as quick to judge as Jonathan, and I dismissed my Yapese colleague as unfit for the work I was there to do. My co-workers were bruised and battered from my disagreements with them. The result of this is confirmation to the Yapese (or African, or Asian) that his western colleague is carnal and unworthy of participation in the ministry.

The African or Asian who comes from a strong group context is also inept at individualistic techniques of open confrontation. When he senses that the confrontational mode of his western colleagues is the only means available to him, he leaps into the fray without the childhood experience westerners have that taught them how to confront, when to raise the voice, when to back down, when to press the point, and when they have gone too far. Lacking these skills, the African or Asian sees the combat as one of open, unrestrained attacks upon one another, and proceeds on this course with often brutal outcomes. The result of this is confirmation to the westerner that his national colleague is carnal and unworthy of participation in the ministry.

Conflict situations challenge our security and comfort with reference to relationships and procedures. As the situation increases in intensity, we tend to rely upon those personal and social strategies that we know best, and respond with either aggression or defensiveness to those challenging us. It is in precisely such situations that we need a deep and intimate walk with God, so that we are able to surrender our fears and anxiety to him and to respond as Jesus did when he was attacked by the religious leaders and ultimately delivered to be crucified. Yet, more often than not we turn to a social formula that we have devised in accord with our cultural biases and rely upon our own strength to finesse or power the outcome.

"Kingdom" Communication

Willard (1993, 127) notes that "some of our greatest problems in understanding and entering into life in the Kingdom of God come from inadequate appreciation of how that Kingdom, like *all* kingdoms, works by communication: by the speaking of words or the use of words for the expression of minds." When the believer is engaged in intimate communication with God, then he or she is able to discern which of his or her motivations come from issues of personal security and cultural bias, and which are responses to the leading of the Spirit and the mind of Christ. We are always able to know from the fruit of our actions whether they were led of the Spirit; as Spurgeon said, when things break down, we know that the Spirit is absent, and we need to address the matter at once. However, most Christian leaders profess a desire to be led by the Spirit and to serve the purposes of the kingdom of God. To accomplish this it is essential that we have vital, effective, and intimate communication with the Father, and that we study to communicate in the same manner within the diverse fellowship of the church of Jesus Christ.

So much disagreement focuses upon the question of what is correct biblical procedure, rather than upon the question of what is Spirit-directed biblical communication. Matthew 18:15–17 is always cited as the clear biblical injunction for open confrontation as the God-given procedure for settling disputes. I will not repeat what I have written on this in other contexts (Lingenfelter and Mayers 1986; Lingenfelter 1992), but rather focus here on the issue of kingdom communication. If we understand this passage as part of the whole of Jesus's teaching about the kingdom of God, we gain some additional insight.

The eighteenth chapter of Matthew opens with a discussion of "who is greatest in the kingdom of heaven" (18:1). Jesus states unequivocally, "Unless you change and become like little children, you will never enter the kingdom of heaven." Jesus then warns his disciples of the dire consequences of causing "one of these little ones who believe in me to sin," and of "woe to the world because of such things that cause people to sin." The application of this text to our discussion is as follows: when you use a procedure to settle disputes and communicate in such a way that causes you and your brother to sin, this cannot possibly be God's intent and purpose. Jesus makes it very clear that we should rid ourselves of anything that causes us to sin (vv. 8–9).

Secondly, Jesus reminds his disciples and us that the Father in heaven is deeply concerned about the least significant person in the kingdom, using the parable of the lost sheep to show how the Great Shepherd seeks the one among the hundred who has wandered away and is lost. The purpose of the text on the brother who sins against you must be understood in the context of the parable of the lost sheep. The Great Shepherd is concerned for the lost, and the restoration of the lost to the sheepfold. Further, Jesus assures his disciples that when they come together in his name to accomplish the purposes of the kingdom "it will be done for you by my Father in heaven" (v. 19). The point here is that the Father does the work. It is not your procedures, your strategies, or your effectiveness in communication that accomplished the deed.

Peter then asks the question that you and many others have asked, "Lord, how many times shall I forgive my brother when he sins against me? Up to seven times?" (v. 21). Jesus answers first with a direct statement, "I tell you, not seven times, but seventy times" (v. 22); and then he tells the parable of the unmerciful servant who is forgiven his debt by his Master, but then goes out and casts a man indebted to him into prison. In the conclusion of the parable, the unmerciful servant is cast into prison, and Jesus applies the story to us: "This is how my heavenly Father will treat each of you unless you forgive your brother from your heart."

In brief, confrontation, whether done directly as in weak group social environments, or indirectly, as is done in strong group social environments, should have as its expressed purpose and outcome 1) avoidance of sin on our part, 2) restoration of a brother, 3) prayerful dependence with two or three others upon the Father to accomplish the work of reconciliation, and 4) willingness to keep on forgiving and working toward reconciliation until it happens. Resignation from the team, voting one out of leadership, shouting matches with one another, and finessing or powering the outcomes are not the "work of the Father." Until we can understand this and begin to build the skills of kingdom communication, we shall continue to employ systems that break down because the Spirit of God is not in them.

Out of Bias: Disciplines for Kingdom Communication

The first discipline needed is that of study with the purpose of comprehending your prisons and discerning the mind of Christ. Applying the criteria presented in this chapter to self and to others is a useful way to begin. Because you are likely to be biased in your self-analysis, it is even better to have a brother who does not share your views examine your values and biases in relation to leadership and conflict resolution. You can provide the same perspective for your colleagues. Careful study of Scripture on these matters is also essential. One must pay particular attention to the total context in which matters of leadership and conflict are addressed, as I have done (with the help of some fine students) in reference to Matthew 18.

While you are researching to gain a thorough understanding of the plank in your own eye and the speck in your brother's eye, and you together are examining the Scriptures to discern the mind of Christ on the subject, practice the discipline of conversational prayer. Prayer with the Father will bring you and your colleagues into a relationship of fellowship and listening for the Master's guidance. Jesus assures you that when two or three gather in his name to implore of the Father on behalf of his kingdom, it shall be done! His directions are for two or three to pray in this manner (Matt. 18:19–20).

The third essential discipline in kingdom communication is submission. Peter, who questioned Jesus as to just how far one should go in the matter of forgiveness, writes:

> But if you suffer for doing good and you endure it, this is commendable before God. To this you were called, because Christ suffered for you, leaving you an example that you should follow in his steps.
>
> > "He committed no sin,
> > and no deceit was found in his mouth."
>
> When they hurled their insults at him, he did not retaliate; when he suffered, he made no threats. Instead, he entrusted himself to him who judges justly (1 Pet. 2:20–23).

We know that submission is taught in Scripture, but we find it so difficult to practice in our daily lives. It is therefore helpful for you to identify specific aspects of the conflict relationship in which you feel frustrated and have become resentful, and practice submission. Submit first to the Lord, and then to the person(s) with whom you are in conflict. If you submit this to the Lord, but not to the person with whom you have the disagreement, the process of kingdom communication is incomplete.

Finally, we must practice the discipline of forgiveness! And practice it without limitation (Matt. 18:22). Team ministry, of the kind sought by UNIWORLD and by Christ for his church, is not possible unless believers, who are committed to his kingdom, practice forgiveness. In the course of our daily activities in any ministry context, different people with different gifts and perspectives will inevitably disagree about how to accomplish the mission, how to complete a task, and even about how to communicate with one another. Forgiveness is not something that you do only when you feel moved; forgiveness must become part of your disciplined spiritual life.

A year or so ago one of my colleagues at Biola and I were discussing plans for one of the schools in the university. As we talked the matter of trust between us became the focus of our conversation. In the course of the conversation, I related to this man an experience of hurt in my life that had, in my perspective, been inflicted by his predecessor. As we talked, I became acutely aware that this hurt was one that I had never forgiven, and it remained a canker in my heart that spilled over into my present relationships. I learned from that experience that unless hurts are forgiven, they remain with us and keep us from being effective leaders and communicators for his kingdom.

How many times shall you forgive your brother? Unless you make forgiveness a daily practice in your life, beginning with the small offenses, and then extending this work of grace to include the vilest ones, you may not, indeed cannot, enter fully into service for the kingdom of God. Jesus said we are to forgive so frequently that we cannot keep count, for such is the love of the Father toward us.

> He himself bore our sins in his own body on the tree, so that we might die to sins and live to righteousness; by his wounds you have been healed. For you were like sheep going astray, but now you have returned to the Shepherd and Overseer of your souls. (1 Pet. 2:24–25)

"Not by might, nor by power, but by my Spirit," says the LORD Almighty. (Zech. 4:6b)

Agents of Transformation

> "Therefore I tell you, do not worry about your life, what you will eat or drink; or about your body, what you will wear. Is not life more important than food, and the body more important than clothes?" (Matt. 6:25)

In chapter 1 we explored how the market, government, mosque, and church were significant external forces for change among people. These changes are characteristic of forces at work around the world. We return now to the subject of change and the role of Christian workers in that process. What does the Bible have to say about Christians as agents of change? What are the biblical counters to our cultural and material agendas? There are many relevant passages, but perhaps the most provocative is Matthew 6:25–34. The text begins by questioning the priority of material life. Jesus then points to the birds that do not plant or harvest, and the lilies that do not labor or spin, arguing that the heavenly Father knows of our needs and will provide. This text should not be interpreted as instruction to live a life free of labor and material investment. To the contrary, many of Jesus' other teachings command that we be committed and faithful laborers. The text addresses human priorities. Jesus is challenging the primacy of the economic agenda. This becomes clear in verse 32, "For the pagans run after all these things, and your heavenly Father knows that you need them."

The priority of wealth in the lives of people has always dominated cultural life. One of the major theoretical paradigms of anthropology is the materialist, best known in the works of Leslie White, Marvin Harris, Eric Wolf (1984), and Richard Adams (1988). Each of these scholars interprets cultural life primarily in terms of economic agendas. Each argues that human behavior is fundamentally material, and that culture, values, and religious beliefs may be reduced to their material foundations.

Much of secular development work by people in the market or bureaucracy is based upon these materialist assumptions; many believe that the solution to basic human misery is material. If we can improve a community's crop production, get more money into the hands of the poor, educate people to follow better health and economic practices, then we have led them to a superior life.

Jesus draws a different conclusion: "But seek first his kingdom and his righteousness, and all these things will be given to you as well" (v. 33). This text challenges the very assumptions of community development, wealth, and health projects. A wealth and health project is described as the agenda of pagans, but is not to be the agenda for Christians. Christians are not to focus attention on property, wealth, or fear for our health and well-being, but rather on the kingdom of God, fearing the One who can kill the soul.

Conflicting Development Paradigms: Toward a Biblical Alternative

The key agendas of the market and the bureaucracy over the last half of this century have been to educate for technological and economic development, to improve public health, and to enable the accumulation of material wealth. Toward that end government officials and private entrepreneurs have also defined social agendas, particularly empowerment to help people to move from situations of passive acquiescence (fatalism), lacking community integration, to corporate integration (hierarchialism) where they can speak for themselves. The goal has been to equip people to be able to articulate their own interests and to have skills, resources, and social power to accomplish what they desire.

In the rare instances when such programs have succeeded, developers have enabled the target population to change their social environment to a new form of corporate integration. Often the task is to help people who are in an authoritarian, fatalistic social environment move into one of the other three alternatives. Sheldon Annis (1987) argues that Protestantism has provided an avenue for Guatemalan Indians to move from the constraining fatalistic world view of traditional Guatemalan society to an individualist, capitalist-oriented economic development. He makes a convincing argument in his book that Protestantism provides the ideology needed to release people from the constraints of their community to take this step of individualism toward economic development. Some take jobs, some begin businesses, some work as farmers and sell their products in the town, but whatever the way, they become independent, individualist entrepreneurs.

According to the economic and communal paradigms of intercultural community work, the desired outcome is to change the social and economic environments of a community into something that more closely resembles the material and social structure of communities in industrialized nations. We help people to change from where they are into a social and economic community with access to more wealth and power. There is nothing inherently wrong with this objective, but it is important to understand the process and outcomes.

What then is the alternative? Matthew 25 provides an interesting paradigm for the church and Christian workers through three distinctive but related parables. The first, the parable of the ten virgins, describes ten girls waiting for the bridegroom to come to call them to the wedding feast. Five have prepared for the wait, having extra oil for their lamps, while five are caught without enough. The five without oil are excluded from the feast; those who were watching and prepared for the coming of the bridegroom were received with joy. Keeping in focus that Jesus is teaching about the kingdom of God, his followers are told to always watch for his coming. Watching means to burn the midnight oil in preparation for that coming, and to work in the interim with that event in focus.

The second parable is that of the talents. In this story the master goes away, leaving three of his servants with five, two, and one talents of silver respectively. This money is their responsibility and opportunity. Two of the servants use the opportunity to double their financial holdings, which they present to the master upon his return. The third servant, acting out of fear, hides the money, earning no gain but returning what he had received. The lesson of this parable is that we are to work as faithful stewards of the resources and opportunities given to us, investing to advance the kingdom. We are to use what he has given us to produce more for his good and for his glory. Productive servants will be given even greater responsibility and reward.

The third parable is that of the sheep and the goats. At the final judgment in the kingdom of heaven, the Lord separates those who claim to follow him. The sheep are those who have served the poor, naked, imprisoned, and hungry; they are recognized and given entrance to the kingdom of God. The goats are those who have turned away the poor, naked, hungry, and imprisoned; they are denied entrance to the kingdom and are cast into outer darkness. The key lesson of this parable is that the servant in the kingdom of God must care for those who are poor and oppressed. Their final rewards are given not on the basis of their preparedness, or on the basis of their good stewardship, but rather upon their compassion and care for those who are in need.

This trilogy of parables sets forth the Lord's teaching on service in his kingdom. All of our work should be done within the framework of our expectation and preparedness for his coming again. We are responsible to work as his stewards, using our resources to produce material results that honor the Lord and his work, investing to advance the kingdom. The resources and rewards that we accumulate from good stewardship, however, are to be used to serve the oppressed in his name.

There is no better paradigm for cross-cultural ministry than that given to us by our Lord. These parables are part of His final instructions before he went to the cross. In them, he provides for us the basic framework from which to consider and do our work.

To follow this paradigm, we are called by Scripture to a social life of pilgrimage. The most powerful life example of the religious pilgrim is Jesus. As the incarnate Son of God, Jesus came into the world, yet he was not of the world; he lived the life of a pilgrim. He had no property, no job, no regular place to sleep. As the master teacher, he traveled from place to place, teaching, healing, and engaging in critical dialogue with members of the society. Like a hermit he lived apart from society, but unlike the hermit He continued to interact with society in a unique and special way.

Jesus recognized that his disciples could not live the autonomous, pilgrim lifestyle that he had modeled. Peter had a wife and family, as did others of the 120 who followed him after his resurrection. But he prayed for them, "not that you take them out of the world but that you protect them from the evil one. . . . As you sent me into the world, I have sent them into the world. For them I sanctify myself, that they too may be truly sanctified" (John 17:15, 18–19).

The five social games and the cultural ideologies by which we rationalize our values and interests constitute the world. The challenge for believers is to deny ourselves, take up our cross, and follow him. While the withdrawal and disengagement of a hermit may have its time and place, believers are called to active service. We may and indeed should engage in each of the five social games, but remain detached in our commitments to the social world. In effect we are called to a life of Christ-centered autonomy, regardless of the game(s) being played around us.

This challenge applies first to those called as servants of the gospel, and then to the community of new believers. Development for wealth, health, and power will not furnish significant gain to any community or society. People may have a slightly longer life, and perhaps more things while they live, but development will, in the final sense, make absolutely no difference. The people will certainly die, and after that face the judgment spoken of in Revelation 20.

What will make a difference is our commitment to Jesus and to his kingdom—watching for his coming, working as his stewards, and serving those who are harassed and helpless with the resources that he gives. In the program of the kingdom of God we promote development to serve as opposed to development to have.

Case Study: Binukid Faith Demonstration Farm

In a workshop (1991) with a mission organization in the Philippines, a pastor from the Binukid churches in Mindanao presented a paper on community development among the Binukid people. He asked: Why do community development projects fail?

Reviewing three different development projects among the Binukid people, he concluded that all failed because of organizational problems arising from the rejection of local leaders in favor of external, hierarchically oriented leaders. In one case a young man who had relevant skills was given authority over the project. In another case a patron who had funds used those funds to enlist workers, and in the third case the government bureaucracy supplied the leaders for the project. This pastor argued that bypassing indigenous leaders in favor of bureaucrats led to their failure.

This pastor also cited three other obstacles to the success of those development projects. First, the new agricultural technology for rice production was something that the people didn't understand. In each case the participants had no prior experience with or knowledge of the complex technology required for the project. Ultimately, they either tired of trying it or they gave up because they didn't understand it and decided it was not helpful.

The second obstacle was the "values" program associated with each project. In each case project leaders promoted values that implied changing the structure of the community, at a minimum elevating the role of women, or, in some cases, giving women authority that they did not ordinarily have. The enthusiastic participation of some women served to intimidate the male participants and the projects died.

The third significant problem arose from the traditional belief system focusing upon the fear of spirits. Among the Binukid, people believe that an incredibly good crop will be the last a person is allowed to harvest. The spirits of the rice crop offer a good harvest to those who are soon to die. As a consequence of this belief, people who have a great crop often refuse to harvest it, preferring to let it rot in the fields rather than let the spirits take their lives. Obviously, this traditional belief undermines community development projects whose goal is a superior harvest of rice.

Seeking to learn from the experience of others who had failed and to articulate a distinctively Christian approach to community development, the pastor related how he and other pastors had determined to establish a "faith demonstration farm." They began by building their project around local leadership, drawing upon their support and expertise. They understood at the outset the fears—the spiritual issues that were a crucial part of the life and work of these people—and they developed a plan to address them. Finally they determined that people don't learn by lectures; they learn by seeing, experiencing, and doing. Thus they designed a model project that would help these people learn new technology and supporting beliefs and values.

Crucial to their plan was their emphasis on faith demonstration in relationship to the farm. They began by praying that God would provide a piece of land appropriate for the development of this farm. After they had trusted the Lord through prayer, the Spirit moved among the people. A member of the congregation gave a piece of land, and others volunteered to work. These Christians agreed to do everything in a Christian, rather than a traditional, way. To empower them for this task, the pastors preached from biblical texts proclaiming that God has conquered the spirits, that in Christ one need not fear the spirits, and that the traditional taboos surrounding planting are void.

In confidence of God's power, they deliberately violated all of the traditional taboos when they began the farm. They did not seek omens as to the proper time to plant. They omitted the traditional ceremonies associated with rice planting, substituting instead a gospel message at the opening ceremony. Pastoral leaders offered a special prayer of dedication that God would bless the project. They also supported the workers at each of the phases marked by traditional ritual; they prayed at the seed sowing, at the weed pulling, and at every key event required for care of the crop. In direct violation of one spirit taboo they further celebrated with cookies and fruit, and at every turn proclaimed a public, visible difference between the Christian project farm and the traditional farm.

As part of their demonstration the pastors also systematically explained to the local populace what was happening. They informed people about new technical information and invited them to watch what was done. With the explanations about fertilizers and agronomy techniques, they also told the story of the gospel of Jesus Christ. The pastor said, "We want to plant seed on the farm and we want to plant seed in people's hearts." In their Bible teaching they emphasized that God is creator and that he provides for people to meet their needs. They taught the parable of the sower and dealt with the issue of sowing and reaping. Emphasizing that God wants us to reap spiritually and materially, they taught the people to wait upon the Lord's provision and blessing.

As one might guess, conflict ensued when they started this farm. Some people were very upset that they did not follow the traditional way. Some of the elders sat down with them and declared, "This farm is going to fail. The rice will not grow because you haven't divined the right time to plant. You haven't sought the omen. You've neglected the proper planting ceremonies." One of the workers subsequently developed a very serious skin rash that wouldn't go away. Seeing this as a sign of spiritual opposition, they prayed for him, quoting proverbs, "The truth will stand forever, the lies will be exposed." As they prayed for the afflicted worker he recovered from his skin rash, but it was a long conflict and a crucial one. At every phase of the development of the farm, people angrily denounced the workers; they criticized, and declared that spirits would wreck their work and attack the workers with illness.

The pastor concluded his report by saying that the farm was doing wonderfully. With the prospect of a tremendous crop, the believers were rejoicing in the blessing of the Lord for their work and in the spiritual victories that he had given over spiritual opposition. They looked forward with great anticipation to the harvest and a celebration of thanksgiving to the Lord.

Analysis

The case study illustrates much of what we have discussed in this and previous chapters. Applying the model of cultural bias, we find the development agenda of the national government and supporting organizations coming from a hierarchist world view. The target community is fatalistic, viewing their lives as dominated by the spirit world and by authoritarian outsiders who set their own agendas and control both the resources and the process. When people from these different social environments and world views attempt to achieve development, their conflicting interests and values have resulted in recurrent failure. When material prosperity is the goal, those who have easiest access to resources exploit them for their private interests.

The Philippine pastor did not have a sophisticated knowledge of grid and group, but he and his fellow workers brought to this project the deep conviction that the power of the gospel could bring about significant change in the community. They began by challenging the fatalism of the traditional world view by preaching the gospel. They also focused on commitment to Christ, calling people to a higher power and agenda for their lives.

The faith demonstration farm had a threefold spiritual agenda. The leaders wanted to demonstrate the power of the Word of God to free people from spiritual oppression, knowing their fears of a good harvest and of dying. They also shared with them both the knowledge of the new technology and the knowledge of the Word of God. Finally, the harvest was for ministry to all the people of the community.

This farm illustrates clearly the difference between the three prior projects—centered on wealth, health, and power—and a project based upon watching for Christ's coming, working for his kingdom, and serving his people. Each of the spiritual objectives—freedom from spiritual oppression, empowering knowledge, and service to others—are essential to Christian intercultural community work. The transformation of the community grew out of its commitment to Christ and to serving one another as fellow workers for the gospel.

In brief, the agenda that the Lord gives us is workable. It is powerful, and through his agenda believers can become instruments of transformation for the church and their communities. Thousands of pastors, teachers, and intercultural workers seek to advance community development projects around the world; in fact most of them will fail. The

Lord's development project is one that will not fail, because in his program, he is building his church.

Agents of Transformation

These Binukid pastors have intuitively understood what it means to become significant agents of transformation in their culture. They examined the leadership and works of others who had attempted to bring about change in their community. Although some of these changed goals were good, they observed quite correctly that the change agents failed to understand community leadership, held critical ideas that became obstacles to the program, and set objectives that, while worthy, did not significantly address the social and spiritual needs of the community. They decided to frame their own efforts in terms of the gospel rather than in terms of the objectives of community development and change. Their solution was an interesting mix of biblically based challenge to accepted ideas and interests and contextualization of their project through complementary social and spiritual relations.

Successful cultural transformation involves challenge of accepted ideas. The gospel is first and foremost a new set of ideas: ideas about God, ideas about man, ideas about salvation, and ideas about priorities and relationships. These Binukid pastors understood that the ideas of the gospel contradict the ideas of the traditional Binukid world. They founded their faith demonstration farm on the premise that they must challenge accepted ideas through the proclamation of the gospel and its theological and practical implications for Binukid life and farming.

The Binukid were motivated and constrained by their ideas about the spirit world, ideas about relationships between men and women, and ideas about leadership. The earlier community development projects structured power relationships in ways that violated their ideas, focusing power on one or two outsiders and ignoring relationships between leaders and followers. These projects also proposed values that contradicted their standards regarding relationships with women. The people in power disdained their ideas about the spirit world and agricultural production. As long as outsiders paid them to participate, the money sustained their interest. But as soon as the funding expired, or the work exceeded local commitments, their interest faded and they dropped the project. No significant change in either ideas or interests occurred as a result of these projects.

270

The Christian pastors set their faith demonstration farm on a biblical foundation, beginning with new ideas. They first challenged many of the traditional ideas about the proper way to plant rice. Then they broke every one of the taboos governing rice planting, in effect undermining old power-causal relationships. When people came and criticized them, they said, "We're standing on the Word of God, we're following God's way, and we are not afraid of the spirits." They used Christian ideas to challenge traditional ideas.

The second key challenge posed by Binukid pastors was to the accepted interests and causal relationships in traditional Binukid society. They understood that Binukid people not only believed in spirits but also saw themselves in significant causal relationships to the spirit world. Their rituals and other activities were their responsible attempts at coping with these causal relationships. Their personal interests were shaped by what they deemed to be the consequences of violating these traditional expectations. These Christian leaders openly challenged the power of the spirits and the power of the social guardians of ritual and tradition in Binukid society. In addition, the pastors engaged believers in the local church to provide support necessary to implement these ideas. Believers gathered; they sang hymns; they prayed; they sought the power of God to do battle with the spirits, praying especially for the man who was afflicted with the skin disease. They employed spiritual power and social power to effect this project successfully. By violating the taboos and substituting Christian practice in their place, they challenged the social structure of traditional farming and spirit-world relationships.

These challenges, however, were offered within the framework of complementary social and spiritual relations. The pastors contextualized their challenge into the traditional Binukid farming cycle. Instead of divining the proper day and seeking the proper omen for planting, they prayed, asking the Lord to guide them as to the time to plant. When the cycle called for offerings to the spirits of the rice fields, the pastors provided offerings to the God who created the rice fields, the spirits, and the people who farm it. They substituted Christian activity for each phase of the traditional ritual process, leading believers in biblically based public events. They organized their activities in the context of traditional, social, and spiritual expectations of the Binukid community. Each of their Christian challenges came at a complementary and significant moment in the cycle of Binukid farming life. They did not utterly reject the old way; rather, they developed corresponding Christian perspectives to address the same issues. At the same time they contradicted the pervasive ideas about the spirit world, and they engaged in a power struggle with the shaman and others who supported tradition and sought to verify its truth in opposition to these Christians.

The power of these pastors as agents of transformation came primarily through their openness to dialogue with the local elders and people in reference to the contradictions and conflicts that people were experiencing because of the faith demonstration farm. When the elders came to declare the absolute certainty of the failure of this project because they had violated taboos, the pastors sat and listened to them and then talked with the elders about their traditional beliefs and the teaching of the Word of God. They discussed the contradictions between the teaching of Scripture and the teaching of their ancestors. They admitted the conflicts between the old world view and the gospel. They discussed the power of God in opposition to that of the spirits and invited these people to receive the freedom that comes in Christ from the power and fear of the spirit world.

Finally, the Christian leaders of this farm attempted to manifest kingdom goals and values in their teaching, actions, and relationships. Rather than seeking wealth for themselves, they emphasized working for the Lord in service to others. These Christians launched the project by giving their resources and ended by giving the produce of their labor. The emphasis of the project was not personal or collective gain, but rather submission to the will of God and service in his name.

These Binukid pastors and leaders demonstrated remarkable insight when they determined that the objective of their faith demonstration farm was primarily for the development of stronger believers, and secondarily for a bumper crop of rice. The goal of these pastors was to disciple farmers, believers in their own congregation, through biblically grounded farming, and to use the farm to share the gospel with the community. Further, they determined that the sharing of the harvest should be motivated by biblical service, rather than upon traditional patterns of sharing and giving, or market patterns of buying and selling.

One of the key questions these pastors discussed was that of meaning and purpose: "Why should the church have a demonstration farm? Is it to make Christians rich?" That question lies at the heart of community development efforts: Are we working to help people buy more things? to acquire economic power? to improve their standard of living? to become a more effectively organized community for greater political power?

These leaders saw material needs among their people, but rejected the idea of community development for more rice or for more money to buy more things. Rather, they asked, What benefit should Christians seek in all of this? The pastor noted that prosperity is good when believers use it to serve others. However, if they use it only to serve their own greed, as he had observed with the three other projects in his area, then community development is not only unworthy, but also impossible. Development for service to others in the work of the Lord had meaning and significance apart from greed; by developing a faith demonstration farm, they hoped to teach people the truth of power and freedom in Christ and service to one another as a community of believers.

In summary, these Binukid men were effective agents of transformation because they were willing to challenge accepted ideas, to challenge accepted interests and causal relationships, to contextualize through complementary social and spiritual relationships, to talk about contradictions and conflicts, and to model kingdom goals and values. In all of this the gospel of Jesus Christ is in central focus, and the objective of these men was to glorify God and to serve in Jesus' name. They were certainly not perfect in their insight into the Scriptures or in their insight into the local society. They experienced tension, stress, and significant social and spiritual opposition. They had personal and spiritual anxieties about the contest in which they were engaged, and yet they were faithful to their understanding of the gospel and its implications for Binukid spiritual and farming life. Finally, they believed that making followers of Christ rather than making better rice farms was the most important objective of their ministry.

Ideas, Interests, and Sociocultural Transformation

The objective of evangelism is to tell a story and to challenge people to respond in faith, believing the message and thereby receiving personal salvation and adoption into the family of the church of Jesus Christ. The story begins with the virgin birth of Jesus, the only begotten Son of God. The story chronicles how he lived among us, the things he taught, the people he healed, and the disciples who followed him. At the climax of the story, he was crucified, raised from the dead, and taken up to heaven to be with the Father. The purpose of this death was the sacrificial offering for our sins. Jesus paid once for all the debt of all mankind for sin. Because of evil in our minds, we were alienated from God, but now we have been reconciled through the death of his son, Jesus Christ, on the cross.

The essence of evangelism is ideas; we want people to understand those ideas; we seek to convince them that these ideas are true; we invite them to believe and receive, to confess Jesus Christ as their Savior, and to enter into a special relationship with God and Christ. If they embrace these ideas, the next step is to engage in a new set of relationships and interests, joining the fellowship and community of believers. When they enter the community of believers, they engage in a new social environment. That social environment will generate feedback, engaging their preconversion ideas and world view with new information, values, standards, and disciplines. The process of becoming a disciple of Christ will transform their world view; to think Christianly becomes central to their social relationships, and their ideas are reshaped by the things that believers teach, the way the believers act toward them, and by the way believers live in the world.

To establish trust in a Christian mission context, we must understand both the fears that stem from ideas and the fears that grow from a threatened loss of social power. If our goal is to build *trust,* we must first recognize the critical contradictions the gospel creates for people. In the Binukid case that contradiction focused upon the power of the spirits and the power of God. Using careful biblical teaching, the pastors argued that the power of God is superior to the power of the spirit world, and that people need not fear, but can proceed with confidence in the power of God. They also noted contradictions about the legitimate way to plant rice, the proper technology, and the appropriate timing. They focused upon relevant biblical teaching and knowledge of new technology to reinforce those working with them who were fearful or insecure.

The pastors also made significant adjustments in their power relationships, engaging in dialogue with the unbelieving leaders about these issues. Every time unbelievers sat down by their field and criticized them, the pastors sat with them and talked at length about the issues. Careful to show respect, they listened to those who disagreed, then explained what they believed and why they felt free to act in this new way. Careful not to debate, they accepted those who opposed, facilitating dialogue but not concession.

The believers also stood solidly in support of one another, celebrating the power and work of God in a way never done before. For the first time believers gathered to celebrate the planting, weeding, and harvesting of a rice field. Through this gathering, believers demonstrated power to sustain and support one another in the social and spiritual battle—a battle about an old way and a new way of planting rice, and about the power of God and of spirits. The pastors established trust by identifying the contradictions, dealing with them openly, recognizing the necessity of complementarities, and redefining the whole planting process in a way that was analogous to tradition, but viewed in a thoroughly new, biblical idea framework.

To conclude, an understanding of how the gospel story may transform people and their cultures is greatly enhanced when we separate analytically the notions of ideas and interests, social environment and world view. By keeping them separate we may examine how they interplay with one another, thereby leading us to a clearer understanding of how the ideas of Scripture trigger significant changes in social relationships, and how social environment feeds back into the ideas and working life of the church. When we conflate them into one functional system, we lose perspective on the tension that exists between them, and the dynamic interplay of influence and feedback that leads to change in the logic of ideas, and in the power, interest, and value structures of social relationships. As Christians our ideas and interests ought to follow from our relationship as disciples of the Lord Jesus Christ. The ideas and interests of our societies stand in contradiction to this call to discipleship. Becoming a disciple is more than a radical transformation of ideas. It is also the transformation of interests and relationships, loving God and loving our neighbors as ourselves.

References

Adams, Richard N.
  1975 *Energy and structure: A theory of social power.* Austin: University of Texas Press.
  1988 *The eighth day.* Austin: University of Texas Press.
Annis, Sheldon
  1987 *God and production in a Guatemalan town.* Austin: University of Texas Press.
Archer, Margaret S.
  1988 *Culture and agency: The place of culture in social theory.* Cambridge: Cambridge University Press.
Douglas, Mary
  1966 (1984) *Purity and danger: An analysis of the concepts of pollution and taboo.* London: Ark Paperbacks.
  1970 (1982) *Natural symbols: Explorations in cosmology.* New York: Pantheon.
  1982 "Cultural bias." In *In the active voice,* 183–254. London: Routledge and Kegan Paul.
Fried, Morton
  1967 *The evolution of political society.* New York: Random House.
Ford, Boris, ed.
  1982. *Medieval literature: Chaucer and the alliterative tradition.* The New Pelican Guide to English Literature, vol. 1, pt. 1. New York: Pelican.
Geertz, Clifford
  1973 *Interpretation of cultures.* New York: Basic.
  1984 "From the natives' point of view": On the nature of anthropological understanding. In *Culture theory: Essays on mind, self, and emotion,* edited by Richard A. Shweder and Robert A. LeVine, 123–36. Cambridge: Cambridge University Press.
Gonzalez, Justo L.
  1990 *Faith and wealth: A history of early Christian ideas on the origin, significance, and use of money.* HarperSanFrancisco.
Goodenough, Ward H.
  1981 *Culture, language, and society.* Menlo Park, Calif.: Benjamin Cummings.
Harris, Marvin
  1964 *The nature of cultural things.* New York: Random House.
Hiebert, Paul G.
  1978 "Conversion, culture and cognitive categories." *Gospel in Context* 1/4: 24–29.
  1986 *Anthropological insights for missionaries.* Grand Rapids: Baker.
Hiebert, Paul G., and Eloise Hiebert Meneses
  1995 *Incarnational ministry: Planting churches in band, tribal, peasant, and urban societies.* Grand Rapids: Baker.
Kraft, Charles H.
  1981 *Christianity in culture: A study in dynamic biblical theologizing in cross-cultural perspective.* Maryknoll, N.Y.: Orbis.

References

Koop, Gordon, and Sherwood Lingenfelter
1980 *The Deni of western Brazil.* Dallas: SIL Museum of Anthropology Publication 7.
Leach, Edmund
1976 *Culture and communication: The logic by which symbols are connected.* Cambridge: Cambridge University Press.
Lingenfelter, Sherwood G.
1975 *Yap: Political leadership and cultural change in an island society.* Honolulu: University Press of Hawaii.
1992 *Transforming culture: A challenge for Christian mission.* Grand Rapids: Baker.
Lingenfelter, Sherwood, and Marvin K. Mayers
1986 *Ministering cross-culturally.* Grand Rapids: Baker.
Mayers, Marvin K.
1987 *Christianity confronts culture: A strategy for cross-cultural evangelism.* Grand Rapids: Zondervan.
Nader, Laura, and Harry F. Todd, Jr., eds.
1978 *The disputing process—Law in ten societies.* New York: Columbia University Press.
Peacock, James L.
1978 *Purifying the faith: The Muhammadijah movement in Indonesian Islam.* Menlo Park, Calif.: Benjamin Cummings.
Ross, Hugh.
1994 *Creation and time.* Colorado Springs: NavPress.
Russell, Walt
1993 "The apostle Paul's view of the 'sin nature'/'new nature' struggle." In *Christian perspective on being human,* edited by J.P. Moreland and David Ciocchi, 207–34. Grand Rapids: Baker.
Sahlins, Marshall
1972 *Stone age economics.* Chicago: Aldine-Atherton.
Schneider, D. M.
1984 *A critique of the study of kinship.* Ann Arbor: University of Michigan Press.
Service, Elman
1962 *Primitive social organization: An evolutionary perspective.* New York: Random House.
Smith, Donald K.
1992 *Creating understanding: A handbook for Christian communication across cultural landscapes.* Grand Rapids: Zondervan.
Thompson, Michael
1982 The problem of the centre: An autonomous cosmology. In *Essays in the sociology of perception,* edited by Mary Douglas, 302–27. London: Routledge and Kegan Paul.
1982 A three-dimensional model. In *Essays in the sociology of perception,* edited by Mary Douglas, pp. 31–63. London: Routledge and Kegan Paul.
Thompson, Michael; Richard Ellis; and Aaron Wildavsky
1990 *Cultural theory.* Boulder, Colo.: Westview.
Todd, Emmanuel
1987 *The causes of progress: Culture, authority, and change.* New York: Basil Blackwell.
Wildavsky, Aaron
1984 *The nursing father: Moses as political leader.* The University of Alabama Press.
Wilk, Richard R., and Robert McC. Netting.
1984 Households: Changing forms and functions. In *Households: Comparative and historical studies of the domestic group,* edited by Robert McC. Netting, Richard R. Wilk, and Eric J. Arnould. Berkeley: University of California Press.

Willard, Dallas
> 1988 *The spirit of the disciplines*. New York: Harper and Row.
> 1993 *In search of guidance*: *Developing a Conversational Relationship with God*. Harper-SanFrancisco: Zondervan.

Wolf, Eric
> 1982 *Europe and the people without history*. Berkeley: University of California Press.

Index

Index